Windows on a War

Windows on a War

The Korean War
as Seen by Peter Koerner,
USAF, 1950–1953

Edited by Mark Koerner

THE BAKELITE PRESS

Madison, Wisconsin

THE BAKELITE PRESS
Madison, Wisconsin

Book design: Sara DeHaan

Printed in the United States of America

Publisher's Cataloging-in-Publication Data

Names: Koerner, Peter, 1928–2012, author. | Koerner, Mark, editor.
Title: Windows on a war : the Korean War as seen by Peter Koerner, USAF, 1950–1953 / edited by Mark Koerner.
Description: Includes bibliographical references. | Madison, WI: The Bakelite Press, 2021.
Identifiers: Library of Congress Control Number: 2021903402
ISBN: 9780578857947 (pbk.) | 9780578857954 (ebook)
Subjects: LCSH Koerner, Peter, 1928–2012. | Korean War, 1950–1953—Personal narratives, American. | Soldiers—United States—Biography. | United States. Air Force—Biography. | United States—History, Military—20th century—Biography. | BISAC BIOGRAPHY & AUTOBIOGRAPHY / Personal Memoirs | BIOGRAPHY & AUTOBIOGRAPHY / Military
Classification: LCC DS921.6 .K64 2021 | DDC 951.04/2/092—dc23

. . . here's one monkey that's going to keep on climbing,
and looking around him to see what he can see,
as long as the tree holds out.

ROBERT A. HEINLEIN

Contents

Preface

Like so many projects of its kind, this one began as a pile of letters in a military footlocker—in this case, my father's footlocker, which sat in the basement of the house where I had grown up. After my father died, I worked on them, off and on, for six years. This book is the result.

I've always been suspicious of the "letters home" format. The letters a soldier writes home are generally interesting only to the family and in any case most of them tell us things we already know: war is hell, the food is bad, and I miss you a lot.

I'd like to think this book is different, if only because my father makes a number of intriguing observations about the Air Force, Okinawa, the Cold War, and midcentury America. But readers will have to decide on that for themselves.

It is impossible to understand Peter's letters without knowing something of his parents, whom he invariably calls "Ma and Pa." Andrew Koerner (1893-1964) was a World War I veteran and an attorney in Portland, Oregon. He had attended Stanford University, where he belonged to the Kappa Sigma fraternity. (Stanford and Kappa Sigma loom large in this narrative.) Cleo Base Koerner (1902–1974) had been Andrew's secretary before they married. Peter was born in Portland in 1928. They had a second child, Ann, in 1930. While my childhood memories of my grandparents are blurry, it is fair to say that they were strict disciplinarians who had high hopes for their only son.

Peter attended local public schools and then Stanford, where he, too, belonged to the Kappa Sigma fraternity. On the verge of being drafted, he joined the Air Force in 1950, graduated from Officer Candidate School, and was discharged as a 1st Lieutenant in 1953. Returning to Stanford, he got an MBA and married fellow student Nan Buland. The couple lived in Palo Alto—not far from the Stanford campus—until 1963, when they moved to Portland. They had four children.

In the mid-1960s, Peter worked for a manufacturer of chainsaw parts. In the 1970s, he owned a business. He later managed a lumber company. He died in 2012 at the age of 83.

My father barely talked about the roughly 36 months he spent in the Air Force. My siblings and I knew that he had been an intelligence officer—whatever that was—and that he had spent much of the Korean War on Okinawa, though he never mentioned the name of his base, Kadena. Occasionally, he let something generic slip about an old case he had worked on, but only once in a long while did he mention any of his ex-comrades. So I got the idea that he didn't particularly like being in the Air Force, an impression that was later confirmed in a phone conversation I had with Eugene Daggett (1927–2016), who had been his cubicle-mate at Officer Candidate School. "No, I didn't think he liked it," Daggett said. Now, at the end of this project, I have a better sense of what might have happened. My father desperately wanted organizations to work efficiently and effectively; waste was always something to be stamped out. And from what he could see, the Air Force exuded waste and inefficiency, so he became frustrated.

I can also see a few previews of my childhood. Peter's brand-consciousness, for example. He writes about Kodachrome film and RCA, the makes of the planes he flew in, the names of government contractors, and so on. This kind of talk never stopped, and it reflected, among other things, his interest in economic concentration—the degree of competition and monopoly in different industries. He had been an economics major, after all. And while he liked movies, he always objected to talk about plots, actors, or specific scenes. That rule had apparently been established early on, for whenever he writes about seeing films, he rarely mentions the names of any of them, much less whether he liked them.

Although Peter never stopped watching movies, as he got older he increasingly watched the same ones over and over, *Mr. Roberts* (1955) being near the top of his list, as I recall. By the time I started elementary school, it was an "old movie," shown weekends on a local TV channel. I doubt my father ever missed it. Mr. Roberts (played by Henry Fonda) is a World War II-era naval officer trapped on a cargo ship that transports toilet paper on some endless loop around the Pacific. My middle-aged father undoubtedly saw his younger self in the main character, even if his had been a different war, and even if he had been trapped on an island rather than a hunk of steel. But whatever he thought and however he felt, my father's personality bore little resemblance to that of Mr. Roberts, who was bored to distraction with life on the *USS Reluctant*. As he writes in a letter to the ship's surgeon:

> But I've discovered, Doc, that the unseen enemy of this war is the boredom that eventually becomes a faith and, therefore, a terrible sort of suicide. l know now that the ones who refuse to surrender to it are the strongest of all.

If Peter's letters say anything, they say that with the exception of basic training and its immediate aftermath, he never encountered that unseen enemy; he always seemed genuinely interested in what was happening around him—and this remained true wherever the Air Force sent him. Dad was the monkey that kept looking around to see what he could, as long the tree held out.

Madison, Wisconsin
January 2021

Acknowledgments

Most of these letters were typed, but they were not typed terribly well. And the typewriters, ribbons, and stationery left much to be desired, which means I owe a great debt to Megan Sharpless, who transcribed them, and to my wife, Amy, who read them aloud as we double-checked Megan's work. Maria San Emeterio did extensive formatting and reformatting.

Toward the end of this project, I was able to contact Kyle McArthur at Kadena Air Base in Okinawa, who was a big help in deciphering some of the more obscure Okinawan terms. He said that the work of an intelligence officer at Kadena today is not all that different than it was when Peter Koerner was stationed there almost 70 years ago.

Editor's Note

To the best of my ability, I have corrected all misspellings and grammatical and syntactical errors. I have also inserted punctuation where it was needed, and the paragraphing is largely my doing. With over-typed or misspelled words, it sometimes took a certain amount of guesswork to decide on the exact word. On occasion, I reordered phrases within sentences so that they would make sense and I eliminated redundant words—without inserting ellipses. Probably the most common changes involved the "really very" combination. Everything was "really very" this or "really very" that. I eliminated lots of reallys and verys, again without inserting ellipses.

On the handful of occasions when I removed phrases or sentences, I did use ellipses.

The book also has some additional wordage. At the top of each letter, I added the day of the week and the physical location of the typewriter and its operator. The subject headings are my own.

Abbreviations

AAA	American Automobile Association
AGO	identification card issued to all military personnel (Adjutant General's Office)
AIO	Air Installations Office
AP	Air Police
BG	Brigadier General
BOQ	Bachelor Officer Quarters
CI	Counterintelligence
CIC	Counterintelligence Corps
CID	Criminal Investigation Division
CO	Commanding Officer
CP	Civilian Policeman
CQ	Change of Quarters
CVA	Clean Vessel Act
FE	Far East
FEAF	Far East Air Force
G-2	U.S. Army military intelligence
GRI	Government of the Ryukyu Islands
KP	kitchen police/patrol
MATS	Military Air Transport Service

MKT	Missouri–Kansas–Texas Railroad
MP	Military Police
MPC	Military Payment Certificate
NCO	Non-commissioned officer
OG	Operations Group
OCS	Officer Candidate School
OJT	On the Job Training
OSI	Office of Special Investigations
PA	Practical Application
PFC	Private First Class
PST	Pacific Standard Time
PIO	public information officer
PM	provost marshal
POL	petroleum, oil, and lubricants
POW	Prisoner of War
PT	physical training
PX	post exchange
QM	Quartermaster
SAC	Strategic Air Command
TAC	Tactical Air Command
TDY	Temporary Duty
USCAR	United States Civil Administration of the Ryukyu Islands
WAF	Womens Air Force

Notices and Postcards, Summer 1950

3072 SW Fairview Blvd.
Portland 1, Oregon
August 30, 1950

No 352828267

Selective Service Board #28,
109 N.W. 10th Ave.,
Portland 9, Oregon

Sirs,
I received your order of August 28, 1950, for a physical examination on
September 18, 1950, after I had enlisted in the United States Air Force
and taken the oath.

I am ordered to San Antonio, Texas, and leave for that place tonight.
I suppose the Air Force will notify you of my enlistment and that you
will make the necessary entries on my records.
Very truly yours,

PETER KOERNER

Application for Air Force Officer Candidate School

August 30, 1950

AC-OC Examining Board
McChord Air Force Base,
Washington

ATTENTION: CAPTAIN DANIEL B. STEDMAN

Dear Captain Stedman,

I acknowledge receipt of your letter of August 26, 1950, directing me to report to your office on September 19, 1950 at 0800 for processing in connection with my application for Air Force Officer Candidate School. I wish to advise you that I have enlisted in the United States Air Force and leave today, August 30, 1950, for Lackland Air Force Base, San Antonio, Texas.

I request that my application for Candidate School be transferred to that base so that I can be processed there.

As soon as I arrive at the base at San Antonio, I will send you my full address, including the organization to which I am assigned. If, however, there is any other procedure that I should follow please let me know.

Sincerely yours,

Peter McColloch Koerner

Postmarked Friday, September 1, 1950

Denver, Colorado, 8:30 a.m.   POSTCARD

Dear Ma, Pa, and Ann,
We are just getting into Denver. We
transfer trains here and leave about
12:30 so we have a couple of hours
to look around. It was quite warm
yesterday but not oppressively so. So
far, the trip has been uneventful, but
I'll write again as soon as possible.
    Love,
    Peter

Postmarked Saturday, Sept. 2, 1950; Fort Worth, Texas

Saturday 8:30   POSTCARD

Dear Ma and Pa,
We arrived here about an hour and a
half ago and are due out in half an hour.
From Denver, we took the Burlington
and here on in we go on the M.K.T.
While it is overcast here and damp,
after a rain last night, it is hot and
sticky. Well, that's all that's new
just now.
 Love,
 Peter

CHAPTER ONE

From Oregon to Texas

Arrival Notice to Lackland Air Force Base

September 2, 1950

I arrived at Lackland Air Force Base this date. Please write to me at my new address:

Private Peter M. Koerner
Squadron 3703 Flight 5571
Lackland Air Force Base

Commanding Officer, his address is

Commanding Officer
3703 Basic Training Squadron
Lackland Air Force Base
San Antonio, Texas

The first letter: he finds a typewriter

Sunday, September 17, 1950
Lackland Air Force Base, San Antonio, Texas

Dear Ma and Pa,

Well, we got off restriction last night and I found a typewriter, so things are looking up a little bit.

While I may not be able to write any more letters, at least those you get will be legible. This last week has been a busy one.

On Wednesday, the group drew KP and I managed to get to go to the WAF mess across the field. It was really a pretty good deal. There was no one around telling you to hurry, the food was very good, everyone treated you nicely, and, above all, they said "please," which made you feel like a human being again. The work was easy; all we had to do was any heavy lifting with no drying or washing of dishes.

It seems that this last week has been full of inspections. We have had to scrub the barracks about five different evenings, but it only takes an hour or so, which isn't too bad. As we did well on the inspections, the corporal let us do what we pleased today as long as we are in by seven this evening.

On Tuesday, we had our aptitude test, which took all day. They told us that we would be told the results in a couple of weeks. The days in between have been mostly classes of various sorts: math, drilling, military conduct, and general propaganda.

Yesterday, we had a typhoid shot—the second one—but my arm didn't bother me very much and feels about normal today. Some of those who had the smallpox vaccination a week ago are quite miserable. I was lucky and can't even see where they scratched the skin.

Last night, the flight had their picture taken and if it is any good I will have one made up for you but the way the bird took the pictures, any similarity will prove quite unusual [i.e., coincidental].

We had no sooner gotten back when we had a rainstorm complete with thunder and lightning. It was quite a severe one but didn't last too long. It calmed down and we went out for a while and then after we got back, it started to rain again and lasted a good part of the night. While it is cloudy today, it is warm and sticky, which is not especially unusual.

I have been swimming in sweat ever since I got here. I have a notion to put in for service in Alaska where it is cool, and you can get a cool glass of good water. I had my first Coke last night and while it was warm, it still tasted good.

One of these days our stuff is going to be sent home, but I have no idea just when. It has been sitting around all packed up ready to go for a week now.

Your dinner party sounds like a nice one, but I hope that you didn't go to too much trouble and get all tired out over it.

I am also writing McChord Field to have my application sent down here.* I am also going to find out when I can take a test for OCS. I should be able to find out about that this week sometime.

Well, I really can't think of too much more to report this time. What I think I'll do is take some type of notes and then type them up for you when I can get over here. I also need some airmail stamps, if you would send them, as the others all stuck together when I put them in my wallet.

Love,
Peter

---

* McChord Field is an Air Force base near Tacoma, Washington.

Basic training: it's a boring life

Sunday, September 24, 1950
Lackland Air Force Base, San Antonio, Texas

Dear Ma and Pa,

Well, it is raining today which is quite nice for a change. It started this morning and is now a steady drizzle.

This last week has been just about the same with a few changes. For the most part, we have had classes in math, warfare, citizenship, and career guidance.

Most of them are pretty boring, especially the math, as it is very elementary. This next week we have classes in gas warfare and have to go through a tear gas chamber, which should be a little different.

This last week in inspection, our flight took first place in the squadron which means we don't have to fall out quite so early in the morning, which is a break.

Friday, we drew the garbage detail for the day, which wasn't quite as bad as it sounds. We got out of classes for the day and were finished by noon, so we had the rest of the day to clean up and do odd chores of various types.

Last night, we all went to what was supposed to be a rodeo in town, but which turned out to be some type of Mexican goodwill program about 10 miles on the other (east) side of town. It was pretty miserable but at least it was something a little different. We got back about 12:30 a.m. and then didn't get up until about 10 this morning.

I went over about OCS this last week and I have to go over again Tuesday to take the test. We have the gas training that day, so I don't know just what is going to come of it, but I will probably take it some other time. I shall have to go over there and get another time or see if I can't get out of classes that day.

As far as sending me anything, there really isn't any point in doing so. I haven't any room to put anything more for a while, but I'll write and let you know of anything that I need. I will be needing that combination lock on my typewriter in the basement fairly soon. When

I left, it was set so all you had to do was to give it a push to take it off. If it won't come off, try our phone number on it. Beyond that, don't monkey with it or you will lose the combination and the lock will be ruined.

As far as the government insurance is concerned, I took out a five-year term policy until I was more settled down and could convert it. I imagine I should get the 30-year life, but I wasn't too sure at the time and this five-year term was the cheapest also. It costs $6.60 a month now which I believe will be deducted from our next paycheck. We get paid just as soon as we finish our basic. Right now, they are finishing up and shipping out during the 6th week of basic. I guess that they are really crowded here.

Well, that is about all for this time.

Love,

Peter

Counting softballs and taking tests

Sunday, October 1, 1950
Lackland Air Force Base, San Antonio, Texas

Dear Ma and Pa,

Well, this has been a pretty busy week. We started out Monday by drawing "detail" which turned out to be a laugh. My job was to help out at the supply building for the OCS area. All I did for eight hours was to fill a water cooler with ice and to help count a couple of hundred softballs for their inventory. It was a pretty good deal as I was inside all the time. It rained all day long.

Tuesday morning, I managed to talk the corporal into letting me off for the morning and going over to take the OCS test. It wasn't a test of knowledge at all but rather a test of preferences, scoring of personal likes, habits, etc. The said that they would get in touch with me later about it.

That morning there were about eight taking the test, all with degrees from various types of colleges. They said that in the last class of about 180 members, all but thirty of them had been accepted from civilian applicants and that the percentage would probably be higher in the January class, which doesn't sound too hopeful.

In any event, it won't be until the latter part of December before I am notified, either one way or another.

I also heard from McChord Field that they had already sent my application down here.

Tuesday afternoon we went through what is called Job Classification to figure out what you are best qualified for, what you would like to do most of all, and, most important, what they feel like assigning you to. It was all based, supposedly, on these tests we took a couple of weeks ago.

There were nine major groupings or classifications listed there. A perfect score on any one of them was a nine but all one needed to qualify was a five.

I got a perfect score on six of them and a seven on the group that dealt with the management of heavy machinery. So at least I am qualified to do about anything, but I'll probably be assigned a large bulldozer.

The job groupings, in the main, deal with radio, radar, engine mechanics and repair, and closely related jobs. There really weren't many that seemed very interesting. When it came down to asking about my preference, excluding the possibility of a discharge, I put down a couple of jobs in the medics and then some type of administration. I was a little bit leery about putting down administration as my first preference for fear of getting a job as a clerk typist or something equally dull and unimaginative.

While my typing certainly leaves much to be desired, it is much better than that of some of the typists they've had around here. As far as the medics is concerned, that sounds very silly for me to be trying to get into, but from what I have heard, they have comparatively little supervision and more responsibility than most jobs and the hours seem to be better and one always eats better around a hospital.

The food here isn't worth a damn for the most part but I imagine that as soon as I get settled anywhere it will improve.

However, as I mentioned before, it will not be until around the first of the year before I hear about the OCS test and in the meantime, having taken it, I will be classified as a 'casual' which means waiting around for bigger and better things while riding on top of several tons of garbage.

But I may be able to talk myself into being some kind of temporary assistant to the supply division of the squadron. They seem to need someone quite often to type and count for them. It wouldn't be too bad for a while. But this, as you know as with everything else, is only how things stand today, so don't give it more than a passing thought.

Wednesday, we had what are called Pre-Mark instructions. They were mostly lectures on how the M-1 rifle functions and how to load it. We also had a couple of hours of instructions on the various firing positions.

In all, we had about six hours of lectures and two hours of practice. The actual sighting and firing were to come later on in the week but didn't. We were also supposed to have gas but that also never got past the instructions stage.

Wednesday night we were selected for night guard duty. We got up at 12:45 so we could go on guard duty at two in the morning. The Army's sense of time is something I shall always wonder at. I guarded a piece of road about twenty feet across and four blocks long from two until six in the morning. I guess that I did a good job for when the sun came it was still there.

We got back, and I was hoping for about eight hours of math instruction, so I could catch up on my sleep but when I got back, I found that we were selected for detail again. Our group was last in arriving and all the jobs had been given out, so we were herded onto a side lawn and someone had an auction of clothes, which lasted about an hour.

Then we were sent over to the repair shops and were assigned as carpenters' helpers over in the WAF area. I wheeled a little cement for about a half an hour and then spent the rest of the day trying to find a little shade to sleep in, but the flies were pretty thick, so I read a Western that I just happened to have with me at the time.

Thursday night we were told that the Army had decided to end basic training for us so that was all as [far as] the math, gas, gunnery, orientation, propaganda, and citizenship classes were concerned.

Friday, we had a couple more shots, an inspection, and a haircut, and general little chores around the barracks.

Yesterday was also quite uneventful. We did get to stay out until twelve, which meant nothing at all since there wasn't anything of interest going on and there weren't any good movies to be had.

Friday night there came word that about a third of those in our flight are going to be sent out to school this next week and more will probably be alerted this next week sometime. Those who were called were for gunnery, radar, sheet metal work, and airplane engine mechanics.

Yesterday we were issued more clothing. We got our heavy overcoats for our blue dress uniform that we got a couple of weeks ago. It is really a nice coat but is very heavy. We also got an "Ike" jacket in the blue. I believe that this just about takes care of it for a while.

As far as the rest of our uniforms are concerned, we have three sets of khaki uniforms, one blue dress uniform, a cap, and a pair of black dress shoes. We also have a couple of pairs of leather gloves and a pair of mittens, a pair of tennis shoes, a ski-type hat, a pair of swimming shorts, a raincoat, and a field jacket. I believe that I have already mentioned some of this to you, but I'm not quite sure.

They said that it might be better if we were to write and tell you not to write anymore for a while until we get settled at the training schools but that was for those who are leaving right away so it doesn't apply to you. If you haven't sent the lock, be sure to do so right away.

It might also be a good idea to number your letters if it isn't too much trouble, so I can tell if I didn't receive any of the local gossip.

Enclosed are the credit cards. I had forgotten all about them.

Love,
Peter

PS: Thanks for the stamps.

The end of basic training

Sunday, October 8, 1950
Lackland Air Force Base; San Antonio, Texas

Dear Ma and Pa,

This last week has been rather dull and quite tiring. Monday, Tuesday, and Wednesday, we sat around while the majority of the flights were getting ready to ship out. We had no classes or anything like that, but we still weren't permitted to get away for any length of time. They left Wednesday, leaving about 20 of us still in the barracks.

Subsequently, about five more have been transferred out, a couple to different bases and some who are going to remain here as a permanent party. This last couple of days we have been on detail, which means if we get caught, we do little odd chores around the base. Friday several of us went over to the building which passes for the armory here and helped put a top on a big workbench. We spent the whole day there, working for five minutes and standing around looking busy for 30.

Yesterday all of importance I did was to stand guard around the swimming pool for three-and-a-half hours. Today is our day off, supposedly, if we do not get caught hanging around when they want someone for guard duty of various kinds.

I have an appointment over at the OCS school this Thursday. I don't know if it is for another test or if I appear before the examining board. At any rate, I hope that I can find out for certain just how I stand as I don't like being listed as a casual. If I find that the January class is full, I have half a notion to withdraw my application. Otherwise, I will be a casual—anyhow, until the next class is made out which will be the first of March. I can always submit my application from another base. Unless you people think differently, I believe I might go ahead and do this.

As far as this base is concerned, it is the main training base for enlistees in the Air Force. All enlistees are brought here first I believe but recently they have been shipping them right out again to a couple of other fields here in Texas. Sheppard is one of them and I believe that

Randolph is another but I'm not quite sure. Every day they are receiving about 750 to 1000 men as near as I can figure it out. They are crowded here and more than a little confused, which is only to be expected.

There is always someone around who will tell you just the exact opposite of what someone told you a few minutes before and the funny thing about it is that they both believe that it is the truth.

Basic training, as I mentioned before, has been cut down this time to 30 days and from there the basics are shipped out to training schools of various types or some are shipped to on-the-job training somewhere. I certainly will be glad to get settled down somewhere as all this confusion and uncertainty gets pretty tiring after a while.

As far as money is concerned, I am pretty well off having only started on the $60 reserve I had with me. About the only large expenditure that may be coming up is $27 for a folding canvas traveling bag I will need if I get moved out of here. However, if I need any money, I shall be sure and let you know. There is no place around here where I can get a personal check cashed which is rather inconvenient.

Last night I was standing barracks guard from 10 to 11 and the corporal called me up and gave me three cans of beer which certainly tasted good. He left today on a 15-day leave and had bought a case of beer and smuggled it in. He and a couple of other flight chiefs had drunk all they could and as he didn't want it to go to waste, I got to finish it up for him. Needless to say, it was the high spot of the entire time I have been here.

Well, that is about all that I can think of to report at this time. Please note the new address. Instead of Flight 5571, it is just plain 'casual'.

Be sure to take care of yourselves and not work too hard in the garden. I wish that some of the rain you have been having would blow down here. It has remained hot and sticky all this last week.

Love,
Peter

PS. Enclosed is a clipping from the base paper I thought you might be interested in and the answer check sheet all checked out for you.

CHECKLIST

1. Are you by chance with any of the fellows who left Portland with you? Yes___ NO _✓_

2. Did you get issued to you a uniform? Yes_✓_ NO___

3. Do you have any leisure for reading? Yes_✓_ NO___ some

4. Have you been able to see all of Lackland? Yes___ NO_✓_

5. Is Lackland just a receiving base? Yes___ NO___ answered

6. Do they have schools for Officers' Training at Lackland? Yes _✓_ NO___

7. Have you been to San Antonio? Yes___ NO_✓_

8. Have you had any time off? Yes___ NO _✓_ not to speak of

9. Is your corporal Big or Little McEvers? Big ___ Little ___ answered (Dorothy and Monty were wondering about this one).

10. Is the WAFs the women's branch? Yes _✓_ NO___

11. Are you able to get magazines, etc, at the PX? Yes _✓_ NO___

12. Are you able to use your electric razor? Yes _✓_ NO___

13. Does your period of isolation count as part of your basic training? Yes _✓_ NO___

14. How long is basic training? 30 days now

15. Is there sagebrush around San Antonio? Yes _✓_ NO___

16. Do you sleep in bunks? Yes _✓_ NO___

17. Do you have access to magazines and newspapers? Yes _✓_ NO___

18. Do you have access to a radio? Yes _✓_ NO___

An airman's life

Sunday, October 15, 1950
Lackland Air Force Base; San Antonio, Texas

Dear Ma and Pa,
I received the [combination] lock this week in good shape. It arrived just in time as we moved back into the tents and I needed it to lock my footlocker. I think we will probably stay in the tents until we move out although they claim that they are going to try and move all the casuals into a barracks soon.

I went over to OCS this week and found out that as soon as I appear for a personal interview before the examining board I will be available for shipment and that if I make it they will take me out of the training school and bring me back here. At least that solves one of my problems. I won't be a causal around here for a couple of months pending admittance.

Monday and Tuesday, I spent all day as a barracks guard in our old barracks. Everything was going along OK until a lieutenant caught me sitting down and doing a crossword puzzle. He was pretty unhappy about that, but I never heard anything else about it. Tuesday, I also had a personal interview about OCS and as soon as that can be processed, I will appear before the OCS board which should be sometime this week.

Both Wednesday and Friday I had KP, which is quite a strain. We have to get up at three in the morning and report at four and then don't get off until about seven in the evening. It is really tiring as you are standing up all the time on the cement floors, trying to look busy.

Thursday, I was called over to the OCS office, but they made a mistake and didn't want me after all, but it gave me an excuse to be gone all day, so I went to the library and did some reading. It was really nice.

Yesterday about 50 of us spent all day cleaning up a barracks. We worked for about two hours altogether and slept the rest of the day. While we had nothing else to do, we still had to stick around. They do that all the time and it sort of gripes me but there isn't much you can do.

Three of us got a pass last night and went to town. We rented a hotel room and went out and looked the town over and then didn't get up until noon today. We ate and went to a movie and then when it got cooler, we looked around and went and saw the Alamo, which was quite interesting. It was really warm in town today.

Well, that is about all that I can think of to report this week. I got a box of candy from Pearl and Dorothy which arrived in good shape, which was surprising, considering how hot it has been this last week.* Be sure to thank them for me as I don't know when I shall have the time.

The way things look I may be out of here in a week or two so please don't send me anything as I don't need it.

Love,
Peter

PS: Let's knock off this "airman" business. I don't like it!!

---

* Peter refers to his maternal aunt, Pearl Base (1913–1984), and Dorothy Monroe, a family friend.

On issuing uniforms, comic books, and Officer Candidate School

Sunday, October 22, 1950
Lackland Air Force Base; San Antonio, Texas

Dear Ma and Pa,

Well, this last week was strangely like the first. Things were about as dull as ever. It is quite easy to see why the Army has never been noted for the mental giants that belong to it.

Monday, I was an orderly-room runner, which meant that I carried various messages of varying importance around the base. It was a fairly good job, but my feet got tired toward the end of the day.

Tuesday's detail was to help over at the building where the new men are issued their clothing. The first thing I knew, I was fitting jackets at the rate of a couple a minute. This sure was a mess as it is all I can do to get something to fit myself even when I have all the time in the world. As a result, I'm afraid that there are a couple of hundred men in the Army that look pretty moldy. It really is too bad as they have to pay for them but the guys that were supposed to do it were smoking in the back room.

Wednesday morning, I was assigned as a plumber's helper, which was quite a laugh. They were, I believe, civilians, and about all I did was hand them a few tools for a while and spend the better part of the morning riding around with them in a truck from one job to another. In the afternoon, I was called to the orderly room and was given an appointment for an interview the next morning for OCS. The guy in charge of the casuals and I then decided that seeing as how I had had a pretty hard day and especially since the guy who relieved me was a notorious goldbrick, I took the rest of the day off.

Wednesday, I had the interview with the deputy commander of the 3700th training group, a lieutenant-colonel. It was interesting and seemed to go along quite well. Among other things, he said I had a high score as far as my background and results from the biographical test and personal interview with the lieutenant were concerned, and that it was only a matter of time, as far as he could say, before I would be admitted to OCS.

But I still must appear before the board which should be either the latter part of this next week or the first part of next week and then I must pass the physical examination. After that, I will be sent on to some type of technical school and will be brought back to OCS when it opens up. There doesn't seem to be much chance for the January class as that is said to be full but there is another one in March and another in June.

In all, it lasted about 20 minutes. As there wasn't anyone around when I got back, I took the rest of that day off and went to the library and did some reading.

It seems that when they took my fingerprints in Portland, they smeared them, so I had to report Friday to have them retaken. As it is a rather complicated procedure, I didn't make it back until mail call at 3:45 in the afternoon. They really have a couple of nice libraries around here and I have been getting a little reading in, so not all of the time is wasted.

Saturday, I got eager and requested detail over at the supply building for the training group. This was the squadron supply, serving just about 1000 men, so there wasn't a great deal to do, especially since there were about eight men working. I worked a couple of hours in the morning and spent the rest of the day loafing around and listening to the various games the numerous Texas teams play.

I'm afraid that it is going to come as a shock when (in the distant future I'm afraid) these people in Texas find out that there are other just as important and much more pleasant sections of the country. It is hard to imagine how completely self-centered these Texans are. As a result, naturally, most of them are living in a haze and are totally incapable of understanding anything more profound than the comic books that seem to be knee-deep everywhere you go. It shouldn't surprise me a bit if the comic book publishers are the leading group lobbying for a large standing army. It is really funny.

About Southerners in general, few of them seem to realize they lost their war 85 years ago. If they were living in the past then as they are now, it is a wonder that the Civil War lasted as long as it did.

Last night several of us went to town, had a few beers, and came back around 12.

Today I mostly loafed around, did a little reading, and went to a movie.

I received the knife this last week and be sure to thank Carl the next time you talk to any of them.* This last Wednesday evening it rained but the last couple of days have been very warm.

Well, that is about all I can think to report for the time being. These last two weeks, they have shipped out about 80 casuals from our squadron so there are about 80 left, with more leaving tomorrow. This doesn't sound too good because I'm afraid that we are due for some KP this next week and the chances of avoiding it are not too good. I shall have to give some serious thought to that problem tonight and tomorrow. I think that I may manage to get over at the supply for the next two or three weeks while I am awaiting getting shipped out of here. KP is one thing that I can't stand. Sixteen hours standing on the cement doing stupid little tasks is more than I like to put in.

Will write again,

Love,

Peter

---

* Carl George (b. 1929) was a paternal cousin. Carl would eventually own George & Son Cutlery, a knife store in Portland, Oregon.

The night of the corporal

Monday, October 30, 1950
Lackland Air Force Base; San Antonio, Texas

Dear Ma and Pa,

This is the stationery I had to get for foot-locker inspection and as I'm out of the other I have to use this. I don't like the looks of it, but I don't like to throw it away. It's too rah-rah for me.

I was going to write last night but decided to go to town, so I didn't get a chance to use the typewriter and I didn't have the energy to walk clear over there tonight—hence the longhand. A shorter letter but a longer one to read. Monday, I had my interview with the OCS board, which was quite interesting. There were a couple of captains and a couple of majors. They asked a few general background questions and then a couple of questions about specific topics of the day. One of them asked about the setup of the CVA program and I was able to give a fairly intelligent answer, which probably helped.[1]

Tuesday, I had the physical examination for OCS, which carried over until Wednesday, so the first part of the week was rather easy and interesting. Because of my mastoid, I had to take some special hearing test which was interesting and which I passed OK.[2] Now all I am waiting for is to be shipped out of here. They will notify me at my next base if and when I go to OCS.

Thursday, Friday, and Saturday I worked supply, which is a good deal, but I don't know how long it is going to last. A corporal in there whom I never saw eye to eye with got mad at me tonight and said as far as he was concerned, I needn't show up tomorrow morning. I think I'll

---

1. The CVA reference is obscure; Peter may refer to the Clean Vessel Act, passed in August 1950.

2. Mastoid operation (mastoidectomy): removal of infected cells of the skull near the ear. Once a comparatively common operation, it became less so with the advent of antibiotics. Peter had had a mastoidectomy as a child.

go talk to the sergeant-in-charge with whom I get along fine and see what he has to say about it. I really don't care too much as things are becoming rather routine in there, anyhow.

Wednesday night, we moved out of the tents and back into the barracks again which makes it more convenient and cleaner.

Saturday night, several of us went to town to the movies and had a couple of beers and came back.

Sunday, I slept in fairly late, got up and ate, cleaned up a little, took a nap and then went to town to the movies again.

I also got paid $30 on Wednesday which helped out, as I was getting pretty low. As soon as we get out of here, we get paid regularly, which will be nice. It seems as if everyone around here is continually broke. It is really funny.

My proofs were no good, so I didn't have any pictures made.

We get a clothing allowance we can draw against—it is not deducted from our pay of $75/month. Our uniforms are just like the officers except, of course, for the insignia.

This last week has been quite warm still but today it was cloudy. Perhaps the weather is starting to change. I certainly hope so.

Well, I've got to take a shower before the lights go out, so I'll close. I hope you don't have too much trouble reading this.

Love,

Peter

Still waiting to be shipped out

Tuesday, November 7, 1950
Lackland Air Force Base; San Antonio, Texas

Dear Ma and Pa,

Well, I'm a day and a half late with this letter. I didn't get back from town until after nine Sunday and last night I couldn't get a chair at a typewriter in the service club so here I am now.

I have night guard now—it is 3 a.m.—but I got a fairly good deal in that all I do is sit around and wait to run messages. For a while, I thought I was going to have to walk a post but managed to get out of that, which is a break. However, as it is, I still only get three hours sleep, which is sort of tough.

As yet, I haven't gotten any shipping orders. Things wouldn't be too bad around here if we didn't have night barracks guard a couple of nights a week. We have to stand three-hour shifts which, as near as I can figure, is the worst deal on the base.

Now for the week's activities, such as they may be. Tuesday about all I did was to water grass for about four or five hours, which, while boring, wasn't too bad as they left you alone.

Wednesday, I white-washed in the morning and just sort of puttered around in the afternoon.

Thursday and Friday, I was assigned to the woodshop, sanding helmets on Thursday—and on Friday I managed to promote myself to some type of assistant so all I did was talk, which was a pretty good deal as there was little work and it was much cleaner.

Saturday, somehow, I got the day off and spent it at the library. In the evening, a couple of us went to town and stayed overnight and came back Sunday evening.

Thursday night a "norther" started and we got up at 2:30 and hammered in tent stakes for an hour or so. (In the morning, they took the tents down). Friday, it continued and got good and cold. It got down to around 34 degrees, according to the papers. What with the wind, it sure was cold.

Saturday and Sunday, it was still cold, as was yesterday. I think that the weather has changed for winter.

I don't know how long my "deal" here is going to last. They took one of the guards away and he's the last replacement here now if anything else should turn up.

Well, I'll try to write on time next Sunday. Don't work too hard!

Love,

Peter

PS: Ma: Out of my account, please get Pa a year's subscription to *Fortune*. Also, if you have any ideas of what you or what Ann would like, please let me know. PK.

The corporal (cont'd)

Sunday, November 12, 1950
Lackland Air Force Base; San Antonio, Texas

Dear Ma and Pa,

Well, there really isn't much to report again this week. Things have fallen into a pattern which doesn't vary much. My guard duty early Tuesday morning turned out pretty well, as I didn't have to do any walking; just sat around so I could be on hand in case any of the other guards got ill. The next morning, we got to go back to bed for an hour or so and then I had to stand more guard in the afternoon.

Wednesday, I painted for about an hour in the morning and laid around the rest of the morning and then in the afternoon I cleaned the paintbrush and helped haul a little plywood around on a truck, so you can see I didn't exactly knock myself out.

Thursday, we had another windstorm from the north. I helped police up the area for about half an hour and then spent the rest of the day in the library. It sure was a nasty day. While there was no rain, it was cold, and the wind cut right through to the bone.

Friday was about the same. Helped clean up the barracks for an hour or so then left and went and read the rest of the morning. In the afternoon we got paid again which certainly was a relief. We got another $30 which makes $90 I have been paid so far. What with going to town on the weekend and buying cigarettes and Cokes, there just isn't an opportunity to get ahead at all. However, once I get settled (if and when), I will get all my pay at once plus that which is accumulating. My base pay is $75 minus the insurance premiums of $6.60. I'm not sure just what is the amount of the other deductions, but I am going to look it up sometime this week.

Yesterday was a holiday. In the evening I went to town, saw a movie, had a few beers, and came on back. I believe that I'll stay here tonight as there isn't anything special that I want to do, and I can't see going to town to spend money just to be doing something different.

I still haven't any idea just what or just when they plan to ship me out of here. I talked to the shipping clerk this last week and he said that as far as he knew my records weren't messed up but that there hadn't been many orders coming through for men from the Army schools. If I get in the Medics, I shall be sent to an Army school at Fort Sam Houston, so it sounds like perhaps that is what I am listed for.[1]

I went over to the OCS headquarters Friday to make sure everything was in order so there would be no danger of anything delaying me. They assured me that everything was in good order so all I have to do is to wait around and hope I'll get alerted sometime soon. The worst part of being a casual is you have to pull guard duty a couple of times a week for three-hour stretches. You can't sit down, read, or smoke which makes it very boring. Our training squadron is notorious around here for being the pettiest in such matters.

Don't worry about my not getting along with one of the corporals, Pa; we just had a difference of opinion and I had to shape him up that I wasn't going to be imposed upon. Besides, he left this last week. Now we are in the midst of trying to shape another one up.

About half of the men in the barracks shipped out this week, so there are about 35 left. As long as that remains so for a few days, I'll have a pretty good chance of working into some semi-permanent detail which is easy and doesn't take too much time.

Supposedly, the Air Force is going to give ten [days] off for Christmas to as many as possible. I have no idea about my chances of getting off or if I do, about getting home via an airplane. I don't believe that it would be easy to get a 'hop'—in fact, almost impossible. What do you think about taking a train? The only trouble with that is that it would take so long to get anyplace. I did get a letter from Bill Koerner in which he mentioned about going over there [Los Angeles] for Christmas if I didn't have enough time to get home.[2] Perhaps you had

---

1. Fort Sam Houston is a U.S. Army base near San Antonio. Peter's many references to the Army reflect the close relationship between the Army and the Air Force. The Air Force had become independent from the Army in 1947.

2. William ("Bill") Koerner (1928–2003) was a paternal cousin; he later became an insurance salesman in the Los Angeles area.

better send me my pass so if something turns up rather unexpectedly, I won't have to worry about transportation.[3]

I don't know if you have heard anything about it, but it seems that the Air Force was given an ex-Navy base in NY—near Rome, I believe. The rumors around here have it that about half of the base is going to move up there to start it going after they get it fixed up, which supposedly will be sometime next March. So, if I don't get into OCS by that time, I suppose there is a small chance of getting sent up there, which would be interesting—for a change.

Well, that is about all that I can think of to report this week, so I guess I shall close.

It got down to 26 in San Antonio the other night. We were lucky and had heat, so it wasn't too bad.

As far as my reading habits are concerned, you will be glad to know that I haven't been reading any Westerns or related tripe. Nor have I picked up the comic book habit. In addition to keeping up with all the magazines, I've been reading some English plays and Greek literature. I have also just about decided to learn to read French just to be doing something different. I can't quite see reading any military literature just yet. Perhaps later.

Love,
Peter

PS: I found out that they forward mail here but just letters and no papers,etc., or packages so don't worry about any letters not reaching me. My typing surely is disgusting today!

---

3. For generations, American railroads distributed free passes (the transport equivalent of season tickets) to favored customers and their families. Peter's father, an attorney, had in all likelihood done legal work for the Southern Pacific Railroad—which at that time was both a freight line and a passenger line.

Men at work

Sunday, November 19, 1950
Lackland Air Force Base; San Antonio, Texas

Dear Ma and Pa,
Well, here it is, another Sunday again. This last week has been just like the others—not much to report. However, I did get some good news yesterday when I went to get my pass. They had a line drawn through my name which meant I was going to be alerted for shipment sometime this next week. I went up to see the shipping clerk before he left for town and he said that I was going to be alerted this next week. That as far as he knew it would probably be Fort Sam Houston or Brooks Air Force Base, both of which are over on the other side of San Antonio, I believe. That would be on the east side, roughly. He also said that he figured I would be wanting to go to town, so he saved my pass, so I got to go to town after all, which was quite nice of him—as I was getting pretty tired of the barracks after a whole week.

As far as work has been this last week, I have been pretty lucky. I have been assigned to the barracks to clean it up in the mornings and by the time that is done most of the work details have already been assigned for the day and all of the barracks guards have been picked. The first part of the week we took off every morning and went to the library for the rest of the day but the bird in charge of us got a little bitter so the past few days we have had to stay around the barracks the rest of the day which is about as foolish as it sounds but about which there is nothing we can do.

Well, as long as I'm getting out of here this next week, I really don't care just what I shall have to do. I also got guard duty twice this last week from nine to twelve in the evenings which wasn't nearly as bad as the next three-hour shift. This weekend I was lucky and didn't have any guard duty nor did I have to go on KP last night, which was a break, to say the least. Well, I guess that just about takes care of the week's activities. Nothing very new.

Monday night I went to a concert they had here on the base. It was the San Antonio Symphony and was pretty good, but a couple of the selections were a bit on the novelty side to appeal to those who had to attend because their training flight had to go en masse. I went to the movies a couple of times and that took care of the limited nightlife.

The weather here this last week has been much cooler and we had a rather heavy rainstorm Monday evening, but it didn't last too long. The rest of the week it has been fairly cloudy with a south wind much of the time. But coming from the south here, it has not been cold, which is nice as that wind from the north is really uncomfortable.

They are getting ready to start sending men on up to New York. They have a system whereby any of the permanent party who want to go can sign up for it. But I don't imagine that any will leave until February sometime. If I don't get into OCS for a while, I imagine that I'll have a pretty good chance of getting sent up there which I think I should try to get if I have a choice and if nothing very close to home comes up. However, I really don't imagine that I will have much choice just where I shall be sent. I only hope that it isn't here in Texas or any place in the South. I certainly get tired of these people.

Now about the rest of the casuals. There are only a half dozen who have been around here longer than I at the present time. Of those, about three are awaiting investigation for fraudulent enlistment of various types. A couple had records, and another had had a medical discharge which he didn't tell them about. Of course, that is what they say, and I wouldn't want to bank on it to any extent. One of the casuals around here a couple of weeks ago said that the reason for his delay was that they had lost his records but that he thought he was going to cook's school. The last time I saw him was in front of a shotgun guard heading for the stockade for six months because of some clothing that he stole.

A bunch around here have been delayed because medical records were lost somewhere in the shuffle. They are all re-enlistees, and someone made a mistake and sent their records to another base, but most of them are leaving in a week or so as near as I can gather. There has been a continual stream of men in and out of the barracks all this last week.

They shipped a couple of flights out and those who didn't get shipped were moved in here so they could make room for new training flights. In this squadron, there are 10 barracks each holding about 70 men when full. All in all, there are about 1000 men when all the staff, etc. are counted, and when all the barracks are full—which they never are, as some are continually in the process of being shipped out.

I guess that I really shouldn't have mentioned anything about getting 10 days for Christmas as that seems to be a very slight possibility, especially when transportation is considered. Please don't count on it. Also, don't worry about mail not reaching me. You can keep on writing me and as soon as I know my next address, I shall let you know. In the meantime, they will forward mail to me.

I have yet to receive the package from Cooper.[1] I imagine that he didn't have time to get it off to me. If you have any clippings of his wedding, I would like to see them. I also thought that it was a kick about the Monroes as well.[2] How did they ever happen to get involved in that and what are they doing about it?

The guy I go to town with was a member of our training flight who, through a misunderstanding, got assigned as a flight chief. He graduated from Iowa State (I think that is the one) this last June. He is quite unhappy about the whole thing. He also has applied to OCS, much to the disgust of the training sergeant. He also is on the basketball team, which means he doesn't have time to do much work around the area. In the office here, they did about everything they could think of to discourage his basketball but he went ahead anyhow and as a result has several of the training non-coms down on him but there isn't much they can do to him because he can turn them into the athletic director if they impose on him. It is really an amusing situation. The only thing is that he doesn't quite know what he is going to do come March and the season ends.

Love,
Peter

---

1. Martin Cooper (1926–2011) was a childhood friend from Portland and a fraternity brother at Stanford University. After college, he settled in Mt. Shasta, California.

2. Marion Monroe, his wife Dorothy (previously mentioned), and their sons William and Gerald, were family friends and neighbors.

He gets the word: accepted at Officer Candidate School

Saturday, November 25, 1950
Lackland Air Force Base; San Antonio, Texas

I'M AT THE LIBRARY AND THIS STATIONERY IS HANDY SO I THOUGHT I'D
WRITE AND LET YOU KNOW ABOUT THINGS IN GENERAL SINCE I HAVE
THE TIME AND OPPORTUNITY.*

Dear Ma and Pa,

I received the box of cookies, etc., Wednesday. It arrived in good shape.
Thanks a lot. They are very good! I also received a box of candy from
Pearl so be sure to thank her for me as I probably won't have much time
to write her myself.

Now for the news of the week. I got alerted this last week for
shipment. I am going to Fort Sam Houston on the other side of town
for eight weeks of training. It is the medics. One of the reasons I didn't
try to get into an office somewhere is that all of those who applied
for clerk etc., are sitting checking individuals' forms as they arrive
and leave. And they will be doing the same thing for a couple of years.
When I have been assigned to some semi-permanent station, I shall
start looking around to see just what kind of a deal I can get but to do
so before I know exactly what I am getting into would be foolish as I
would run too great a risk of getting placed in an obscure corner.

Today I "processed" which means a final check to see if all my
records are in proper order. They were, so there won't be any strain
as far as that is concerned. I shall be paid $30 Monday and will leave
some time Tuesday probably. Knowing the way they do things, it will
probably be in the middle of the night. From the $30, I'll buy a traveling
bag to pack my uniforms and what with the duffle bag, I'll have enough
room without having to carry loose odds and ends.

Thanksgiving we had the day off, which was quite pleasant. We had

---

* Handwritten note on American Red Cross stationery.

a good meal for a change and they even gave us a package of cigarettes, which was very welcome.

This last week, outside of Thursday, has been just about the same as the week before except I haven't had any guard duty at night, which is a relief, but I shall probably draw it tonight as I haven't done anything today.

Guard duty here is determined by the training officer(s) of the squadron (3703), as is the entire program for the casuals. For our squadron, this man (or men; I haven't been able to place the blame on any one person) must be pushing for a promotion as he has (they have) us all over the base doing various details and his (or their) regulations covering barracks guards are about the strictest I have come across.

While there is absolutely no need for night guard duty walking the streets (as they are patrolled by AP's in jeeps) the barracks guard does perform a useful function in keeping out unauthorized personnel from the barracks and thus cuts down chances for theft. In addition, each barracks is connected to the orderly room by an intercom system and he answers when they might want someone—which is quite often. But this business about not being allowed to sit down, smoke or read is strictly a local ruling that has absolutely no valid reason behind it.

I have no idea just what it means, but when checking through my records this morning, I saw where I had been accepted for OCS and would not be sent overseas. As near as I can figure, I won't be shipped overseas for some time (for sure) and that business about being accepted for OCS probably means that I am just another qualified applicant they can call on when and if the occasion warrants. At best I know they have my name down, which is something around here.

I also received the pass, Pa, and thanks. I'll see just what I can find out about Christmas and let you know. Keep writing here and I'll let you know my new address as soon as possible.

Love,
Peter

Interim training as a medic

Thursday, December 7, 1950
Company B, Third Battalion, Medical Field Service School
Fort Sam Houston; San Antonio, Texas

Dear Ma and Pa,
I have this free stationery, so I thought I would write and help straighten you as to my present position. I guess that the telephone connections sometimes left something to be desired—hence the confusion about the address.

The course here is under Army supervision—the Air Force having some sort of training arrangement whereby we are trained under the Army program and then sent back to Air Force assignments. We have eight weeks of courses, eight hours a day; there are a variety of courses: atomic energy, anatomy and physiology, emergency medical treatment etc., plus courses in Army procedure and property and supply, which are pretty interesting for the most part.

Here we get up at around 5:15 to 5:30, eat at 6:00 and fall out for class around 7:15 to 7:30; clean up the area and start class at 8:00. Lunch is at 12 and classes again from 1 till 5. We have to dress up for dinner which certainly is a pain. Lights go out at 9 but we don't have to be in until 11. In all, it is much better than over at Lackland because we are busy all the time and are learning something. Also, they let us alone to do what we want in the evenings.

So far, most of the instructors (1st lieutenants and captains) have been good, which is a blessing. But right now, we are supposed to be having anatomy and haven't had a thing to do with it for an hour. The captain is really a fool. I have never heard of such a stupid person who passed himself off as an instructor.

Tuesday and Wednesday, we had a strong north wind here again and it really was cold. Last night the wind dropped down which is a good thing because it got down to 16 degrees last night which was the low for the season so far. From what I have been able to gather, there is a drought here this year and we are more than due for some rain.

Now, about the plane. I received the bank draft, Pa, yesterday evening, so there is no trouble there. Thanks a lot. I had planned to go to town this Saturday to see the ticket agent about the extra section. But I have some type of guard duty then, so I shall call up there tomorrow between 5 and 6. If they have no word yet, I'll call Sunday sometime, and then Monday. If they don't know by that time, I'll call some other time and if that doesn't work out, I'll call you up to see just what you can do at that end. However, if I find I do have a reservation, I'll go to town on Monday at five and pay them before they close at 6. However, by the time you get this, I probably shall have called you, so all of this will be old news.

Well, I have a quiz tomorrow, so I had better study. Take care of yourselves.

Love,
Peter

The logistics of Christmas

Wednesday, December 13, 1950
Company B, Third Battalion, Medical Field Service School
Fort Sam Houston; San Antonio, Texas

Dear Ma, and Pa,
I thought that I would write and give you the word about some of the questions you have asked in the last letter.

First, addresses for the Christmas cards. I would like the addresses for the following people:

Doug Graham,

Couch,

Strowbridge,

Phaon,

Colin MacKay (his home in town would be OK),

the Georges.[1]

I think that I have all of my friends (of my age) but I was wondering about some of the older people I should send a card to. If you could make any suggestions, I would certainly appreciate it.

If Father has his heart set on *Holiday* instead of *Fortune,* I suppose that you had better go ahead and get that for him. I just thought that *Fortune* was not only entertaining, but at the same time somewhat enlightening. Just about everything that comes out in *Holiday* is also to be found in some issue of *National Geographic.*

About Ann's present: I think that it should be fairly easy to find something nice for around five to six dollars. If you could get her a couple of good books whereby she could improve her mind, and at the same time would prove interesting to her, I think that would be just fine.

Am I correct in assuming that I still have an account with you? If so, will it cover all these expenses? And if not, please tell me how much I am in debt.

---

1. Peter refers to personal and family friends, as well as his cousins.

About Father's Christmas gift to me. For some time, I have been thinking about the war bonds and lately, I have come to the conclusion that I would just as soon stop having much to do with them. If you want a reason, I have two which seem to settle the matter as far as I am concerned.

FIRST: The general overall effect of war bonds upon the economy is strictly inflationary. To aid this general trend would be foolish because it would further tend to decrease the relative value of those already in my possession. If the government needs more money (as it certainly does and will continue to need in greater amounts), let it secure this money by less inflationary methods.

SECOND: In times of inflation, my fixed investment is an especially poor one for obvious reasons. Since I rather doubt if there will be any chance of any counteracting deflation, I would just as soon get out from under and have my limited means tied up in some sort of investment that would tend to follow general economic trends. If Father wants to buy me something useful for Christmas, a presentable pair of blue suspenders would come in very handy here as my trousers do not fit well with a belt. If he further has his mind set on a present, a share of some type of good stock would be very practical and welcome. I guess that just about takes care of Christmas and the general economic situation of the country, so I shall turn to more varied subjects.

Life here has settled down to a fairly regular routine but as we are busy most of the time and as I have a little more time for sleep and myself, it is much more bearable. We have our regular seven hours of classes every weekday and the inspection on Saturday morning. Last Saturday, the general inspected us and it couldn't have caused more excitement and panic than the second coming of Christ. It was really funny, how perturbed some of the people get around here; even the older non-coms.

The high spot of the whole thing came Friday evening when the first-sergeant came around checking to make sure we had waxed our floors. (They are of composition tile and take a nice shine). He came in muttering in his beard and slipped on the floor. Needless to say, he didn't get after us for not having waxed the floors.

One of the birds in the barracks flew the coup last night and the first-sergeant was rather perturbed about that today. What with

Christmas leaves being cancelled, I suppose there will be a decided increase in that sort of thing for a couple of weeks.

Today, our battalion had to stand retreat parade for the general. While it was a lot of trouble changing clothes and standing around, it was something a little bit different, so it wasn't too bad but I hope they don't make a practice of it. It is awfully dusty tromping over the fields around here. The weather remains fairly clear and dry. Nor does there seem to be any prospect of rain in the near future.

I forgot to mention over the phone the other night that I would also like you to send me my belt along with my clothes. It is rather essential, and I do not want to have to buy another one.

Your trip sounds like could be a lot of fun and I'm glad that you have found someone like the Wilcoxes to go along with.[2] I'm sure it will add a lot to your trip. But I don't want either of you to go climbing around various steep places. To do so would be extremely foolish. Just take it easy and do all of your sightseeing sitting down. It is much easier that way. I only wish I knew where I will be at that time, but I have no idea, nor could I find out. I shall just have to let you know somewhere along the line, I guess.

Well, they are closing the place, so I shall have to close. I haven't anything else to report this time anyhow.

Love,
Peter

---

2. The Wilcoxes were family friends.

Christmas in Texas

Thursday, December 28, 1950
Company B, Third Battalion, Medical Field Service School
Fort Sam Houston; San Antonio, Texas

Dear Ma and Pa and Ann,

Boy, I really have been disorganized for some reason lately. I don't know where the time has gone but I simply haven't gotten around to writing, for which I feel badly. Maybe the extra stamps will speed things a little. I've been trying to call you ever since Saturday but with no luck. All we have here are about three telephones for several thousand men, which is inconvenient, to say the least.

Christmas was rather uneventful—went to town and got caught up on my sleep. Here I had been bothered by a cold in my eyes for several days and as a result, I wasn't feeling too hot. But they are all right now. However, now I have a lulu of a cold, so I think I'll probably stay around again this weekend. I feel quite poorly but I will probably be OK in a few days.

I received all the packages you sent. They were fine. Thanks a lot. I don't know how much longer we will be allowed to wear civilian clothes, but I'll try to get them home in case they are forbidden. The food was especially good and was a good arrangement.

Yesterday I received the suspenders; they are just fine. The trousers I have are a bit too big but will be just about right when I wear them.

I also received cigarettes from the Monroes and the Strowbridges. Would you please thank them—as I rather doubt I'll have the time to write.

Your presents for Pa and Ann seemed especially good, Ma. Thanks a lot. I only wish your choice of Christmas cards was as appropriate but maybe this year they were presentable.

I also received the candy and check from Pearl and tell her that I'll write later but not to hold her breath. In addition, you will find a check from Bill Test.* Would you please deposit it to my account? It is just about impossible to get a personal check cashed around here. I only hope I'll never have to get one cashed in order to get along. Anything in uniform in this town is mud, but then seeing some who are in the Army, I hardly blame anyone for their attitude toward the services.

It never ceases to amaze me the great number of absolutely worthless people—a great number of them coming from the South. It should have been permitted to secede. (I think you had better send me my dictionary. I continually feel lost without it.)

I also got the French flashcards Ann sent. They are very good. Thanks also [for] the Chappies. I certainly have been hitting the jackpot lately so as far as the mail is concerned. I only wish I had done better as far as my correspondence was concerned.

I have barracks guard today and am writing this on a footlocker, which accounts, to a large degree (I hope), for the scrawl.

As far as companions are concerned, there really isn't anyone special with whom I have been going around. Don't worry about it for fear I'm missing out on things, because I'm not. I already told you about Rickert.

Well, I can't think of much else to report so I guess I'll close. It is getting to be about lunchtime. The food here continues to be much better than at Lackland. Last Friday, I had KP for the first time. However, there isn't any difference in KP. I just can't seem to adjust myself, I guess.

Will write later,

Love,

Peter

---

* William A. ("Bill") Test (1914–1994) was a paternal cousin. Family legend had it that during World War II, Bill's commanding officer received a letter from Mrs. Test saying that her son needed a good pillow.

"From what I hear, Lackland is really a mess."

Tuesday, January 2, 1951
Company B, Third Battalion, Medical Field Service School
Fort Sam Houston; San Antonio, Texas

Dear Ma and Pa,

Well, after last week's mistake of not writing more often, I thought I would get on the ball and write a little early.

The weekend was rather uneventful so far as any "big doings" were concerned. However, I did manage to amuse myself in such a manner that time did not hang heavily on my shoulders. I have always had plenty to do so I am never at a loss for some type of activity which certainly is something to be thankful for.

Friday night, as always, we spent shining shoes and straightening footlockers in preparation for inspection from eight to ten Saturday morning. We have two hours of class and then are free for a day-and-a-half. Saturday evening another fellow and myself (Bill Rehm by name but I don't see that that makes any difference at all) went to the symphony here in town. It really was quite good; I suppose you read where the regular conductor died here a couple of weeks ago. Strohovsky was the first substitute—having already been signed up—and last Saturday, the first violinist conducted—and considering everything, seemed to me to do a good job but for all I know, he may have been quite poor.

It seems to be the custom here to pass out free tickets to servicemen—by people who can't make it but have already purchased their tickets. I lucked out and got a front seat which in addition to a saving, was quite pleasant. Had a couple of beers afterward and came back.

Sunday, the same guy and I went to the movies in town, ate a couple of times, checked around the tattoo parlors, drank some beer, and came back. The other guy had been wanting the tattoos—not me, so don't worry. I'll let you know when I get one.

It rained quite hard here Sunday night which made things nice and fresh the next day. It was a good thing as they need water here in the worst way. Everything sure is dried up here. It came from the south, so it was nice and warm.

From what I hear, Lackland is really a mess. They have tents all over. They also have men in all the classrooms, a couple of the warehouses, and have even converted one of the two big service clubs for barracks. Basic training there—or rather what is left of it—is now two weeks, so you can imagine just what they do with them; I guess it is little more than shots and clothes and the articles of war before they ship out. They are sending quite a few of them overseas for OJT (on the job training). I got out of there just in time, it seems.

I got paid today—$70, which puts me just about right when I consider the $1.20 from last month and then something for the 30th and 31st of August. I wish I knew just who figures out the payroll, so I would find out just where I stand. I'm afraid they will find out something is wrong and pay me something like $27 some month. That really would be a blow.

I'm going to try and buy a radio tomorrow. All anyone who has a radio ever seems to play is damn cowboy music. I don't mind telling you I'm all through with that stuff. There ought to be a law against it.

We leave here the last of this month. Don't worry about not knowing where I'll be for I'll at least be able to drop you a postcard before I leave and may be able to call you. I'm afraid I won't be able to find out just where I am going until a day or two before I leave—and probably not my address until I arrive, judging from what I have been able to gather. It would be a help if you could give me some idea where I could get in touch with you so if I am stationed somewhere in this neck of the woods, you would know about it before you finish your trip.

In past classes, there seem to be about one-third of classmates being assigned to air evacuation of the wounded—quite a boom in that, these days. Others are being assigned overseas via ports of embarkation and then to bases here in the U.S. About one-third each, if I were to make a wild guess. Will write lots.

Love,

Peter

From paycheck to paycheck

[Undated letter postmarked Saturday, January 6, 1951]
Company B, Third Battalion, Medical Field Service School
Fort Sam Houston; San Antonio, Texas

PAY

Sept 5 . . . . $30.00   insurance @ $6.60/month for Sept, Oct, Nov, Dec
Oct 25. . . . $30.00
Nov 10 . . . $30.00
Nov 27 . . . $30.00 $26.40
Dec 11 . . . $84.00   Pay @ $75 / month for 4 months = $300.00
Jan 2. . . . . $70.00
            $274.00
            $26.40
            $300.40 total = $300.00

The 40 cents difference I believe can be accounted for by the 30th and 31st of August during which I drew pay at the rate of approximately $2.50 a day. ($75/30 days)

Therefore, I still have $4.60 due me but which I doubt I'll ever see. However, I do believe they may be carrying a couple of dollars on my account, as they do not pay any change—just to the dollar.

Enclosed is a clipping I thought you would be interested in, in verification of my last letter.

Love,
Peter

In case I don't get a chance to
call you or if I do and you can't
understand well, I've been
transferred, and my address is now
    O/C Peter Koerner AF19382126
    FLT B OCS
    3700 OC TGN. SQ.
    Lackland Air Force Base
    San Antonio, Texas
Will write lots as soon as I have
time, am busy!
    Love,
    Peter

POSTCARD

Back to Lackland

Tuesday, January 16, 1951
Lackland Air Force Base; San Antonio, Texas

Dear Ma and Pa,
When I wrote and said I was busy, I didn't know the half of it. This is the first time I've had to myself in a week and even at that, there are several things I have to do this evening. Arriving here late as I did—by a week—made things pretty difficult but I think I'm just about caught up at the present time. Classes didn't start until yesterday, so I didn't miss much there but in the previous week, there were orientation lectures and policy discussions that I missed.

What is especially difficult are the inspections—I don't seem to be neat enough for them but I'm gradually shaping up, I hope. I've been trying to phone you the last couple of nights but there has been either no time or a long line.

It is quite a long story about my sudden transfer. The Tuesday morning before Christmas, I was told over at the other place that I was being transferred over here and that my orders would arrive either that day or the next Friday. I thought I would wait until I actually received them before I notified you. Well, I waited but nothing came of it and since it was such a late date before I was notified, I figured I was an alternate and that in the meantime that other bird had decided to accept or something like that and I would not hear.

I was quite discouraged about the whole thing and did not feel I should bother you about it, so I didn't say anything about it at the time. I did finally receive the orders on the 9th. It turns out that they were not made out until the 2nd of January; why the 7-day delay, I don't know, but that makes no difference now.

The barracks here are of the same design as those over at Fort Sam Houston with the exception that here they have been partitioned off into cubicles with two to a cubicle of about 12 feet by 15.

In case you are interested, here is a rough design.* There are 12 such arrangements on both floors (downstairs a little different)—six to a side. While it seems to be a little small on paper, it is huge when it comes to cleaning every morning. They are really strict about the displays in the footlockers and shelves—and tomorrow all the demerits start counting.

They work the school on a class system—an upper and a lower. On March 10, the present upper-class graduates and then we became upper-classmen. Although this is less than three months, they have been here the full time—just due to some kind of a change-over in times past. It is up to the upper class to shape up the new men. They are quite fair about everything, which makes things much nicer than they otherwise could be.

The others here in the lower class (#51B) are a good bunch of guys— about five or six of them are married—about half come directly in from civilian life and a couple of others have been in the service two and three years. But I'll write more about them as I get to know them better.

As far as classes are concerned, so far they have been more or less introductory, and I haven't been able to find out just what we do have and how much of each. We do go to class about six or seven hours a day and then have drill and parades a few hours a week, but as yet there doesn't seem to be any set pattern that I can find out. This, too, I'll let you know about.

Make out a list of questions and I'll answer them for you, as I'm sure there are many things you are wondering about that I wouldn't think to mention.

As yet, I haven't received any of the old mail, but I did get your first letter. It won't be long before you leave. Perhaps you had better send me another itinerary in case the other gets lost. Don't work too hard getting ready. Will try to write this weekend.

Love,
Peter

---

* Drawn sketch of the cubicle with a handwritten note: "Furniture is a little too small."

Early impressions of Officer Candidate School

Tuesday, January 23, 1951
Lackland Air Force Base; San Antonio, Texas

Dear Ma and Pa,
I thought I had better get on the ball and get a letter off to you. First, about the names of the hotels you should stay at in San Antonio. The Menger seems to be about as nice as any and it has a nice quiet location—across the street from the Alamo and about three blocks from the center of town. Or you could try the Gunter which is in the center of town– also nice but probably much noisier than the other. Both are centrally located, so there isn't too much strain there.[1]

However, I would certainly advise your making reservations in advance. If you could give me an idea just when you would be here, it would be easy to get accommodations for you. I could phone in and then send them a check. I would have plenty of time so there is no worry there.

The town, needless to say, is very crowded so you would be wise to tend to this sometime in advance. I've had a little bad luck on the inspections lately—things keep coming up I've not heard of before but I'm not getting caught on many things more than once or twice so in a couple of weeks I shouldn't have anything to worry about. They certainly are fussy—takes about an hour each morning.

As far as the classes are concerned, there is no set time for them. We don't know from one minute to the next exactly what we are going to have. So far, we have had quite a bit of drill and several hours of PT (which isn't too bad). As for class—academic—we have English, maps, mess management, organization of the Air Force, and teaching procedures.

---

1. These two San Antonio hotels survived into the 21st Century, although at some point the Gunter had become the Sheraton Gunter.

Later we will be having other classes. They keep us on the go all the time which makes it nice, but we go to between 10 and 10:30 and get up at 4:30 so I'm not getting as much sleep as I'm accustomed to by any means. There is no one here whom I ran across before. Most of the fellows in this flight are from the East or the South. Salt Lake or Santa Fe being as far west.

I got the dictionary—thanks—it arrived in good shape.

You mentioned that Tom Sammons announced his engagement but neglected to say to whom.[2]

Well, outside of the weather, which is from 30 to 45 in the evenings and night to the 70's in the daytime—there is little else to report. I'll send you more news when I get more of your questions.

Love,

Peter

---

2. Thomas Knapp Sammons (1929–1967) was a family friend. He would become an insurance agent—and die in a plane crash.

An impending visit from his parents

Sunday, February 11, 1951
Lackland Air Force Base; San Antonio, Texas

Dear Ma and Pa,
Well, by this time I imagine that you are fairly well rested up, what
with two weeks on board the ship, with a little exercise in the way of
gardening, etc.

Well, this last week (or rather two now) has been much busier than
any of the preceding. The classes have become a little more involved
and hence I have had to study more than the first two weeks. We
are still taking about the same courses with one exception: we are
now in military geography (in place of maps and charts). It is a new
course here, but it is very interesting. It is just about the same thing
as geo-politics. This next week we start in on Supply, which takes the
place of Mess Management. That will certainly be a relief, as the Mess
Management course was rather dull, and the instructor was not at
all interested in teaching the course; he just read the course from the
outline they handed out to us.

This Supply course is one of the main ones here and will carry us
through for quite a while. I believe that there are around 70 hours of it,
but I am not sure.

I made your reservations at the Menger Hotel for Saturday and
Sunday nights. The man I talked to over the phone said that you would
be able to take over sometime before noon in case you arrived here
before then.

I had a little bad luck last week, so I am working off hours today, but
it really isn't too bad. I think that this should be about my last week
for that kind of business, as I seem to be getting organized all of the
time. I managed to pick up a lulu of a cold yesterday and have run out of
handkerchiefs today but outside of that, I am in pretty good shape.

I suppose that you heard of all the bad weather we had the other day.
I can't seem to remember if I mentioned that to you when I talked to
you or not. If I did, you might just as well stop reading this paragraph.
It got down to 5 degrees here and was below freezing for about three

days. Needless to say, it was quite uncomfortable; it even snowed here. While it was less than an inch, it did stay on the ground for two days, so you can see how cold it was. From all the noise made in the newspapers and over the radio, you would think that this was one of the wonders of the world. Real funny.

This typewriter belongs to the barracks as near as I can figure and is probably one of the last ones of its model in existence. The keys are continually getting stuck. And most of them are bent to a degree, which accounts in part for the mistakes. Also, my nose is running, which seems to make it harder.

Strange but I can't seem to think of much to report today. However, I shall write later and tell you everything I forgot. Don't try to do too much. Have a good time.

Love,

Peter

A fountain pen, a dance, and a dictionary

Monday, February 19, 1951
Lackland Air Force Base; San Antonio, Texas

Dear Ma and Pa,

I received your letters mailed from Balboa.* It took them just three-and-a-half days which is pretty good considering everything. From what I gather, the trip seems to be very restful, but I hope the seas were not too heavy for you.

As you might gather, I lost my fountain pen and am using a borrowed one. It really gripes me to lose something like that!

As far as things around here are concerned, they are about the same and I'm just as busy. Last weekend, I did not have any extra duty, so I got caught up on a little rest which was quite welcome. Went to town and did a little shopping and came back. Went to the movies here in the evening and had a couple of drinks over at the OCS club. I've never lived so close to a bar before and find that it does have its advantages—convenient, to say the least!

The present upper-class graduates in just 18 days. This Saturday we officially become upper-classmen, so we won't have to go through as much funny stuff as far as they are concerned, which will be a relief. We will have a lot more time for ourselves. As it is now, a couple of nights a week we have to do an hour's work around here. The new class will move in about the 2nd of April. So, we will be to ourselves around here for a couple of weeks.

Last Wednesday there was a Valentine's dance here that was the main event of last week. I didn't think too much of it, though, but it wasn't too bad.

The weather here has been a little different lately. One day it will be clear and up in the 70's and the next day it will be cloudy with a chance of rain.

---

* Possibly Balboa, Panama.

Right now, the papers are forecasting more rain, which will certainly be a relief. Last week we also had a big sleet storm. It turned cold, so it lasted on the ground for a couple of days. The weather certainly is variable here.

Well, that is about all I can think of to report for this time. I shall probably be seeing you before I get another chance to write. Have a good time and take it easy.

Love,

Peter

San Antonio: "strictly small-time"

Tuesday, March 20, 1951
Lackland Air Force Base; San Antonio, Texas

Dear Ma and Pa,
I seem to be more than behind schedule this week. I'm sorry—I don't have any idea of just where the time has gone.

Car trip to Houston was very pleasant. While we didn't have much time, we managed to do a fair amount of sightseeing. Houston is a much cleaner city than San Antonio. It seems to have been built with some planning behind it.

San Antonio is strictly small-time in comparison. One nice thing about it is that there are very few service personnel wandering about town. However, we cut the time-estimate a little close for comfort on the return trip. We made it back with just six minutes to spare, which is pretty good considering it is a 200-mile trip.

This last week has been rather uneventful as far as anything new is concerned but I have been pretty busy with the courses. We had our regular test yesterday. I spent most of the last week getting ready for it.

I got a letter from Ann today, and I was quite amused by her description of her courses and term paper. Somehow, she just doesn't seem the type to be writing a large paper on foreign policy. She sounded almost as if she were interested in it. I only hope she doesn't start any World Rescue organization.

I received the candy you sent today. It arrived in good shape and tastes fine. I also received the wallet! Thanks a lot for both.

I was quite surprised to hear of all the snow that greeted you on your return. I hope that by now your colds have run their complete course.

I think that there is something about this locality that is conducive to colds.

Well, it is getting late. I'll write later.
Love,
Peter

"Pink forms" for background checks

Wednesday, March 21, 1951
Lackland Air Force Base; San Antonio, Texas

Dear Ma and Pa,

Big Deal. I am Officer Candidate Officer of the Day tonight, so I have plenty of time and the facilities to write you a letter. The one last night was rather sketchy. I imagine you were wondering just what was the deal having two letters in a row. I admit it doesn't happen very often.

My duty here entails mostly just making sure that everything-in-general is in order. If the occasion should present itself, I could make out emergency-leave papers but that is about all that can happen, I hope. This together with OG and CQ are the main duties we all have to draw but as there are a couple of hundred to draw from, we don't get it too much.

This weekend it seems that almost all of the AP's are having some type of party somewhere and will not be able to assume their regular duties, so we all have to draw it for them. I have no idea just what that will entail but I hope that I don't get a walking or a directing traffic detail. We are on duty from Saturday afternoon until Sunday morning at 7:30.

One of the things I forgot to mention when you were here was that when I first came out, I had to fill out some personal history forms (the so-called "pink forms") and on them, I had to give some references.

For references, I gave Mr. Sammons, Mr. Buland, Mr. Stevenson, Monty, and Mr. Cooper.* Do you think that I should write and tell them that I took the liberty of giving them as references or should I skip the whole thing? However, I imagine that by now there is a pretty good chance that they have already been contacted. One of the men in the next barracks had his pink forms bounce somehow and he was

---

* Peter refers to family friends, among them his future father-in-law, George L. Buland (1897–1975).

immediately removed from the school. It was quite sudden, and he certainly was the last person I would ever have guessed to have had something wrong with his past or something. It was quite interesting what with the speed they moved him out and all the rumors that were spread about it. No one seems to know for sure just what was the trouble.

A couple of weeks ago, we filled out a form that stated our preference for assignment after we graduate. We got three choices of jobs in various fields. The last class got the same deal and about 80% got one of their three choices, which was pretty good considering everything.

For my first choice, I put in for a special investigations officer in the intelligence field. It is supposed to be a good job and very interesting.

For my second choice, I asked for transportation officer, which I thought would be a job with some fairly practical sides. It supposedly has to do with the arrangement of both air and rail transport. It too should be pretty interesting.

The third choice was exchange officer—who does the purchasing and manages the operations of a PX. One of the men in the upper-class barracks got this job and he said that from what he heard it was supposed to be a good one and also quite practical.

Of course, it would be rather silly to count on any of these assignments, but I do hope I can get them. We are rather limited in our range of jobs when we get out of here. There are only certain fields they will let a 2nd lieutenant enter. Procurement would have been the ideal one but there are absolutely no positions available. I only hope that I don't get assigned a job in the training command. That would be really miserable.

Starting this week, we dropped a couple of courses and started a couple of new ones. Rather, I should say that we finished a couple. We are all through with Military Management for a while. When we get to Practical Application about the last 6 or 8 weeks, we will have some management audits. In its place we have a course in military leadership, which has the earmarks so far of being a pretty good course.

We also finished our Intelligence and Military Geography and now have Air Defense, which is very interesting. The Air Force is absolutely sure, according to this class, that we will be attacked, and that more than likely it will come over the North Pole.

Well, that seems to be about all that I can think of to report for the time being. I guess that I am just about caught up with all of the past news that might interest you.

Pa, I have been wondering about the income tax correction we talked about when you were here. Did you decide that it wouldn't be enough to bother about or just what? I thought that you mentioned something about sending me another form to sign and send in. But I imagine that it is a little late to be thinking about that now.

I can't think of much else, so I shall close. I'm trying to get caught up on a little correspondence this evening.

Love,

Peter

PS: I haven't forgotten about Ann. Is there anything she especially wants? Otherwise, I shall send her a book the first time I have the chance. —PK

AP duty

Monday, March 26, 1951
Lackland Air Force Base; San Antonio, Texas

Dear Ma and Pa,

I couldn't find any stationery envelopes for the other letter so that is the reason for its delay.

The AP duty came out pretty well. They called for volunteers for the various posts and there were enough to take care of all the jobs, so I didn't have to pull any guard.

I just happened to think that I may have neglected to thank you for the wallet. It is very nice.

It started raining last night and has rained hard most of the day. Everything sure is wet as there is absolutely no drainage here—big puddles all over the place.

I tried to call home yesterday, but all of the circuits were busy, so I'll try again, anyhow.

Had quite a restful day yesterday—slept till around 10—went to town around noon and went to the smorgasbord at the Sunta and ate for a couple of hours, saw a movie, ate again, and came back and went to bed.

Well, I can't think of much else to report this time. Over the last two weeks before the test last Monday I came up from 140 to 61, which isn't too bad.*

Will write later.

Love,

Peter

---

* Possibly a ranking system.

A bad day—and listening to General MacArthur's farewell speech

Wednesday, April 18, 1951
Lackland Air Force Base; San Antonio, Texas

Dear Ma and Pa,

Little news this week, but I thought that I would write you while you were on your trip. By the time you get this, I'm afraid that you will be just about ready to leave for home but better late than never. Since I last wrote, it has continued to be warm with this afternoon being about as hot as any day so far.

The second class is getting fairly well squared away and we don't have to spend so much time on them. They got club privileges last weekend, so they could get rid of a little of their money over there. This evening most of them are out to the movies—which is a good deal for them as they have only been here a couple of weeks. They started regular classes this week, so they don't have to be watched all the time.

This last week I ordered both of my uniforms—a set of blue gabardines and a set of the new silver-tans. I got them at the PX as they were cheaper and were not worth the extra amount having them tailored downtown. A week or so ago I ordered a set of tailor-made slacks and shirt which look pretty good. I'm going to pick them up tomorrow if they don't need anything done to them. I also got a pair of shoes. This should leave me about enough to get a new hat out of the $250 uniform allowance we get when we graduate from here.

It is now the next day. I got delayed. Right after I wrote you last, I ran across Dick Schutte.[1] He got a direct commission and is here being processed for his assignment, which takes about a month what with all the tests and interviews they give them. He came over last night

---

* Dick Schutte (1926–2008) was a fraternity brother at Stanford University. Schutte would later have a career in radio broadcasting before becoming a stockbroker.

and we went over to the club for a few beers and by the time I got back, there wasn't much time to do anything but get ready for bed.

Last night he said that he heard that Pete Mohler was enlisting and should be down here in a couple of weeks. He went over to Houston last weekend to see Dick Shelton, who is going to navigators' school at Ellington Field there.[2]

Today was very miserable as it got up to 99 this afternoon.

I had a really bad day today. The tactical officers came around and threw a purge. They really went through the place with a fine-tooth comb. I ended up with about five [demerits] which will put me on the ramp next week if I get any more, or if a couple come through that were due last week. They have been doing this to all of the other flights this week. I would like to know just what they are trying to prove by putting everyone on the ramp, but I can't quite figure it out. As it was, I came out about a little better than the average but that is slight compensation.

They don't have any more than an hour's work a day over there and they are really pressed for something to do. Everyone is really disgusted.

Three of those gigs were for a postcard that I left on the top of my wall locker and that I overlooked this morning when I was cleaning. Don't send me any more of them, as they are too easy to overlook.

Last Sunday afternoon and Monday I had CQ (charge of quarters) which meant that I answered the telephone in the TAC office and sent out various and sundry messages to anyone in the organization. It was quite a pain in the neck but not difficult in the least.

Tomorrow afternoon, we have the afternoon off. As near as I can figure, it is to allow us to go to town and see the San Antonio Festival. It is supposed to be pretty good, but I don't think we will take the time out to go to it. We have a paper coming up in one of the courses and are planning on going to the library in town and see what we can dig up

---

1. Dick Shelton (1929–1999) was a fraternity brother at Stanford University, as was Peter Mohler (1929–2018). Ellington Field later became Ellington Field Joint Reserve Base, shared by various military units and one civilian agency, NASA.

for it and then to go and pick up our uniforms. Anyhow, it is quite nice having the extra time off. I just can't figure out what prompted them to give us the time off. I sure will be glad when we get out of here as I am getting rather tired of it. Things are beginning to get a little on the old side.

I got your letter from New York today. I'm glad that you arranged it to have a little extra time to check around the city a little. I wish that I were able to be there with you. I imagine that the parade tomorrow will really be something and I hope that you will be able to see it from a fairly non-congested spot somewhere. I heard his speech today. It was really something. He certainly is a good and forceful speaker for a man of his age.[3]

I just wish he had laid it on a little thicker, but I imagine that it wouldn't have done any good as Truman is too thick to figure out anything more profound than a cold-water faucet.

Well, that is about all that I can think of to report at this time. Too bad about the mix-up in the reservations but it was fortunate that everything worked out as it did. How did that happen anyhow?

As long as things were not going too well with Suzie I'm glad that she gave him back his pin.[4] I thought that he was a little too much on the strange side anyhow.

We have been having PT about four hours a week lately and what with the nice weather, I should manage to pick up a tan, but I would just as soon do without and not have to take PT. It is a lot of bother washing clothing afterward. In addition, they are organized just enough to make the entire program confusing. I've just about reached the conclusion that anything to do with the government is completely and hopelessly a mess. I don't believe that there will ever be any great

————————

3. The references are to General Douglas MacArthur (1880–1964), who had recently been relieved of his command by President Truman and was about to be feted with a ticker-tape parade. The parade actually occurred not on April 19 but on April 20; presumably, Peter's parents were visiting New York for the occasion.

4. "Suzie" was a nickname for Peter's sister Ann (1930–1993). The "pin" in question refers to a courting ritual.

reformation that amounts to anything. Too many people have too many soft jobs as is well illustrated by the tactical officers around here.

That's about all for now. Thanks for the hairbrush but I haven't been able to find out yet just where I should display it, so I put it away for a while.

Love,
Peter

MacArthur's ticker-tape parade

Thursday, May 3, 1951
Lackland Air Force Base; San Antonio, Texas

Dear Ma and Pa,

I certainly am ashamed of myself for not having written sooner but this last week seems to have been exceptionally busy. Most of last week was spent studying for the phase test we had this last Monday. I did fairly well on that so that is one thing I don't have to worry about unduly.

Today we had a paper that was due for our English course and I spent the better part of a couple of evenings attending to that. I also had to write another paper and give a talk for our leadership course yesterday, so you can see that time certainly has not been dragging on my hands, at least this last week or so.

Today we went out on the firing range. We fired only for familiarization today and tomorrow for score. We fired 50 rounds with the M-1 carbine and 25 each with the .45 and the .45 caliber "grease gun," which is a machine gun.

In all it was interesting, but it was quite hot to be considered comfortable. The weather here these past couple of weeks has been warm-to-hot with a couple of showers and a little thunder. It is interesting. One day the humidity might be around 95 while the next it may be around 16. With the same temperature there is all the difference in the world. Today it was very high and as a result quite uncomfortable.

Your trip sounds like it was a good one and that you managed to get quite a bit of sight-seeing worked in along the way. It certainly was nice having someone like Mrs. De Nyse to show you around the area. You must have gotten a lot more out of it than if you had tried to do all of it yourself. Too bad Pa had to work as much as he did, but I guess that that is part of the deal.

From what I gathered here from the papers and the radio (both of which would be considered an absolute disgrace in any halfway-civilized community) the parade for MacArthur was one of the greatest spectacles of the century, with the great crowds. We all managed to hear his speech, which was one of the best I have ever heard or heard about.

It was quite interesting to get the reaction here of our instructors. They naturally were quite hesitant about making any comment on the entire situation but those that seem to be the most alert and intelligent of them seemed to be in more or less complete agreement. They really aren't in much of a position to say much that is not included on the study plan.

Everything is pretty well regulated and controlled around here. We have just 50 more days to go but it sounds better to say, "just next month." It certainly will be a relief as things have reached the point where they are assuming a rather ridiculous aspect.

For all intents and purposes, we are through with the more formal aspect of the training of going to classes six hours a day. Starting next week, we go on Practical Application, which is mostly a study of the various activities about the base. We get graded on this, but we are on teams which go out to the various organizations and study their functions firsthand.

In the past, this has been a rather easy program, but as far as anyone is able to figure, this time it had been more difficult as the word got back to the academic department somehow.

Texas is not on daylight savings time. However, in a couple of decades the word will probably reach them about it, and they might decide to look into it.

Last night we had a Phase Dance over at the non-coms club, which is just down the street from us. It was quite nice and was something different for a change.

From what I gather from Ann, she is still seeing Dave quite a bit. Perhaps I shall have to write her and give her a little good advice. I was glad to hear that she did quite well on grades this last quarter. I think that she has finally found the secret to success and she won't have too much trouble from now on if she doesn't get too careless.

My ears are really ringing from the firing range this afternoon. I hate to think what they will be like after tomorrow.

I'm glad to hear that Pa is finally venturing out with the car alone but I hope that it doesn't reach that point where there is the problem of who is going to get it next.

I received the candy and the handkerchiefs that you sent me, and I enjoyed them very much. The candy was very good, and the handkerchiefs were just what I needed, and they arrived just in time to save me a separate washing.

Saw Peter Mohler the other day. He is in a temporary basic squadron over on the other side of the base prior to being sent on up to Sheppard Field (about 300 miles to the north of here) for his basic training.[1] Schutte is leaving in a few days for March Field outside of LA for his assignment as a personnel officer.[2] He is about the luckiest person I have ever come across.

As it turned, I didn't get on the ramp last weekend. One of the offenses was not my fault and the other one did not count as much as I thought it would, so I came out of that OK. Starting today we are on a three-demerit week which really puts the bind on us all, but as we have gotten fairly well used to the program, and barring many surprises and tough inspections, there shouldn't be too much strain. Especially since we do most of the inspections ourselves.

Starting this week, we also have Open Post every night of the week until 11:30, which means we can go to town if we feel like it from 4:00 to 11:30, which is quite nice. I went in Monday. We also got paid Monday. I can see what they mean when they say it is impossible to save any money in the service. I deposited $50 in the bank and spent about all of it before the month was over.

Well, that seems to be about all that I can think of to report this time. If there is anything that you would like to know, I'll try and straighten you out.

I'm enclosing the money for the steak knives. Thanks a lot. Ron said that his mother was quite delighted with them.

Love,

Peter

---

1. Sheppard Air Force Base is near Wichita Falls, Texas.

2. March Air Reserve Base is located in Riverside County, California.

Logistics of a trip home

Sunday, May 13, 1951
Lackland Air Force Base; San Antonio, Texas

Dear Ma and Pa,

Well, there isn't too much to report this week, especially after talking to you last night. I figured that I had better try and get the call through then as I didn't know if there would be much of a chance today. As it was, I had to wait about an hour for it. Telephoning from around here is really a strain, as there are only a couple of phones handy here.

As far as the school is concerned, we are now on Practical Application—which I mentioned previously. This last week we made a tour of a supply room of one of the basic squadrons on the other side of the base. For PA we are divided up into teams of five, each with one of the members acting as captain each week. It is his duty to assign various aspects of the problem to the members of the team for them to report to the instructor when it comes time to present the study.

I was captain for the first week; I am glad, as that is one thing that I have behind me. As far as I am concerned, the presentation was very good but then I am not giving out the grades and the instructor wasn't telling what he thought about the presentation, which seems to me to be a little ridiculous but then so does a lot of the stuff around here. He is a civilian instructor (of which there are about three in the English department) and didn't know a thing about supply, so it wasn't much of a strain as for some whose advisers were continually asking embarrassing questions all week through the presentations. The one problem or observation took all week.

This next week we have a small problem each day. We solve it in the morning and then give our solution in the afternoon. As yet we don't know just how they are going to explain it to us the first thing in the morning.

At the present time, we have just 40 days left here and then I'll be home, so you can tentatively figure on getting the appointment sometime during the week following the 22nd of June. As yet, I have no idea of just where I am going to be sent but it should be made known in about two or three weeks at which time I'll give you a more definite schedule. I imagine I'll fly home but how long I'll have will depend upon how much delay en route they will give me to my next base in addition to the 10 days leave that is usually allowed. At that time, I shall have accumulated 25 days leave-time, but they would not allow my taking all of it then.

I imagine that I still have to ship some of my stuff home via the RR or Express and take the rest of it with me. A lot of it I won't be needing so I shall leave it at home. I'll take what civilian clothes I want with me in the car when I leave. Right now, I am afraid that I am going to be pressed for room once I get the new uniforms that I have ordered.

Well, that is about all I can think of to report this time. The days are beginning to drag a little, so I got a book from the library the other day. I sure will be glad when this is all over as things are beginning to get as dull as anything.

Love,
Peter

The upcoming management audit

Tuesday, May 22, 1951
Lackland Air Force Base; San Antonio, Texas

Dear Ma and Pa,

I have a lot of work to do so this will of necessity have to be a short one. Besides, there is comparatively little to report on this last week. I was sorry to have not been able to talk to Pa the other night when I called but as you were way down in back I thought that I wouldn't bother you. I hope you had a nice birthday. I want to get you a book, but I couldn't find anything that I thought you might enjoy. I will just have to wait until I get home. As near as I can figure it, I must have a year's presents to get caught up with.

All of last week we worked on the Practical Application problems that they gave us. There are five of us on a team and we have a problem every day, which we divide up so each one has something to do. This week, PA is just about the same. However, instead of giving a problem each day we are grouping them up and giving them in two settings, so we have a little free time. However, I have to write a staff-study today, so I have no extra time. While we have been pretty busy this past week or so, it has been fairly interesting, so it is not too much of a strain.

Next week, for PA we have what they call the management audit. It is a survey of an organization with regard to good management principles as we learned in the Management course earlier here. It is a more formal report than what we have had heretofore and thus will be a little more work, but it only lasts about 3 days, so that is not too bad.

Here we work in teams of four. Each person is assigned some specific thing to look for and then we compile our findings and present a written observation upon the efficiency ratings of the organizations we observe. The organizations are notified ahead of time that we are coming. As a result, they have time to get out all of their work and organizational charts, etc., so it is usually fairly difficult to find anything terribly in error. It is sort of a laugh.

Our team is going down on the flying strip and observe a flight of medium attack bombers, which should really be interesting. It is a good thing that we didn't draw supply, as that is so complicated and boring it would be almost impossible to get out a decent report on it.

I heard yesterday that almost all of the assignments are in, but they are not going to give any of them out until they are all in—which should be sometime around the first of the month. They are waiting so there will be a big crowd when they finally decide to give them out. At least that is the only reason I can think of to hold off.

Well, outside of the weather, which has been very hot and sticky the past few days, that is about all that I can think of to report for the time being. We had a fire-drill last night and I lost a little sleep, so I am a bit tired today. Too bad I have so much to do; otherwise I could get a little nap in this afternoon. I'll write later and tell you just what has been going on when there is anything to report.

There are just 30 more days left. Tomorrow the number will be in the twenties, which will sound a little better. After the PA for next week we go to class for a couple of weeks to pick up a bunch of unrelated subjects like the organization of the Army and Navy and probably some more military law. There has been a big revision in the manual for courts martial and military law.*

Don't either of you try and do too much.

Love,

[Peter]

---

* Probably a reference to the Uniform Code of Military Justice. The UCMJ was passed by Congress on May 5, 1950 and signed into law by President Truman the next day.

The management audit—and a trip to Corpus Christie

Friday, June 1, 1951
Lackland Air Force Base; San Antonio, Texas

Dear Ma and Pa,

This last week sure has been a busy one and that is the main reason for the delay in my weekly letter. Last week we completed one of the more academic phases of Practical Application. It was strictly the classroom type of work. This week we had what is called the management audit—where we go out and observe an organization as far as their management is concerned.

For an organization to observe, the team I was on drew a maintenance squadron down on the flight line. It was very interesting. The one we visited maintained the two-engine-attack-type bombers that have been converted for carrying passengers and for pilots to maintain their flying proficiency. We were down there a couple of days and got to observe all of the various activities. It was about the most interesting phase of PA.

Our job was done Tuesday, for the most part, with a little to do yesterday. But as others had not finished and were using the typewriters around here, I did not have a chance to write you.

Last weekend, having stayed around here for a couple of weeks, we went down to Corpus Christie for the weekend. It was a lot of fun. We spent most of the time on the beach and as a result, I picked up a fairly good tan as I had been out a little during the PT program. The beaches are not as nice as on the West Coast. They are rather dirty, and they smell rather poorly. Everyone seems to fish around here, but judging from the numbers of dead fish, they don't eat any of the fish or even throw them back in. They do keep the sea trout and a couple of other kinds, but they don't catch many of them in proportion.

The surf is quite poor, the waves being small but as the water is warm it is nice to swim in. The only thing is the possibility of stepping on a stingray. They have a spine on the base of their tail that is long and narrow and sharply barbed, which makes it a poor thing to have rammed into you. In addition, they are a dirty fish, so there is usually poisoning along with the wound. We saw a man catch one of them. I think that was the first one I had ever seen. They certainly are ugly things.

We had the day off Wednesday and decided at the last moment to go down again for the day. It is about 150 miles from here, which really isn't too bad.

That is very interesting about the investigating they are doing on me. However, I don't think that it is an unusual amount. They really give a thorough sifting of everyone's background around here. I thought that it was funny about them going to the women. They seem to know their business!

As yet there is no word on the assignments. Now it seems that contrary to previous rumors, they are not in and that no one knows for sure when they are due. Someone said that we may not find out until the week we graduate. It is rather poor, as a person can't make any definite plans, even for when to leave here.

If the new station is not ready for us right away, so the leave and travel time come out even, there is a chance that we may have to wait around here a couple of days. That happened to a couple of guys in the previous class.

We got paid yesterday, which was a break, as I did not have a single cent left after going to the beach on Wednesday. I went into town last night and bought more socks and had dinner and then a couple of beers and came back to go to bed. Outside of that, there is little to report.

Love,

Peter

Days of rain and softball

Sunday, June 3, 1951
Lackland Air Force Base; San Antonio, Texas

Dear Ma and Pa,
Well, having written just a couple of days ago there really isn't much
to add this time but I thought that I would try and get on the schedule
again.

Friday, we had little to do except a short class on the management
audit and what it showed, which was actually little. In the afternoon
we had a couple of hours of PT and that was about all.

Saturday, we had a small parade in the morning, which was a
short one, and then we had what they called a field day. Each flight
participated in a track event, which was a lot more pleasant than the
usual inspection. There was also a softball game between one of the
flights and the tactical officers, which was a laugh.

In the afternoon, a couple of us went over to Randolph Field to see
a couple of cadets whom Masters knows, stopped downtown on the
way back, and did a little shopping and then came back and went to the
movies.* In all, quite a restful day.

This morning it started raining at about three and rained very
hard until about noon. From the radio reports, it was one of the worst
rainstorms in some time. There were about six inches of rain up to
noon in town, with it still raining a little bit. Things look very wet out
here. What with the rain, I slept late and stayed around here most of
the day.

I packed my duffel bag and shall try and get it off in a day or so. I
think that I shall have enough space for the rest of my uniforms. As it
was, I had to include my issued blue uniform in there, but it will be OK
again after a cleaning and pressing. It was dirty to begin with so there
isn't much harm that can come to it.

---

* Ron Masters (1926–2012) was in Peter's flight group at Officer Candidate
School. According to the class book, he was from Salt Lake City, Utah.

I heard yesterday from the personnel officer that some of our assignments are in for sure this time, but he has no idea when the rest will be in, so they can announce them. Almost all of the WAF assignments came in last week and they were given out. Almost all of them drew recruiting service in their own neck of the woods. What a deal they got, and they don't deserve it. They are so stupid that I don't see how they will ever get their quota even by lying. They really are a disgrace to the Air Force and everything else.

Well, we start classes again this week but only for about four hours. I'll write again if anything of interest comes up. I imagine that Ann is just about finished with school for this year.

Love,

Peter

Waiting for a permanent assignment

Monday, June 11, 1951
Lackland Air Force Base; San Antonio, Texas

Dear Ma and Pa,

Well, still no assignments but today there is an especially hot rumor to the effect that they will be in sometime before Saturday. In fact, some of them came through today. A couple of the men here in the barracks got theirs today. They both applied for Weather Officer. They are going to go to civilian university (MIT or UCLA) for a year and then serve three years after that so it amounts to about four-and-a-half years altogether.

I talked to a couple of the men who work up in the personnel office and they both said at different times and places that there were 29 of the assignments received today but that was about all they had to say except that five of them were going overseas. Later this evening, they said that it was Puerto Rico. But then they may very easily have gotten together and decided to start a good story. That is about the main sport these days around here. It is really funny.

Last week was very quiet in all respects. I went to town a couple of times to do a little shopping and took in a couple of movies. That was about all that was out of the daily routine. I sent off my barracks bag about Monday or Tuesday, so you should be receiving that fairly soon. I sent it by RR Express and the cost was about $9.50. I reversed the charges, so you will have to take care of it.

This last weekend was a comparatively tame one. Masters knows some cadets over at Randolph Field, so we went over there Saturday afternoon and went swimming in their pool. It was very pleasant as it is a lot larger than ours and not nearly so crowded. In the evening, we checked around town for a little while and then came back to the base.

Sunday, I stayed around here and napped a little while and then went out in the evening and had a steak.

The weather here last week has been very uncomfortable. While it is not especially hot in itself, it is the humidity that really gets a person down. I don't believe that it has gotten below 80 for some time now. It doesn't get much below 70 degrees all night long, so it is rather poor sleeping weather. It is a good thing we don't have a very heavy schedule.

Today we saw a movie on the Africa campaign, which, considering the hot weather and the stuffy theatre, was extremely realistic. We had a couple of hours of administration during which we read outlines that he handed out and spent a couple of hours filling out forms. Filled out the discharge and the history forms today.

Saturday, we signed our AGO cards and clothing allowance records; we are fairly well along in getting out of here.

Well, that is about all that I can think of to report this time. We went swimming for a couple of hours in the afternoon and then to a movie this evening.

Love,

Peter

Peter's assignment: Office of Special Investigations

Sunday, June 17, 1951
Lackland Air Force Base; San Antonio, Texas

Dear Ma and Pa,

Well, outside of what I mentioned on the phone yesterday, there really isn't much to report. I got word of the assignment late Friday afternoon and I only found out by nosing around a little bit. They have yet to make any official announcement of the majority of the assignments. The only way is to nose around and take the chance of not getting caught bothering anyone.

Outside of knowing where I will be sent and vaguely what I will probably be doing, there is little I know about it for sure. They said that the orders for us should be out sometime this week, probably Wednesday, but I doubt it seeing the way they get things out by the time they promise them.

As mentioned, I have 25 days of leave coming to me. I shall take 15 of them now. In addition, they allow traveling time at the rate of 250 miles per day, which should add to about six more days. That is based on travel by the shortest common carrier, which in this case should be around 1500 miles from here to Travis AFB. In all, I should be home around 18 days.

About the assignment itself… I really don't know too much about it. It comes under OSI (Office of Special Investigations) and my job description is very general. It is supposedly a special investigations officer, as probably was the man who investigated me a couple of weeks ago. However, the job description lists everything from investigating automobile accidents to counterespionage. At any rate, there is a good chance of getting to travel around quite a bit after I have been taught the job.

The assignment officer attached to this group said that we would probably be sent to Washington D.C. after about three months for a training course of about six weeks and then return back to Travis. At least this is what he told another one of those who were assigned the same job but at another base. From what I gather, they try and assign a person to the locality he is most familiar with, so there is a good chance of my remaining in that area for a while which would be very pleasant, to say the least.

The OSI man they have stationed here said that he hasn't had a uniform on since 1945, which if at all applicable to the job I get, would also be rather convenient.

About the base I am going to be stationed at, I have managed to pick up a few things. Daggett (my cubicle-mate) was stationed there before he came here.* He said that it really isn't a bad base at all, and the living facilities were in pretty good shape. However, at present it is a SAC (Strategic Air Command) base, which might mean that I will have to work seven days a week as is the policy of that command.

However, they also have a MATS (Military Air Transport Service) group there and I may be assigned to that outfit which seems a little more likely. I probably will be assigned more to the base as the center of a locality than to an outfit as such but most of this is just plain speculation. I won't know any of the details of my assignment until the orders come out and I find out definitely just when I report and to whom, etc.

This next week is going to be a full one what with a couple of final parades and all the last-minute instructions and the processing we have to complete before we can leave the base. We also have some kind of testing tomorrow morning for some type of survey or other.

The weather here this last week has remained very sticky and warm. In addition, there have been a lot of mosquitos to contend with, so we have to sleep under a sheet at night to keep from being chewed up.

I leave here at 10:22 a.m. Saturday, arrive in Dallas at 12:43 p.m. and leave there at 1:25, arrive in San Francisco at 5:35, and leave there at 6 p.m. and arrive in Portland at 8:25 p.m.

---

* Eugene O. Daggett, Jr. (1927–2016) was in Peter's training group in Officer Candidate School. According to the class book, he was from the Bronx, New York. He later settled in the Los Angeles area.

Well, that is about all that I can think of to report again. I shall try and drop you a card Thursday morning.

Don't try to do too much work in the yard. I hope that you are feeling better.

Love,
Peter

Graduating from Officer Candidate School

Thursday, June 21, 1951
Lackland Air Force Base; San Antonio, Texas

Dear Ma and Pa,

Just a quick one to let you have something to read more than anything else, as you know about everything there is to know—or about everything I know.

As far as I know, I shall still be coming home Saturday evening but what with the strike I may be delayed a little while, while I try to get another line home. If they do not go back to work and I have a change of plan, I shall wire you as soon as I get to San Francisco to let you know what's what.*

Last night, we had our graduation ball over at the officers club. It was a nice dance and everyone seemed to have a good time. They have a new club, a very nice one.

We just now got paid all of our back pay which amounted to about $87. Tomorrow, after the parade and the graduation ceremonies, we get our $250 uniform allowance, so after I take out what I owe the PX I shall have about $100, so I am in pretty good shape as far as finances are concerned.

Well, that is about all that I can think of to report for the time being. I imagine that this will get there Saturday morning, just in time. At least I hope so. I have to get this posted so it gets there.

Love,
Peter

---

* At that time, the Brotherhood of Railroad Trainmen was engaged in a nation-wide rail strike.

CHAPTER TWO

California

Travis Air Force Base

Thursday, July 19, 1951
Travis Air Force Base; Fairfield, California

Dear Ma and Pa,
The reason for the delay is that my immediate status has been in quite
a bit of doubt—and still is, for that matter, but I figured that I couldn't
delay any longer.

I arrived on the base about nine on Saturday morning, having stayed
in a motel in Woodland. It was air-conditioned so it was nice and cool
while the rest of the country was very hot and especially so coming
down the valley. I was assigned a bed in the BOQ right away and was
told that I didn't have to report until Monday morning, so I didn't have
anything else to do as far as they were concerned.

I went to the city and came back on Sunday evening. I met up with
the other two men who were assigned to OSI Sunday evening. When we
reported Monday morning to the office, we were told that while they
did not know just what the story was on our arrival, they did know
something was up because they had a little mail for us that had been
forwarded from Lackland but that they had not received any orders
giving any of the particulars.

They thought that they could send us right off to Washington to
school and sent a wire asking to have us admitted to the class starting
this coming Monday. But it was a little too late and the class was full so
that fell through. However, they are going to send us out to some of the
various field offices in the district (which includes all of Nevada and all
of California from a little north of Bakersfield).

I shall either be sent to Sacramento or Fresno. As yet, they haven't
quite decided, but I shall let you know this weekend sometime. In any
case, I shall probably leave here Monday and report to the new station.
This will be probably for a month's time until the new class starts, and
we can go to that.

From what I gather, I am sorry I bought so many uniforms with
my uniform allowance as we shall probably have no occasion at all to
wear them.

As far as doing anything so far, we have been reading various publications on the policy and procedure of the OSI and some of the various types of cases that they handle. While it is interesting, time is beginning to hang a little heavy as we have just about exhausted the supply of reading material.

Also, as far as all of the things I forgot, and I imagine that you must realize by now that they are fairly numerous, I shall tell you later just where to send them to me when I get my new address. Until then you can send any mail to:

19th OSI (IG) District
Travis Air Force Base
California

And as they do not like to have any of the agents (which I shall be after I go to the school in Washington) referred to by rank, you can omit that if you want to right at first.

Well, that is about all that I can think of to report for the time being and since I am getting a little tired, that is about all that I shall write just now. I shall write later after I get settled again.

Love,
Peter

Moving to Merced (Castle Air Force Base)

Wednesday, July 26, 1951
Castle Air Force Base; Atwater, California

Dear Ma and Pa,
I am now stationed at Castle Air Force Base which is outside of Merced a few miles to the north and east. I was sent down here yesterday. It is a very nice base; small and compact so one can walk to wherever one wants to go. There are also a lot of trees for shade which makes it nice—as the weather here is quite warm.

I have a room in the BOQ all to myself which makes it nice but is quite a small room with no adjoining bath as I had at Travis.

As far as I know, I shall probably be here about a month or until I get sent to school. After that, I may be stationed back here but that is much too far in advance to be making predictions. I am working around the office learning the various procedures so that makes it nice. At Travis, there was absolutely nothing for me to do and I was under-foot all of the time as they were very crowded; so I am glad that I left.

However, I am sorry that I am so far from the city. It is around 140 miles. I haven't decided whether I shall try and get there this weekend or not. Last weekend I went in and stayed with John Matthews.* I got caught up on all of the gossip and had a good time.

The working hours here are one hour earlier than they were at Travis, which means we have a longer late afternoon and evening which is a little more agreeable. Time there went quite fast after I got off. Here we get off at four. In addition, usually there won't be any work to do on Saturday; the whole base closes down—which seems strange as it is a SAC base but not as large or important as Travis.

As far as clothing is concerned, I am going to send all of my uniforms home probably the first of next week as I am definitely not

---

* John Matthews was a fraternity brother at Stanford University. He would be the best man at Peter's wedding.

going to be wearing them. I shall be needing more white shirts, so when you get the suitcase, you can load it up with everything I forgot and send it on down, together with the shirts. What with the warm weather here, I shall probably find that the suit I bought at home will turn out to be handy.

I also believe that I must have left my traveler's checks in my top dresser drawer. You might look for them for me and send them on down, although I won't be needing them, I imagine.

The car worked fine on the way down but something is wrong with it now. I think it is a sticky valve so I shall have that taken care of at the first opportunity. At present, I don't have any identification I can use outside of my AGO card and I can't use that as it has my rank on it. So be sure not to use my rank on any of my mail. They seem to stress that around here a lot.

I received all my travel pay and all pay and allowances including the one for the 15th of July. I get paid next Wednesday for the rest of July (they will take the whole month's deductions out of that so it won't amount to very much). I shall also get paid for travel from Travis to here as soon as my pay record arrives here.

We pay for the meals as we eat them. (The meal allowance of $1.40 a day is added to our pay each month). Needless to say, it is pretty difficult to live on that amount; especially at Travis, where they had a cafeteria in the officers club. Here, they have what they call some type of supplemental field rations, so we can get by on the allowance.

Love,
Peter

Firing range

[Undated letter postmarked Saturday, August 4, 1951]
Castle Air Force Base; Atwater, California

Dear Ma, Pa, and Ann,

Well, not a great deal to report this week. There isn't too much that I can do around here until I have gone to school, but I do manage to keep pretty busy and everything is interesting.

Tuesday, we went out on the firing range and that took up most of the time. We fired the .38, which I have never done before. It was warm and uncomfortable that day, but it has since cooled down somewhat. Wednesday, I went down to Fresno with one of the agents, which was quite interesting. It certainly was warm down there. It isn't such a bad town. Well laid out and pretty but too warm to be really nice.

Just what do I have to do to be a godfather? I trust that it won't be any trouble and all I have to do is give my consent. It is nice of them to ask me, so thank them for me.

As yet, I haven't gotten around to sending the uniforms home, but I did pack them up and they are ready to go. Perhaps I shall get them off tomorrow.

Neither of the other two who were assigned to Travis came down here with me. One of them stayed there and the other one was sent to San Francisco to work in that detachment for a while. But I imagine that we shall all go back to school together.

I just received the car registration and thank you for sending it on to me. I am just about set as far as identification is concerned so there is nothing to panic about, Mother.

I am planning on going on up to the city this weekend. It is nice not having to work on Saturdays. I can leave a little earlier. I don't think that I shall be needing the old tweed suit just now but the rest of the things on the list are OK with the exception of washcloths, which I definitely do not need.

Well, that is about all that I can think of to report now.
Love,
Peter

PS: Pa, have a good time on your fishing trip but don't try and do too much.

On the road

Monday, August 13, 1951
Castle Air Force Base; Atwater, California

Dear Ma and Pa,
Well, the latest news today is that I will not go back to school for
another month. Instead, I shall leave sometime in the middle of
September. I guess that that news must have come down here Friday
when I was down in Fresno and as we don't work on Saturday and
as I didn't see anyone, I didn't hear about it until today. I hope that
the rush in getting the suitcase off to me did not cause you too much
inconvenience. I got the traveler's checks today. Thanks for sending
them on to me.

I went to the city over the weekend. The weather was nice and I
had a good time. Last week, in addition to going to Fresno, I went to
Modesto but I believe that I mentioned that when I called you about the
suitcase.

I hope that the fishing trip turned out well. From what I gather, the
weather has been pretty good which would make it a little nicer but I
imagine that the water must have been a little low what with the dry
year the country has been having.

About storing the car, I thought that I would store it here and then
send Ann the ticket and she could get one of her beaus to drive her over
here soon after school starts and take it back over there. They will fly
me back to the San Francisco airport and it would be easy to go down
there and pick it up. That way, it would be cheaper and it would be
better to have someone turn the motor over every once in a while.

Well, it is time to quit, and besides, there is nothing else to report.
The weather here has been warm. Will write later,

Love,
Peter

Heat wave

Tuesday, August 21, 1951
Castle Air Force Base; Atwater, California

Dear Ma,

Well, I didn't get a chance to phone you last night as I had planned, for which I am very sorry. But I shall try and call you tonight.

Yesterday right after work, I drove up with the detachment commander (the 19 OSI District is divided up into detachments scattered about the various districts; there are about eight of them in this district and every other Tuesday morning they go on up to the district office at Travis and have a meeting) to pick up a different jeep for the office here.

Our present detachment commander is getting transferred over to the new detachment they are opening up at Camp Parks (which is going to be the instruction and training center for basics east of Denver) this week and he is taking the jeep we now have here so we had to get another one for this base.[1]

The new CO here arrived last week. He was recalled last June and put into the OSI. He seems like a pretty sharp person, so things are going along quite well.

We drove up to Stockton last night and then on to Travis this morning. I left there about 10:30 and got back here about two. It was a rough ride as there are no cushions to speak of and the springs leave much to be desired.

I leave from here for school about the 1st or 2nd of next month, the school starting the 4th. I got a letter from John Bonsac in which he said that he is going to be there at the same time, which will be

---

1. Camp Parks was a U.S. Army facility in Dublin, California, later renamed Parks Reserve Forces Training Area.

nice. I believe that I have mentioned him to you before. I'm glad that he will be there so there will be someone I know.[2]

This last week or so, I have been helping writing up cases after the information has been gotten from interviews. I have been pretty busy, and it is very interesting and will become more so.

This last week has been quite warm. Last Tuesday it got up to 105, which is plenty warm for me but it is a dry heat which makes it a lot better than it could be.

This last weekend I stayed here on the base. As I thought I would be leaving for school, I didn't make any plans to do anything in the city. I went swimming most of the time and saw a couple of movies. Outside of that, there was little to do. It is dull around here on the weekends, apparently, but then I wasn't so tired yesterday morning.

Well, I hope that you had a nice and restful birthday and I'm sorry I didn't get to talk to you last night but that is one of those things.

I bought a hat on Saturday for $2.84. It was pretty good-looking until I put it on and then it looked rather silly, but I guess that I am going to have to get used to it, as much as I dislike it.

Well, that is about all that I can think of for the time being. Nothing much to report from one week to the next. I shall write again and let you know just what I am going to do with the car. I had thought I might store it here and then send the ticket home so when Ann gets back down to school, she can get one of her friends to drive her over here and pick up the car and take it back to school. That way, it would not cost so much for storage and it would not be sitting idle for two whole months. I could come down and pick it up when I fly back to San Francisco after I finish school and then drive it back over here. Does that sound OK to you?

Will write later,

Love,

Peter

---

2. John W. Bonsac (1927–1986) was in Peter's training group in Officer Candidate School. According to the class book, he was from St. Petersburg, Florida.

On to Washington—

Friday, August 31, 1951
Castle Air Force Base; Atwater, California

Dear Ma and Pa, and Ann,
I leave here tomorrow for the city and I thought that this would be the last chance I would have to write for a few days until I get settled back in Washington.

This week has passed quite rapidly as I have had a lot to keep me busy. The other day we went out on the firing range again and that is about all that I have done this week out of the office.

We have an inspection coming up sometime this next week and I have been spending most of my time getting the files and things in order and requisitioning stock that we are authorized to have on hand but which we did not have. Not that we are planning on getting most of the stuff but just so we can say it is on order.

That certainly was terrible about Mary.* I guess that she is very lucky to have gotten out of it alive. If you find out any more about it, I would be interested in hearing about it. I have to write Bill one of these days, so if you would send me his address, I would appreciate it as I seem to have lost their address.

I am planning on leaving here early tomorrow morning and driving on up to Travis where I shall pick up my ticket and then go on over to the city and leave the car and the things that I am not planning on taking with me. I shall let you all know just where I leave my things so Ann can pick up the car when she gets down to the city when school starts. What with her having a car for herself, I imagine that she will have quite a time keeping two of them around for a while. What a wheel, having two cars at school.

---

* Mary Koerner (1929–2019) was a paternal cousin and at that time a student at Stanford University. She had been injured by an exploding automobile air conditioner—an explosion that killed at least one other woman in the car.

I think that I leave about 10 p.m. tomorrow but I am not sure just which plane they got the tickets on.

The weather here this last week or so has been very nice—quite a bit cooler than it was a couple of weeks ago.

I got a couple of letters from Bonsac this week and he seems to have everything all lined up for me as far as a place to stay is concerned. I think that we have a room at some boarding house where a couple of people he knows are staying.

I shall let you know the exact address as soon as we are settled down.

If we don't like it we are going to try and get a room at the hotel that I was telling you about the other night when I called.

In any event, you don't need to stop writing as they will forward my mail from here. I shall wire you as soon as I get in Washington which I imagine will be sometime Sunday morning. As school doesn't start until Tuesday, we shall have a chance to look around a while before.

Well, it is 5:30 and I have to leave so I can eat and start packing as I have not done a thing yet. I sure hate to pack. I never seem to have enough room but then I always seem to have too much stuff with me once I get there.

I get paid today and sent some to the bank so you can see that I am taking good care of my money. The big thing will be to try not to draw it all out before I get paid again.

Will write later,

Love,

Peter

CHAPTER THREE

Washington, DC

"As yet, I haven't got a permanent room . . . "

Tuesday, September 4, 1951
Bolling Air Force Base; Washington, DC

Dear Ma and Pa and Ann,
This will have to be quick, but I thought I had better get my address off to you:

LT Peter Koerner
OSI TNG School
1005th I.G. SIU
Bolling AFB
Washington 25, D.C.

As yet, I haven't got a permanent room, so until I do, this address will be OK.

We started today. It seems as though it will be very interesting—and as there are quite a few here I know, it makes it much nicer.

I shall write again soon and give you more details, but I am in a hurry now.

Love,
Peter

The Arrival

[Undated letter postmarked Saturday, September 8, 1951]
1644 21st St, NW; Washington, DC

Dear Ma and Pa,

I am not sure if this is going to turn out too well as this machine is on its last legs as must be quite apparent to you. They issue one to every two people to type reports out and this must have been the first one the government bought. As yet I haven't gotten mine–but I hope it is better than this. This is Ernest Willhelm's, who was in the same flight as I in OCS—but I hope it is better than this.[1]

Well, to give you a few details of my trip. The plane was supposed to leave at 10 p.m. Saturday but it was late, and we didn't get off until about midnight and then instead of going to Chicago as scheduled, the plane developed a bad engine and we went to Los Angeles—where we were transferred to another plane and then proceeded to Chicago. We got there about four hours late; and then there was a thunderstorm over the airfield here, so we circled around for about an hour, supposedly to wait until it had passed but when we finally did land, we hit the storm right on the nose.

The rain was really coming down. I have seldom seen it rain so hard as it did here and on top that, it was very hot and sticky.

I went out to the place that Bonsac had arranged for us but it was too far out—being in Maryland—so I came back and got a room at the Manchester for a couple of days but that was only temporary and I had to move out of there and I am now at some sort of Officers Club which

---

1. Ernest V. Willhelm, Jr. (1928–2017) was in Peter's training group in Officer Candidate School. According to the class book, he was from Seven Oaks, Texas. He would serve with Peter on Okinawa, and, after the Air Force, have a career in the oil industry, working first for Humble and ultimately for Exxon.

is much nicer than the Manchester, so I think I shall stay here instead of moving back over there when they have a room available.[2]

Here the rent is $48 a month with no meals and while it is a little more expensive than the Manchester, it is much nicer and cleaner and in a much cleaner and nicer neighborhood. It is also a bit cooler as there is no building quite so close to the windows and a breeze does manage to get in.

This past week has been warm but not nearly so bad as it was when I arrived here.

We started school out with a bang on Tuesday and have been going right at it ever since. So far it is mostly administrative in nature and some background information but today we did have three hours on photography which was very interesting. The course is very good, and I think that I should be able to work a camera by the time I finish it.

I think that we have eight hours of it altogether.

We go to school from 9 a.m. to 5 p.m. with an hour off for lunch and then have Saturday and Sunday off, which makes it nice. This weekend I am planning on taking in some of the sights.

I seem to be getting closer and closer to a bar every time I move. This time I don't even have to walk across the back alley. There is one downstairs. This is quite a social place what with a dance here every evening but as yet I have to take one in. Seeing as how I don't have any school tomorrow, I may drop in later this evening.

Well, I can't seem to think of anything else to report for the time being and this machine is beginning to get me down, so I guess this will be all for now.

I shall write soon.

Love,

Peter

---

2. John W. Bonsac: see p. 93, note 2.

1644 21st St., NW

Sunday, September 16, 1951
1644 21st St, NW; Washington, DC

Dear Ma and Pa and Ann,
Well, to get down to answering some questions:

1. If you want to send the mail to a different address try 1644 21st St. N.W. That is the address of the place I am staying, and it should get to me a little quicker as it won't have to go through the sorting, etc., over at Bolling. If not—the other address is SIU, not SIV, but that doesn't make too much difference.

2. Bonsac is still out at the other place and I think he is planning on staying there.

3. I don't really need the coat. However, it did rain here on Friday afternoon. If it looks like it is going to rain, I'll get a plastic raincoat. It is too hot even when it rains here for that other coat. Besides, I don't know how I would get it back. I'm going to have to send some of my stuff back pretty soon. As usual, I brought twice as much as I'll ever use.

4. Paid my automobile insurance the other day. But it seems to me I should be able to get some for a little less money.

5. Let me know the address of your friend in Arlington and I'll get over to see him.

6. The first chance you get, please pick up a carving knife, and fork sets from Gerber's for me. Jim Munger is getting married one of these days, soon. Please just forward any mail. Don't censor it.[1]

---

1. Gerber was a knife manufacturer, later to become Gerber Legendary Blades. Jim Munger was a fraternity brother at Stanford University. As of 2020, he still had the carving knife.

7. Enclosed is a list of instructions for Ann about the car. You had better supervise her packing, so she won't forget them.

8. School is coming along just fine. This last week we had about eight hours of photography which was interesting and instructive. We have been spending most of the time on report-entering which is really important because as far as anyone knows, the only thing they know about us is in the written reports we have to turn in on each case. We also started in on the Articles of War—mostly the rules of evidence. We will have quite a bit of that before we are through. We also had classes on physical surveillance and parachute jumping.

9. Yesterday I went to the Smithsonian and finished that (the new building only; haven't been to the old one yet) and saw the rest of the art museum that I wanted to see. Today I have quite a bit of reading to do and a report for Tuesday, so I think I'll stay around. The weather the last couple of days (except for Friday's rain) has been a bit cooler.

10. I moved across the hall Friday evening and got a much nicer room— the other one had no cross-ventilation.

11. Last night my roommate (a lieutenant in the Air Force who is stationed here) and I went down on the wharf (such as it is) and had some seafood, which was very good.

12. Herman Spun is in the class which just started today.[2] They now have two classes of about 56 each and our class of 35. All are OSI. The instructors are either Air Force or civilians with occasional guest lectures from all sorts of organizations—government and military.

13. Well, I guess that just about takes care of all the questions.

14. Class is over October 26th.

Love,
Peter

---

2. Herman Spun was probably a family friend.

Plans for the week

Monday, September 24, 1951
1644 21st St, NW; Washington, DC

Dear Ma and Pa and Ann (if she's still home),
Well, as I did very little this last week and as I have a lot to do this week, this shall be very short.

We had a test this morning which I passed without much trouble. Studying for that took care of last weekend as far as doing anything interesting was concerned. This next Monday we have a big report due and as I may be busy elsewhere, I am going to be busy all of this week, so I won't have to study over the weekend.

I came down with a cold yesterday but doubt it will prove fatal although it is a great nuisance.

The weather is quite a bit cooler—changed with the seasons, or so it seems—and very nice.

Well, I'll write later when I have something to report.
Love,
Peter

PS: Hope you got to see the game. I understand, though, that Stanford couldn't quite make up its mind whether it was playing football or soccer.

Weekend in New York

Tuesday, October 2, 1951
1644 21st St, NW; Washington, DC

Dear Ma and Pa,

Well, as you must have surmised by this time, I went to New York over the weekend. Bonsac and I both went up together Saturday morning and returned late Sunday evening. Didn't do a great deal to speak of but did manage to do some sightseeing. Saw Ron Masters and his wife, which was nice.[1] He is stationed out on Long Island.

The weather was very nice all of the time which is something to be thankful for as they said that most of last week it was pretty warm. It was a lot of fun; I don't think that I would like to live up there for any great length of time as it is much too expensive and there are too many people. Also, too many exhaust fumes.

Finally got a typewriter issued to me last week (I share it with another fellow who lives here and is in my class). It seems to be a pretty good machine, but it does skip at times. Also, it is a portable but then I guess that I am lucky to have one at all.

I would have written last night but I went to the movie and by the time I returned I didn't have the urge to start a long letter.

About the wedding presents: as you know I have a couple to get at this time so if you would get them for me, I'll see you in a month or so and you can give them to me then and I'll take care about delivering them then. . . .

I got the copy of the letter Pa sent to Colonel Woolnough.[2] I think that I shall call him sometime this week and see if it would be all right

---

1. Ron Masters: see p. 75 note.

2. Peter probably refers to James Barton Woolnough (1879–1958), an Army colonel who likely served with Peter's father in World War I.

by him to call on him sometime during the weekend when I have the time to fight the bus situation around here.

I went over to Bolling AFB today to get paid. What with waiting and the riding, it took me about two hours to get over from here and back to the classes.

I received the gas bill you sent me today and thanks a lot.

About the place I am staying: it is supposed to be a non-profit organization that provides rooms for officers of all the armed forces. There are two sections to the organization. One, the old one, is a plain common-garden-variety house for Washington with perhaps accommodations for 20 or more. The other, and the one I am in, is three stories high and is built like a lighthouse, complete with a spiral staircase. It is unique, to say the least, but it is comfortable. On each floor are 10 rooms, (except the ground where there are eight), pie-shaped, with two to a room.

They are really nice rooms, clean with good beds and a complete rug. Each room has a washbasin and then there is a toilet and a shower that is shared with the next room adjacent.

For this, the rent is $48 a month, which is about right for Washington as far as I can figure. There is no dining room for eating in the building, but there are several good places to eat just a block away, on Connecticut Ave. It is in the N.W. section of town and Bolling is across the river and then some away; I would say about five air miles. But so you know, we do not have the classes over there but rather down on Pennsylvania Avenue, across from the ICC building.[3]

It takes about 15 minutes to get down in the mornings and a little longer to get back in the evenings. The bus and streetcar pass just a block away, so it is quite convenient.

They have been giving us plenty to do lately so that we have to study several nights a week, mainly writing reports. Monday, we had

---

3. The Interstate Commerce Commission (1887–1995) was the first federal regulatory commission, charged with regulating the rates and routes of railroads. The ICC building would eventually become the home of the Environmental Protection Agency.

our spy case to turn in and then next Monday we have a personnel-background type of case to turn in. They all necessitate quite a bit of work.

I worked almost every night last week to get it done so I could leave for the weekend.

By all means, tell Pearl that when she comes to Washington I shall see her. Just what weekend is it? Please let me know as soon as possible so I won't have too much else to do then. Masters is coming down in about two weeks.

Well, I think that that is about all of the outstanding questions that I can find, reading over what few letters I have received this last week or so.

Love,
Peter

OSI training

Wednesday, October 10, 1951
1644 21st St, NW; Washington, DC

Dear Ma and Pa,

Well, I've had a busy week or so, thus the delay in writing but then again, I supposed that you will appreciate it more this way. Besides, I was getting in a rut writing every Sunday.

Last Monday (day before yesterday), I had a report due that took the better part of the weekend and then yesterday we had our second examination. Which leaves just one more report and one more examination to go before we graduate. Both of these will be the week after this coming one.

We graduate on Friday the 26th which leaves just 12 more days left of going to class. Of these, one is spent with graduation (we graduate in the morning and get out around noon); one day we have Moot Court upon which there is no examination.

Thursday the 25th a test is given in the morning and then we have yet to spend three days on the firing range, which leaves about six more days of actual class, which makes it seem much better. I am getting rather anxious to get out of here and back to Castle. While things are still quite interesting, I nevertheless shall be glad to finish up here.

I only wish that I had more time to look around here than I have had or that I am likely to have before I leave but that is just one of those things.

I got a letter from Pearl today in which she stated that she will arrive on Friday evening and will stay at the Mayflower Hotel.* I imagine that we will have some time to do a little sightseeing together.

Tomorrow, we get our criminal report, which from what I can gather is going to be quite something. About 14 pages long when it is finished,

---

* The Mayflower Hotel is located at 1127 Connecticut Ave NW, Washington, DC 20036.

which may curtail my activities these next two weekends. However, on the weekend after next, I shall call up Colonel Woolnough and go over and visit him.

The weather here this last weekend turned cold. It has been in the 40s during the night for the past couple of days, which is nice for a change.

Well, that is about all that I can think of to report for this time, so I shall close.

Love,
Peter

Moot Court

Wednesday, October 17, 1951 7:00 a.m.
1644 21st St, NW; Washington, DC

Dear Ma and Pa,

Well, this last week has been a rather busy one what with the report that's due Monday. I spent almost all of the weekend on it and every evening so far this week, so I shall be more or less free this weekend coming up. It is a long report, but I think I shall be able to finish it in a couple more evenings.

We don't have much more time around here. Today we have Moot Court for our criminal problem. I think that about Friday we go to the range for three days and then on Thursday morning we have our last test and then graduate and turn everything in on Friday morning.

The weather this past week has been cool, except for the last two days when it has been warm, but I think that was just a last spurt of summer.

This week I have to make arrangements for my reservation back—I have the ticket but have to make my reservations on the plane. I think I shall try to arrange it to arrive in San Francisco sometime Saturday morning. I believe there is a plane leaving here Friday evening which would give me plenty of time to get squared away so I won't have to hurry.

About the first of next week, I am going to ship my suitcase out by rail, so I won't have any extra air freight to pay for the over-weight.

Well, as near as I can figure, that is about all that is even half-way interesting. For the most part, the classes remain interesting, but I shall be glad to get back.

Love,
Peter

CHAPTER FOUR

Back to California

Return to Castle

[Undated letter postmarked Saturday, October 30, 1951]
Castle Air Force Base; Atwater, California

I assumed that Pearl briefed you on my activities, so I didn't write last week. Besides, I was very busy! Got in safely today around noon. My address is still:

> Box 1107
> Castle Air Force Base

I shall try to write on Monday or Tuesday.
    Love,
    Peter

Leaving for Travis

Monday, October 29, 1951
Castle Air Force Base; Atwater, California

Dear Ma and Pa,

Well, I have a little time left this afternoon so I thought I would try to get a short letter off to you. I arrived in San Francisco about noon Saturday. I left Washington about five on Friday and got to Chicago around seven. The plane should have left there around nine in the evening, but it broke down, so they had to fly another one in from some other place.

As a result, it was about a quarter to two in the morning by the time we left there. We stopped once for food and gas in Albuquerque. It was a coach flight with no food served. From there we came to San Francisco. McCord was in town so I stayed with him.[1]

By this time, I imagine Ann wrote and mentioned that she picked me up at the airport and from there we went and picked up the car. McCord is being stationed in Alameda which is pretty nice for him, being so close to home. He thinks that they will place him on a ship and that he will be going out sometime fairly soon for about-two-month cruises.

I left the city this morning and came down here only to find that I have been stationed back up at Travis for a while. Beyond that, I have had no other particulars about what I'll be doing or just how long I am going to stay there. I am going to stay here tonight and then drive on up there the first thing in the morning. I sort of hate to leave here as it is nice, but I shall be a little closer to the city. I only hope that they don't do too much on the weekends as I would like to see a couple of ball games.

---

1. Frank McCord (1928–1994) was a fraternity brother at Stanford University.

I saw Pearson in the city.[2] He left this morning and drove South and from there he is going to fly East for school for seven weeks and then come on back to Treasure Island.[3]

Well, I can't think of anything else to report for this time. I guess that you can send any mail to the old address that I had up there. In care of OSI Travis AFB California.

Will write later,

Love,

Peter

19th OSI District
Travis AFB
California

---

2. Donald C. Pearson (d.1998) was a fraternity brother at Stanford University. He would later become an insurance salesman in the Los Angeles area.

3. A man-made island and neighborhood in San Francisco.

Small-town legwork

Tuesday, November 6, 1951
Travis Air Force Base; Fairfield, California

Dear Ma and Pa,

Well, I have a little time today, so I thought that I had better try to get a letter off to you. The reason I had missed yesterday is that I spent the day running down leads in Vallejo and I didn't get back until just about the time they close the office and hence didn't get much of a chance to get a typewriter.

So far all the work has consisted of contacting references. The area here is comparatively small in size with most of the work centering here on the base or over in Vallejo. There are a few small towns nearby that we cover but they are comparatively simple and few.

About Colonel Woolnough: Pearl has told you that I did get over. He was fine and I had a nice visit with him. He asked about you and sent on his best wishes. He was fine.

Pa, I assume that you are getting into San Francisco 9:30 a.m. on Thanksgiving Day. As yet, I have no idea if I shall have to work that weekend, but I shall try to find out sometime this week and let you know. If I have to be duty agent that weekend and stay around the base, I shall try to trade off with someone, but it will be about a week before I know exactly where I stand on that score.

I need a ticket to the Big Game, and I hope that you will be able to get one.* Not belonging to the Alumni, I have no source for tickets, and the way things look now, it doesn't look too hopeful, but I shall see what I can do. I have a few people working for me, but they don't seem too hopeful.

I saw the game last weekend and Stanford looked pretty good, but I am not so sure about this coming game with USC.

---

* The football game between Stanford and the University of California, Berkeley.

I have a nice room in the BOQ but I think I shall see what I can do for a room in town so I can get my rental allowance. What with losing the rental allowance by staying in government quarters and paying the maid service on top of that, it is costing me $80 a month which is too much, although it is a nice room. If I can get a room or apartment with someone else I should be able to come ahead on the deal.

The suitcase I sent from Washington via RR Express at government expense has not arrived yet so it will be sometime before I send anything home. I think that I shall buy a cheaper suit as I don't like to wear the two good ones that I have to work in every day.

Well, that is about all that I have to report this time. I shall write later and let you know about Thanksgiving. Please let me know what you can find out about a ticket for me for the game.

Love,
Peter

A night full of rain

Monday, December 3, 1951
Travis Air Force Base; Fairfield, California

Dear Ma and Pa,

Sorry I'm late with this week's letter but I had a busy weekend.

Saturday morning there was a meeting of all the agents in the district which took until after noon and then something came up and as I was duty agent for the weekend, I had to attend to that and as a result, it was around five by the time I got back here.

Friday evening there was quite a storm here—I imagine that you heard of it—and when we got to the office Saturday morning, there were about eight inches of water in the building. The rain really came down.

Sunday I helped clean the place out a little and then this morning it rained again and started to flood the place again. It was a mess, but things have cleared off now and it looks like it might be nice tomorrow.

The countryside is really damp. Several places along the local roads are under a couple of inches of water. On the base here, what with the construction of the new housing units, it is terribly muddy and not having grass planted, there is a terrific runoff.

I got my orders granting me leave for 15 days commencing on or about the 15th, so I imagine that I shall leave here after work on Friday. I shall have to get in touch with Ann and see just exactly what her plans are. I hope that I won't have to drive down to pick her up, but I don't see how that can be avoided. Perhaps she will want to take the train home when she gets off, but I shall have to talk to her and find out.

This last week has been busy and this next shall undoubtedly be also which makes it a lot better. The only trouble is that with the rain, it is pretty hard on clothing and shoes.

Well, that is about all that I can think of to report this time. Nothing much has happened. I hope Pa is feeling better and is over his cold by this time.

Love,
Peter

Office Politics—and preparations for Christmas leave

Monday, December 10, 1951
Travis Air Force Base; Fairfield, California

Dear Ma and Pa,

Another rather uneventful week so this shall be another short letter. Ann and I are leaving here Friday sometime—whenever I get to Berkeley to pick her up. She is leaving her car there with someone. We shall be in Portland sometime Saturday afternoon, I should imagine, depending mainly on road conditions. But in any event, don't expect us until you see us.

This last week has been a busy one, what with all the little odds and ends and everything— but nothing too unusual or especially interesting. We are getting a new CO sometime after the first of the year, which will undoubtedly prove to be interesting.

One of the most interesting things about the whole job here is watching a couple of the people in the office trying to outfox each other for the good graces of the colonel. It is really a laugh and what with the new man coming in, the competition could become just that much more intense and grimmer. It is quite interesting and amusing, since as far as I can tell, no one is really doing it very well.

The weather here the past week has been clear but quite a bit colder. I got some anti-freeze Friday just in case it gets any colder here and in case it is cold at home.

I hope the weather stays clear here so there won't be any snow in the mountains on the way home. From what I gather, there isn't any to speak of on the way north from here, but I shall call the AAA or the highway patrol just before I leave to make sure, so don't worry about us.

Well, that is about all I have to report this week. I spent the

weekend over at Bob Peterson's home in Orinda which was very
enjoyable and restful.*

See you next Saturday.

Love,

Peter

PS: This paper is a bit brittle!

---

* Bob Peterson was a fraternity brother at Stanford University.

On the Road Again

Thursday, January 10, 1952
Travis Air Force Base; Fairfield, California

Dear Ma and Pa,

This is really a late one, but I have been getting more and more to do every day. I guess that I can't plan anymore to get my typing done at the office. In addition to all of the background investigations for the area, I have been assigned a couple of criminal cases which take up quite a bit of time and energy. They are quite interesting, so I don't mind any of the extra work.

Our new colonel was due in here yesterday, but he didn't make it. A telegram arrived this morning stating that due to weather conditions he was in Denver and expected to get in here sometime tomorrow. He is driving his own car. It is really a laugh, as his orders read that he was to report not later than yesterday.

The trip down was without event. We stopped over about an hour and saw Cooper in Grants Pass and then drove on through.* Switching off every couple of hours made it easy and we weren't too tired by the time we arrived here. And then over the weekend, I didn't pull any duty, so I was free to do as I pleased and didn't have to report at the office until Wednesday, which made it nice. Too bad I couldn't have had the extra time at home but that is just one of those things. It certainly was nice to get home for Christmas vacation. Besides, New Year's couldn't mean much less to me anyhow. . . .

The weather here had been nice until yesterday when it started to cloud up and then today it rained most of the time. The mornings have been quite cold for about a week with ice on the puddles and frost all over the windshields in the mornings.

---

* Peter probably met his friend Martin Cooper in Grants Pass, Oregon—about 60 miles from the California border.

Had a lead up in the mountains above Calistoga, [California] a couple of miles earlier in the week and there were a couple of inches of snow along the road. It was really pretty. That was about the first time I think that I have ever been that far up the Napa Valley. It is pretty country. Last week I was up as far as St. Helena, [California] and as I wasn't as rushed then, I went through the Beringer Winery in St. Helena. It was interesting.

Well, that is about all that I can think of to report this time. I shall try to see Ann this weekend and find out about her plans for her trip this next summer. Will try to write about next Monday.

Love,
Peter

The new boss

Thursday, January 17, 1952
Travis Air Force Base; Fairfield, California

Dear Ma and Pa,
Well, I seem to be a little late again this week with my letter. One of
these days I have great plans to get back on the old Sunday schedule of
letter writing.

This last week has been really wet around here, but so far the office
has managed to stay dry—which is a break. Today it was fairly dry for
a change and this evening it is clear, or at least was when we got back
from eating; but the weather forecasts predict more rain so I imagine
that tomorrow will be wet again.

Last weekend, as you must be well aware, I went down to the city
and spent the weekend with a friend who works in the San Francisco
office. Nothing much doing but it was fun. Saw Ann and she said
she thought that the trip was shaping up and that she was going to
Oakland or Berkeley to talk to Audrey's mother about it, or some sort
of story like that. I hope that everything turns out all right for her.

The new colonel turned up Monday morning after being snowed
in for a couple of days along the route from Washington. He seems
like he might turn out to be pretty good. I certainly hope so, as the
organization could stand a decent commanding officer. At least I think
that this one will be trustworthy.

This week started out to be pretty slow but it is picking up and the
past couple of days have been pretty busy. Just about the same old
stuff, but just enough different to make it interesting.

Tomorrow night the office is having a party for the new CO down
in Vallejo, which ought to be pretty interesting and enjoyable. This
weekend I am the duty agent and thus have to stay around here in
case anything happens. After next week, there will be only four of us
drawing it so it will come up quite a bit more often. Well, I guess that
that is about all for this time.

Will write again. Your trip sounds like a good one and I shall see you again on your way through.

Love,

Peter

Party in Vallejo

Wednesday, January 23, 1952
Travis Air Force Base; Fairfield, California

Dear Ma and Pa,

Well, another busy week and hence the delay again but I am a day ahead of the last weekly letter.

Last weekend I was duty agent and hence stayed around the base and Vacaville where I could be reached if need be but nothing important happened, so I had an especially dull and uneventful weekend. About the only thing I have managed to do is catch a cold, but it is much better so there is little to even comment about that.

I got a letter from Bill the other day.* He didn't have much to report except it has been wet down there and hence not too good for the cotton crop. He said that this year he should have had vegetables.

We haven't seen too much of our new CO as he has been out touring the district the past few days. However, the district had a party in Vallejo—a combination going-away- and welcoming party. It was pretty good, and everyone seemed to have a good time, although I don't think there was too much thought behind it.

Saturday morning, we had a training program here on the base which did not turn out too well for about the same reason—same bird behind both of them.

Can't think of much else to report this time; I shall have to start taking daily notes, I guess, in order to write any kind of decent letter. Enclosed is an invitation I wish you would take care of for me.

Love,
Peter

---

* Peter likely refers to either Bill Test (1914–1994) or Bill Koerner (1928–2003), both paternal cousins. Given that Bill Koerner was roughly Peter's age and that Peter knew Bill Koerner better, it seems likely that he means Bill Koerner.

Criminal cases and judo lessons

Monday, February 4, 1952
Travis Air Force Base; Fairfield, California

Dear Ma and Pa,

Well, another week just about like the past one. I am becoming busier all of the time but with nothing out of the ordinary. I have had a couple more criminal cases, but they haven't been too spectacular.

Most all of it is new; however, there is always the big problem of writing up the cases. The actual fact-finding is only a small part of the task. The reports have to be written up just so, and as everything is continually different all of the time, the report writing tends to slow up the process.

This last week has been pretty good as far as the weather is concerned. Friday it rained but that has been about the only day. Today it was clear and quite warm, very lovely.

I suppose that by this time, you will have heard about last weekend, so I shan't go into any of the details, but it was pleasant. I stayed with Frank [McCord]. He is leaving for Coast Guard OCS in New London, Connecticut this Friday. It is four months long and he seems to think that there is a good chance of his being assigned back here after it is over.

We had judo lessons today for the first time. While my legs aren't stiff yet, they are certainly going to be in the morning. We are going to have two hours of it twice a week. It is a good thing I am leaving here—I don't think that I could take much more of it.

This next weekend we are going to move our office. I only hope they won't decide that we have to help and thus stay around, but I don't think they will as they have arranged for a bunch of convicts from the stockade to help do all of the heavy work.

Well, that is about all that I can think of to report for the time being.

As I shall be home in a couple of weeks, I don't see why I shouldn't wait until I get home before I figure out my income tax return.

Will write later,

Love,

Peter

A time for cleaning

Thursday, February 14, 1952
Travis Air Force Base; Fairfield, California

Dear Ma and Pa,

Well, getting ready to leave this Friday has me pretty busy these days so this will have to be a short one; I have been busy this last week trying to get everything ahead of schedule so there won't be anything to do in my department for a week or so after I leave.

Over the weekend we moved the office and getting ready for that put me behind a little. The new building is quite a bit nicer, but everyone is still trying to find things that were lost.

Last weekend, I went to the city and stayed with John Matthews.* Went out in the evening and that was just about it. Nothing of unusual interest.

I still haven't any word about just where I shall be stationed nor will I be able to find out until I actually report to headquarters in Japan. From there I shall be assigned my permanent duty station. From what I gather, the tour of duty over in that theater is about 18 months but it would be very foolish to accept that as the final word.

I plan on leaving here Friday after work and driving on up the valley that evening. I think that I shall drop in and see [Martin] Cooper if he is there so there is no telling just when I shall arrive home, but it shouldn't be any later than Sunday.

I have to have the car greased sometime this week before I leave— and the tires rotated. I am just a little bit unhappy about the work I had done on it when I was home on Christmas. I still have the rattle and there is something definitely wrong with the steering but nothing to worry about except that the tires are not wearing evenly.

---

* John Matthews: see p. 87 note.

This week I have to get all packed up—both my stuff and McDermott's, as we are going to give up the apartment and I am going to bring the stuff that he left out here to the office where it will be stored. In addition, I have to clean up the room, which is not a small task in itself. I was nearly late this morning for work as I had a hard time finding the door to my apartment, but I think that I shall be able to get everything shoveled out in time to leave Friday evening.

The weather here last week has continued to be clear and fairly warm during the days. But last night it got a bit cold and frosted up the windshield.

Well, that is about all that I can think of to report this time and I shall be seeing you in about a week.

Love,

Peter

At Stoneman

Wednesday, March 5, 1952
Camp Stoneman; Pittsburg, California*

Dear Ma and Pa,
Well, outside of the fact I arrived safely, have all my luggage, and am
through processing (this morning), there is little to report.

A recent change in policy someplace now makes it mandatory for
all security personnel to fly. All I need now is new orders cut for me
and I shall be on my way. It shouldn't take more than another day or
two at the most as they seem to have plenty of planes for transport at
present. I shall try to get a card off prior to leaving but I may not have
the opportunity.

Love,
Peter

---

* Camp Stoneman was a U.S. Army base. It was decommissioned in 1954.

Goodbye, California

Friday, March 7, 1952
Camp Stoneman; Pittsburg, California

Dear Ma and Pa,
Got our orders today and should be leaving sometime after tomorrow afternoon. We will be flying from Travis. Got the trunk off this afternoon and outside of packing up, some errands, and turning in the bedding, I am all set to go. Sitting around here is getting rather dull, to say the least. Well, will write again as soon as possible.
    Love,
    Peter

Honolulu, Hawaii   POSTCARD
March 10, 1952

Dear Ma and Pa,
Left Travis at approximately 0220
this morning and arrived here at 1220
Hawaiian time—12 hours flying
time elapsed. Leave here at 1500 this
afternoon for Midway.
Love,
Peter

CHAPTER FIVE

Tokyo

A plane lands in Tokyo

Wednesday, March 12, 1952
Tokyo Electric Hotel; Tokyo, Japan

Dear Ma and Pa,

As I forgot to write "Air Mail" on the card I sent from Hawaii,
I shall start from the beginning. We left Travis at about 2:20 a.m.
on Monday, 10 March. We were on a DC 4 chartered by MATS from
Pan American—came clear through with it.

We arrived at Hawaii at approximately 1426 PST or 1226 hours
Hawaiian time—10 hours elapsed flying time. We had a box lunch on
the way and then were fed there at the airport again. It was a warm
day—about 80, I should imagine—with a few clouds and a fairly
strong wind.

We departed at about 1500 hours for Wake and arrived there about
2400 hours Hawaiian time or 0200 hours Wake time—about nine
hours elapsed flying time.

But as we crossed the international date time we lost a day, so it
was early Wednesday morning when we arrived. It was warm (about
80°) and very humid with a slight wind. From Hawaii to Wake we had
a couple more box lunches; one was supposed to be for the last leg of
the trip, but the stewardess didn't let us know about that.

We left Wake at about 1:30 a.m. their time and arrived at Haneda
Airport—near Tokyo—at 12:30 Wake time or 9:30 Japanese time—
lost three hours this time. This last bit was very rough in a couple of
places, but it was OK by the time we arrived. From the airport, we
were taken to a processing organization about 25 miles across Tokyo
and then back to OSI HQ in the city. We had a little more processing
there and then were assigned places to stay. Most of us are at the
Tokyo Electric Hotel, which is supposed to be one of the better ones in
town. There are about 30 beds in this one large room, but it is more or
less partitioned off, so we have enough room and ample closet space.

Tomorrow afternoon we are going to get cleared with the OSI for
the Far Eastern Air Forces (FE AIR FORCE) and then probably get our
permanent assignment on Friday.

The weather here today was clear and fairly warm, but it got quite a bit cooler this evening. There were about six inches of snow here a week ago and there are still a few traces of it despite the comparatively warm weather.

Well, as I haven't had a great deal of sleep the past two nights, I think I'll get to bed. Will write in a couple of days.

Love,
Peter

PS: Plane carried about 45 passengers plus a crew of four.
You can write at:

6001st I.G. Special Investigations SQ
APC 925
C/o Postmaster
San Francisco

Tokyo with eyes wide open

Saturday, March 15, 1952
Tokyo Electric Hotel; Tokyo, Japan

Dear Ma and Pa,
Well, we finally got our assignments on Thursday and I am going to be
sent to Okinawa—probably about Wednesday—depending upon how
soon we are to finish getting processed here. Of approximately 18 in
our shipment, only myself and a major are being sent there. The rest
were scattered all over the area quite evenly.

I am quite satisfied with the assignment and hope that it works out
to be as good a deal as it is supposed to be.

The weather here—outside of Friday when it stormed and rained
all day—has been clear and warm but I understand that it is rather
unexpected for this time of year.

The past couple of days we have been walking about looking at the
shops and doing a little shopping. The various stores and shops are all
very interesting—and the people even more so. Just about everyone
you see is hurrying down the street—you seldom see a Japanese who
seems have nothing to do—everyone is hustling someplace.

One of the most interesting things here is the way everyone drives.
Though they seldom go over 35, you have the impression of traveling
at breakneck speeds. The streets are for the most part made of
cobblestone and hence often quite rough. There are also cement streets
but more often than not, they are quite uneven. Of course, everyone
drives with a horn which adds to the confusion.

What with traffic keeping to the left, things seem even more
unusual. It is amazing the way everyone manages to scamper out of the
way of an oncoming vehicle at the last possible moment, and the way
the drivers tear through crowded alleys without a moment's hesitation.
The children are exceedingly well-trained by our standards and keep
out of the streets. Of course, in the city here, one doesn't see too many
of them but in the outlying villages, there are children everywhere.

The streets are quite congested with traffic. I would judge that
approximately 2/3 of the vehicles are of American manufacture;

about half of these are new cars and the other half are of middle '30's vintage—mainly Fords. The rest (1/3) are foreign-made cars (to the U.S.) of many various types—but mostly all quite small.

Then there are the motorcycles with two-wheeled carts on the rear. There are many of these which for the most part take care of much of the commercial freight shipments. The loads carried by these are unbelievable. There are also many bicycles—also often very heavily laden down.

Here in the city, most Japanese wear Western clothing—usually black or gray and rather drab. Very seldom do you see a man in the old-style dress although women in kimonos are fairly common. It is really too bad they do not wear kimonos as they are much more colorful and becoming to the women than Western dress.

In the rural areas, just the men wear Western clothing and even then not entirely.

Well, that is about all that I have time for now and this pen doesn't seem to be working too well.

Will write later,

Love,

Peter

The Layover

Friday, March 21, 1952
Tokyo Electric Hotel; Tokyo, Japan

Dear Ma and Pa and Ann (if she is home),
Well, I am still here in Tokyo, but I shall be leaving Sunday morning at 0900 for Okinawa—via plane.

After my last letter, we were told that all the assignments had been canceled and that about 70% of us would be sent to Korea—seems that the CO had just gotten back from there and that the man in charge over there had managed to impress upon him the great need for more men. But as soon as he got back, the other seven district commanders must have put up arguments equally good, so there were no great changes in the original plans.

However, there was the delay. One of us left last night and there are several more leaving this evening, and by Sunday we all should have left with the exception of those who are remaining in the general vicinity.

The past few days have been cold and wet and hence we have not been able to stir around much.

The other night we went to a cocktail party for the new CO which was quite interesting. Had a chance to meet some of the people in the district.

Now—in answer to Mother's letter of 10 November 1952:

1. All phone calls are mine.

2. The other two showed up on schedule so you don't have to worry about that.

3. My other letter took care about the question on Hawaii.

Father's Letter:

1. Tuesday your time and Wednesday Japan time—nice clear warm day.

2. Plane—DC–4—4 engine—about 12,000 feet and about 240 MPH (usually less than about 220 MPH). Time of fights explained in previous letter.

Tokyo and the surrounding area are flat but there are snow-covered bluffs to the north—about 25 miles, I should imagine. The central business area is fairly clean. There are quite a few new buildings under construction but none of them are over 9–11 stories tall—most of the buildings outside of the banks and main offices are 3–5 stories.

The bank buildings are typical bank buildings seen everywhere as are most of the larger office buildings. It is only the oldest buildings and smaller stores that could be considered to be of "foreign" design.

I have rather hesitated to do much shopping just now. On Okinawa, there may not be the bargains, but I shall be getting on up here from time to time and then I'll try to get some things. Is there anything special you think you would like? Will mail this and write later.

Love,
Peter

Please note new address:

OSI District #3
APO 239

Peter Koerner, official Air Force photo, June 1951

Peter Koerner, OSI office, Kadena Air Base, Japan, circa 1952

Peter Koerner, OSI office, Kadena Air Base, Japan, circa 1952

Unknown children, Okinawa, circa 1952 (Photo by Peter Koerner)

Unknown children, Okinawa, circa 1952 (Photo by Peter Koerner)

CHAPTER SIX

Okinawa

Okinawa, finally

Sunday, March 30, 1952
Kadena Air Base; Okinawa

Dear Ma and Pa,

I lost my other stationery somewhere along the line; thus this new stuff with the map, such as it is.

Well, I think I am just about as settled now as I shall ever be. Wednesday, I moved from the transient BOQ to my permanent quarters. It is a one-story building with four single bedrooms (about 8 by 12) leading from a living room of about 10 by 16. In addition, there is a large bathroom and a refrigerator in the living room. My furniture consists of, in addition to a bed, a desk, chair and dresser, and a large built-in closet. In all, it is very comfortable.

Of the three other occupants, two are also agents, which is a help. I was very lucky to get settled so soon, as people are currently waiting up to six weeks for their permanent quarters.

The mess hall is just about a half a block away, which is convenient.

The office is a Quonset hut about a half-mile away, but as there are about seven jeeps for 10 agents, transportation is not too great a problem.

Had a little excitement yesterday. We picked up a man who had been AWOL since last July. It was interesting hearing how he had managed to elude capture for nearly a year. He claims he is going to write his memoirs and he should have plenty of spare time to do it.

Today Willhelm and I in one of the jeeps went on up to the north end of the island—to Okuma where a rest camp, so-called, is maintained.* It is 56 miles by road from Kadena up there—both routes—see map.

Toward the north from Kadena, it is mountainous with shrubs, tall grasses, and scattered pine trees. The foliage is very thick. Most of the farming is carried on along the coastal sections. The roads are mainly

---

* Ernest V. Willhelm, Jr.: see p. 100, note 1.

dirt and rock and not well laid-out but passable—no mud but along the coast there were places where it had been washed out by the ocean. The northern end of the island is quite pretty. Down around here it is not as interesting.

Naha is the big city of Okinawa with, from what I can gather, about 400,000 people. The field where I landed is some distance from it and I did not have a chance to see it. In all, there are around a million natives on the Ryukyu islands with the majority living on Okinawa.

While they are separate from the Japanese people, they are not too dissimilar—a bit larger perhaps with a heavier bone structure. I understand that while they have their own language it is not too different from Japanese, which is commonly spoken. For the most part, they are friendly and clean. There does not seem to be a very great difference in social status judging from the homes—at least in the northern part.

Well, I will write later as it is getting late.

Love,

Peter

The lay of the land

Friday, April 4, 1952
Kadena Air Base; Okinawa

Dear Ma and Pa,
Well, this last week has been rather uneventful. Except for this
morning and early afternoon when it rained hard, the weather has
been warm with a rather brisk breeze blowing. It rained very hard this
morning but cleared up this afternoon and things were just about dry
by evening.

Nothing of unusual interest has come up at the office outside of the
usual burglaries. I can't make up my mind who is the most to blame for
them, the natives who seem to be kleptomaniacs or the stupid people
who don't lock up their valuables. I am beginning to think that the
latter are more to be blamed than the thieves themselves.

For the most part, I have been riding around with some of the
other agents becoming acquainted with the base and the surrounding
area. Just to the south of us about five miles, the Army has a very big
installation which is the main headquarters for the island, being under
Army command. But in back of the base are ammunition dumps that
extend a goodly distance. In between everything are native vegetable
and rice sections.

The government is spending a terrific amount of money on new
construction on the island. Everywhere you go, they are tearing up the
roads to lay pipe, or making new roads or constructing new buildings. A
good deal of the construction is dependent housing which seems a little
out of place as there are quite a few men living in tents, but most of
them are plane crews who are only here for about three to four months
before they complete their required number of missions and get moved
out again.

Outside of the Vinnell Co. [a private corporation with military
contracts], ownership unknown to me, and Morrison-Knudson [a
civil engineering firm], almost all the construction work is handled by
Japanese contractors. There must be a dozen or so of these. Almost all
of the labor is native, with some Japanese and Philippine. Concerning

the number of Americans on the base (and the islands) I could not even venture a guess but there are a lot of them.

It does seem rather strange, though, to see natives living in thatched huts (about two-thirds of the native huts) driving big earth movers and steam shovels. But I have heard that on this base alone there are about 1300 maids, which gives you a pretty good idea of the size.

Each officer has a maid full-time that costs $10.80/month which is a great deal. They take care of all cleaning of the rooms, laundry, and sewing, and keeping all the clothes washed, mended, and ironed. It is really a deal. My maid came with the room as she did not wish to leave her friends when the person who was here before me changed his quarters.

As near as I can figure it, they work a couple of hours and then visit with other maids in the area and listen to the radio and generally gossip. I have a good one as she doesn't use my toothbrush as many of them do but I think that she has been wearing my sandals, so I think that I shall have to buy her a pair the next time I get to one of the villages.

Well, that is about all that I have time for tonight, so I shall close. Willhelm and I are going to the bullfights sponsored by the Red Cross this weekend down toward the southern end of the island which should be rather interesting. They fight one bull against the other. Will write and tell you about it later.

Love,

Peter

Life—and death—at the base

Sunday, April 13, 1952
Kadena Air Base; Okinawa

Dear Ma and Pa,

Well, this week certainly slipped by on me and I hardly know just
where it went. Last Sunday, as I mentioned in my last letter, Ernie and
I went to the bullfights about seven miles south and east of here. It
was sponsored by the Red Cross and lasted all weekend. The spot is
marked on the chart. It was near the top of the main ridge of the island
running north and south in that area. It was near the ruins of an old
castle built in the 15th century by some ruling prince of the islands.

The bullfight itself was interesting but there was really little action.
Two bulls were pitted against one another and the main purpose was
to see which bull could exert the most pressure. There was no stamping
and rushing. The bulls were kept snubbed by a handler and only tried
to push the other one to the rear. Each one lasted about a half an hour
before one of the two yielded.

The bulls were quite large—weighing around 1300 pounds—and
were kept especially for fighting. As yet, I have to see any livestock
raised on this island. The view from this old castle is really good.

I should imagine that the elevation at this point is about a thousand
feet and it looks down on both the East China Sea and the Pacific
Ocean or the Philippine Sea, as the maps and charts refer to it. As it is
closer to the west side of the island, the view of the China Sea is much
the best one.

All along the coast, there are scattered wrecks of landing craft and
looking up toward Buckner Bay are the larger cargo vessels and the
main naval anchorage of the island.

The port of Naha is too small to accommodate all the shipping and
will not take the larger two-stacker cargo vessels. I think that many of
the wrecks along here are as much the result of typhoons as of battle
damage. As near as I can gather, the main landings were made on the
east side of the island around Kadena and met comparatively little

resistance at the time. The main battles were fought south of here around Naha and below.

The weather Sunday was very nice and as a result, the view was good but in the evening, it began to cloud up and it started to rain during the night.

Monday and almost all of Tuesday, it rained steadily and hard, and about six inches came down bringing the yearly total to around 16 inches which as I understand it is below the yearly average for this time, and that we can expect more rain just about any time. Before the bullfights, we went down to Naha and looked around and I bought a pair of rain pants, which came in very handy Monday and Tuesday.

Tuesday evening Willhelm and I started taking Japanese classes. The beginning class meets two nights a week for five weeks and then we advance to the intermediate class. I don't know if we are going to be able to learn enough so that it will eventually help us in our work, but we thought that we would give it a try. The course is taught by a Chinese who seems pretty good. Each class is two hours.

Wednesday evening, I was going to write you but I couldn't get a typewriter so that was that. Thursday was a bad day for just about everyone—or so it seemed. It started off early in the morning when a couple of Japanese guards in the munitions area got jumpy and started shooting with the result that one of them ended up with a belly load of buckshot. And then in the afternoon, a crew of painters was riding around on their paint truck when one of them must have lit a cigarette which resulted in nine of them being burned to death. And then in the evening, we had our class again, so I wasn't able to get a letter off to you. Friday night I went to an army camp about seven miles to the north and looked up Alex Chilton and talked to him most of the evening, which was very interesting.* From what I gather he has a pretty good deal and seems well pleased with it. He thinks that he will be moving on to Tokyo around the end of this month.

Saturday morning, or rather sometime Friday evening, the deserter we picked up a couple of weeks ago broke out of the stockade and

---

* Alex Chilton (1918–2004) was a family friend and career Marine.

managed to get away without anyone knowing about it for several hours. Luckily, we weren't called out to beat the bushes for him.

He was picked up about seven the next morning when he broke into the civilian jail in Naha, so he could talk to his girl. And then it was only by accident, as he had all the civilian police backed up against the wall with a lead pipe. Never a dull moment.

Saturday evening, several of us went over to one of the agent's homes and played cards and it was rather late by the time we got home.

This morning, we went for a drive and then this afternoon, Ernie and I and another fellow who was in our lower class at OCS went down to Naha to see about when Ernie's car would be unloaded. There is a place down there where they manufacture fairly good lacquer-wear if you are interested in anything. If Pearl uses a nameplate on her desk at the bank and if she could use a new one, I thought that one might be a rather nice gift for her.

Well, that is about all that I can think of to report this time. This Wednesday evening, I am the duty agent, and if nothing comes up, I shall try and get a letter off to you then.

Love,
Peter

Of snakes and diseases

Saturday, April 19, 1952
Kadena Air Base; Okinawa

Dear Ma and Pa,

Well, the big news this week is that I got my footlocker which was a bit of a surprise—not that it wasn't due—but rather because there wasn't a big delay when someone lost some of the orders, though goodness knows I left copies of my orders all over Tokyo when I was there.

Everything arrived in good shape except for the metal edging along one side of the end.

This week has been a fairly busy one. I got several cases and managed to finish one but another one—a burglary—is a bit complicated and I can't seem to get ahold of everyone without a big delay.

I think that eventually I am going to more or less take care of all the counterintelligence cases for the office when the agent presently in charge of them leaves—or at least those are the plans now. And until that time, I shall be working more and more with him.

It is a pretty good deal as most of it is rather interesting.

The weather here this last week has been good except for Monday when it rained all day. The past several days it has been rather warm and today I broke down and bought a small fan because from what I can gather, later in the season, they are almost a necessity and the PX is just about out of them and they probably won't have any in for some time.

One of the men in our lower class at OCS is an assistant PX officer and I get a little information from him on how things are holding out there. Quite a few things are often in short supply and a person has to keep a rather close check on the PX to come out OK on the supplies. I have great hopes that this is just about my last big expense as far as getting settled is concerned and I shall be able to start saving a little money one of these days.

Speaking of weather, I am enclosing a clipping from the local daily newspaper concerning the weather here that I thought might be of some interest to you.

I also have a map but if I can't get another, I shall have to trace it, so I can have one of my own.

About the snakes, they are called 'habus' (pl.). I believe that they belong to the same family as the moccasin, but I am not sure. They are a poisonous snake, but they are not as bad as some reports would have you believe. They had another article in the paper, but I lost it, so I shall have to rely on my memory concerning them.[1] Last year some 300 people (white and native) were reported to have been bitten by them. Of this number, there were about three fatalities and about six amputations, so you can see they are not as bad as the encyclopedia would have you believe.

I have also heard that there is a little malaria—but very little. There is also some encephalitis but that is quite rare. They spray by airplane here and we sleep under nets, which reduces the number of mosquito bites. However, somehow I manage to get chewed fairly regularly. I have a grass rug in the room that has numerous fleas. I also saw a mongoose the other day, which just about ends the discussion of the fauna of the island.

They also have what I believe they call schistosomiasis, a parasite of the bloodstream, carried by the snails that are common on the island, but the only way to get it is to wade around in the freshwater streams, or at least that is what Alex Chilton was telling me when I saw him. There is also amoebic dysentery on the island. Colin MacKay got it when he was stationed here during the war and afterward.[2]

However, I don't believe that any of these are considered a threat to the safety and well-being of the occupation personnel, as the deserter

---

1. As Peter notes, *habus* is the plural of *habu*, a catch-all term used for several species of poisonous Asian snakes.

2. Colin MacKay was likely a family friend. Peter also makes a reference to a Douglas MacKay, presumably a relative.

who lived out in the hills for eight or nine months was very healthy when he came in.

Am also enclosing a picture of approximately a quarter of the office. It was taken about two weeks ago when I somehow had extra film in the camera that had to be used up before the rest and more important pictures could be developed.

Well, that about all that I can think of to report this time,

Love,

Peter

The duty agent

Saturday, April 26, 1952
Kadena Air Base; Okinawa

Dear Ma and Pa,

Well, I have duty agent again today, so I thought that it would be a good time to get some letters written. With ten people pulling the job, it isn't too bad. I also had it a week ago last Wednesday, but luckily nothing happened. However, the way things have been going the past couple of nights, I wouldn't at all be surprised if something came up and I would lose a night's sleep.But better to lose Saturday night's sleep than any other night's, as we still have to work the next day. I guess that my last couple of letters must have been delayed somewhere along the line, judging from the letters I received from the both of you today.

Got five-day [mail] service coming this way, which isn't too bad. I hope that by this time they both arrived. I can't remember just what I reported in them to be able to go over them again.

This last week has been a busy one for just about everyone in the office. Two of the men had to go to Tokyo, which leaves us a little short-handed. On top of that, the PX had its inventory yesterday and I wouldn't at all be surprised if they found shortages and we had another couple of cases there come Monday. It seems that just about everyone on this island has some kind of a deal—and most of them are illegal.

It is quite interesting, some of the things that come up. The other night, 900 feet of three-inch pipe were dug up and carted off without a trace. It sounds impossible but there was nothing but a trench the next morning. It had been in the ground only a couple of days.

The weather here this last week has been just about the same. A couple of rainy days, and the rest of the week has been pretty good. It dries out quite rapidly once it stops raining so there isn't the big fight against the mud for a week or so.

Willhelm got his car a couple of weeks ago—I can't remember if I mentioned that or not—and last Sunday five of us took a trip around the southern end of the island which was very interesting. We went down to Suicide Cliff where the Japs jumped off instead of surrendering at the end of the campaign for the island.[1]

It was really interesting. There are quite a few blasted-out caves down there and in one place there is a big pile of bones. There are also lots of grave markers in a couple of places. I got some pictures of them I shall send home one of these days—as soon as I get them back.

For all the heavy fighting that took place down there, there is not a great deal to see outside of the monuments that they have here and there. About anything that was left on the battlefield that could be moved was carted off by the natives. Occasionally, a farmer will come across an old shell, and the civilian police will hear about it and bring it in but that is about all.

The beaches are all strewn with wrecks of various kinds that I mentioned before, but they are mostly due to typhoon damage.

That certainly was too bad about Ed Strowbridge and Charlie Wegman. I was also very much surprised to hear about Peter St. Pierre. Did they ever find out just exactly what had been bothering him?[2]

The price for the car seems to have been a good one. About my bank statements, please send them on to me so I can check them. However, as I established a checking account with American Express over here, there wouldn't be a great deal of activity there, although from time to time I shall send some of that home.

Well, that is about all that I can think of for this time. Will write again,

Love,

Peter

---

1. Peter refers to events of the Battle of Okinawa (April–June 1945), one the last major battles of World War II.

2. Ed Strowbridge was a family friend; presumably Charlie Wegman and Peter St. Pierre were, too.

Crop report, radio programming, and seeing a movie

Saturday, May 3, 1952
Kadena Air Base; Okinawa

Dear Ma,

Well, this week has gone very fast and here it will be Mother's Day, so I thought that I had better get this off to you wishing you a good day.

I am also sending a couple of newspaper clippings and a few pictures that I thought you might be interested in. I have been meaning to compile a list of questions that you have sent me but as I neglected to do so, I shall have to try to recall them as best I can. As far as staying someplace off the base, there is no occasion to do so as we always come back here in the evenings or at least since I have been here. I can't imagine under just what circumstances that problem would come up as long as we stay on the island.

I believe that Pa was wondering about the radio. There is a military radio station here on the island that is 24 hours a day. While there isn't very much good music, there is no advertising at all but rather lots of advertising on matters pertinent to the service. Not advertising as much as campaigns to get people to be more careful, etc. Right now, the big campaign is getting people to register for absentee voting.

The only other question that I seem to be able to remember is the one about the vegetables. They have gardens here on the island under military supervision from which we do get some vegetables, such as lettuce, cabbage, tomatoes, and radish. Also, there are some cucumbers and peppers.

According to an article in the paper here about a week or so ago, they are increasing the acreage so there will be more locally grown vegetables in the future. They also grow carrots. The vegetables are all pretty good, but I think that they are inclined to pick the tomatoes a little too late and hence they are often overripe. The carrots are very nice to look at, but they often don't possess much flavor.

You will probably notice, in the pictures, all of the Easter lilies in front of the monuments. There are great numbers of them just about all over the island. They all grow wild and are sold quite extensively in the villages on Sundays when people do some sightseeing. For the most part, you have to go to some of the more remote areas before you see any great numbers of them growing as the hills are pretty well scoured by the natives. The maids usually bring a few and put them in the rooms. There are also quite a few gladiolas around the villages. They are also a hardy-appearing flower, but I haven't seen any of them growing wild in the fields and I rather imagine they are grown in the villages exclusively.

In addition to rice, the natives grow quite a few potatoes of the yam type, I think. They do have other things they grow but as yet I am not quite sure. There are a couple of experimental agricultural stations here on the island and I think that I shall have to go to one of those sometime to find out just what crops they do grow here on the island.

Before the war, quite a bit of sugar cane was grown; in fact, it was one of the principal industries, with several sugar refineries. The war destroyed the refineries, although as I understand it, there are a few rather crude ones on the southern part of the island.

As near as I can find out, the area where Kadena is located was one of the main areas for the cane fields. Over near Kadena village on the north side of the field are ruins of an old refinery. Judging from the size of it, the refinery must have been quite an important one. There was even a small railroad before the war, mainly for the sugar industry.

I had dinner over at the Rycom Officers Club last Sunday with Alex Chilton. On Tuesday he was to fly on up to Japan where he will be doing more training for a while. I shall have to get some pictures of that club. It is situated on a hill overlooking the China Sea. It has a tremendous view. It is made of reinforced concrete and is three stories tall. It has four bars in it and is quite elaborate. They claim it only cost a couple hundred thousand but if it cost less than three-quarters of a million, I would be quite surprised.

Had a rather quiet weekend. Saturday afternoon a couple of us went to the movies here and in the evening, I painted a couple of the walls in my room. Today Ernie and I went to Naha to see the Japanese movie *Rashomon*. It was pretty good. It was showing at an Okinawan theatre. The building was a new one and in pretty good shape. On the lower floor, there were ordinary seats. The balcony had seats in the center section and around the sides (the balcony was shaped like a horseshoe) there were mats on different-level platforms for people to sit. It was quite interesting, seeing everyone sitting on the mats with their shoes off. It was a warm day and many people had fans and were fanning themselves, smoking and chewing gum. The natives are great gum-chewers.

The road from here to Naha is—or rather was—paved, but they are widening it to four-lanes, and for the most part, it is pretty rough. The traffic is quite slow due to the detours and the two-wheel horse-drawn carts. While many of the carts have old iron wheels, most of them have GI wheels and tires on them—probably most of them stolen, if the truth were to be known.

These carts are often very heavily laden, and you wonder just how the horses can pull such great loads over the rough roads, but I don't believe that I have yet to see a horse that did not seem to be in good shape. In fact, I don't ever believe that I have even seen a horse that was sweating. Just about all of the horses are sorrels. I don't believe I have ever seen a white or a gray one since I've been here. They are a little smaller than our riding horses but seem to be a little stockier.

The only milk we get here is what they call recombined milk. It comes in the regular cardboard containers which are bottled here on the island someplace, but it is made out of powdered milk and isn't too good. They also have chocolate milk and due to the chocolate, it doesn't taste too bad.

There are eggs for breakfast, but I haven't been eating breakfast except on Sundays. In all, the food is pretty good. Occasionally we get canned beef that doesn't taste too good. We have ice cream several times a week.

Cabbage is one of the main dishes here. A lot of it is grown on the island. The cabbage they grow here is really beautiful—too bad I don't like it cooked but we get it raw in salads quite a bit of the time.

As far as sending me packages, you can use the same address. Cookies would be very acceptable, and they seem to arrive in good shape. I think that airmail postage is not too much if you were to send them packed in coffee cans. They arrive in good shape in about a week.

I ordered myself a lacquer cribbage board the other day when I was in Naha. It is a nice one with inlaid mother-of-pearl and with my initials. Most of it is custom work and takes some time to get it done.

When I feel wealthy someday, I am going to order some bookends that are pretty nice.

Tell me what you would like, and I shall see if I can't get it for you. Just let me know.

All of the ordering for our PX is done through a central Army PX office. As a result, the selections are not always too good. Like a great deal of the other activities the military has undertaken on this island, it seems to lack common sense in the operation.

Well, I can't think of a great deal else to report this time. Let me know your questions and what lacquer you would like—colors black and red.

Love,

Peter

Japanese–American ("Nisei") interpreters

Sunday, May 11, 1952
Kadena Air Base; Okinawa

Dear Ma and Pa,
Well, this has been a rather uneventful week although I have been busy, and it has gone quite rapidly. That, coupled with the letter I wrote last week in which I exhausted nearly all information I possess at the present time, will tend to shorten this letter.

First—about my bank statements—please forward them as I have my records here. I thought that I had answered you in regard to this matter, but I guess it slipped my mind.

I received the absentee ballot; returned it right away but I'm afraid it arrived too late. I'm a little unhappy about that. At the time I registered when I was home, I was told I would receive the ballot in plenty of time. I am going to write those people a letter!

As Papa has a birthday in another eleven days, I had better wish him a happy birthday in this letter if it is going to get home by the 22nd. Happy Birthday, Papa! I'm sorry, but due to the rather slim pickings in the PX, I'm afraid you are going to have to take a rain check on a present for some time.

Ma, would you be able to get Ann something for me for her birthday? As for *The New Yorker* for me, that would be very nice.

The natives in the background of the pictures are called translators-interpreters. While they are better than nothing at all, sometimes they are pretty worthless. In addition to these two, we have two Nisei on the same job.* One of these is a civil service employee and the other is a PFC who just got assigned a week or so ago. The civil service employee is the best one of the bunch but if given a chance, he will try to run the investigation. The PFC can't read or write Japanese, but he is pretty

---

* Americans of Japanese descent. More precisely, a *Nisei* is a Japanese–American who was born in the United States and whose parents were born in Japan.

good at speaking and is a smart boy and is trying to learn more and eventually I think he will become very good.

The weather here this last week has been quite warm and humid. Today was about the warmest but this evening it clouded up and we had a thundershower which helped it cool off.

This weekend, I've stayed around and read and napped a little bit. This last week, as I said before, has been uneventful so I shall close.

Love,

Peter

The base without a fence

Sunday, May 18, 1952
Kadena Air Base; Okinawa

Dear Ma and Pa,

Well, another busy week but there really hasn't been too much worth reporting. I was duty agent Friday night. A guard shot himself through the hand, but he did it at eight in the evening so it didn't mean any loss of sleep.

This last week Ron Masters arrived here at Kadena.* Although all of his previous military training and schooling was as an exchange officer, they assigned him to a supply squadron, a rather typical act on the part of these people around here. And then they wonder why people don't like military service.

This afternoon we went down to Naha to look around the markets and see what was new. Nothing was, but it is always interesting to go through the market areas. A person sees more government property down there than he does on the base. At one time, the military government released property to the natives and made no provision to mark it. Now it is possible to steal things from the base and claim that it was part of the property that had been issued to the natives. The only thing that the natives cannot have in their possession is any part of the blue Air Force uniform. Mere possession is a felony with the establishment of true ownership not necessary for a conviction. However, this is only a very minor matter when one considers there is no one wearing blue uniforms here during most of the year.

As nearly as I can tell, the main fault lies with the military government in their lack of planning and control. A rather interesting example of their lax administration came up this week. It seems that right after the war was over, there was a lot of equipment that the government had no use for and that lay abandoned about the

---

* Ron Masters: see p. 75 note.

island. A system was set up whereby any native could buy it from the government by locating it, describing the item, and then paying a token sum for it and receiving a bill of sale from the military government to establish ownership.

This setup is still in effect. Now, due to a complete lack of fences on just about all parts of the island, and a lack of care taken by the different organizations possessing equipment, equipment often lies for some time in rather isolated places. An Okinawan found a Caterpillar [tractor] in a field that was fairly-well grown over, went to the military government at Naha, described it, and paid $100 for a bill of sale.

The army has a lieutenant-colonel down there who is charged with the responsibility of making sure it is abandoned property before signing it over to a native. He didn't do it, so the native got the bill of sale and immediately turned it over to a Japanese for about $1200. All of this in a day or two and he didn't even have to touch it. On top of that, the loss wasn't discovered for a couple of days by the organization responsible for it.

The security on this base is terrible. There is no fence around it and even the Air Police don't check the trucks as they leave. It isn't their fault entirely as they do not have enough men to take care of it.

I think that enough property leaves this base every six months to almost pay for the construction of a barbed-wire fence around it, to say nothing of the security value of a fence with roving patrols. I certainly would be ashamed of this base if I were the commanding general. One of these days there is going to be a big stink about it.

The weather here last week has been pretty good for the most part, but it is getting a little warmer all of the time.

I was thinking that after you get through with *The Saturday Evening Post* and no longer want it, it would be nice if you were to mail it to me. As there is no hurry about it, send it by boat mail. We get the Pacific edition of *Time*, which is pretty current, so current events are fairly well taken care of.

As I was thinking of buying a good camera and what with all of my clothing, I think it would be a rather good idea to get some insurance on my things. Mainly fire and fire damage, theft, and wind insurance. I shall look into the matter here, but as I am not sure if I can get any insurance here, would you mind looking around and see if there is any I could get there and if so just what it includes and exactly what the cost would be? I think that I should get some soon as the typhoon season will soon be here and if there is a bad one, the shack may leak.

Well, I can't seem to think of much else to report this time. I guess that the mail has been delayed this week, so I haven't got any of your questions to answer.

Love,
Peter

Nago and Yonabaru

Monday, May 26, 1952
Kadena Air Base; Okinawa

Dear Ma and Pa,

I'm sorry this letter is late, but this past week has been a very busy one. The weather through Sunday was pretty good. Hot in the daytime and rain several evenings. Yesterday and today, while it has been cloudy with a few showers, it has been quite humid and uncomfortable.

Last Tuesday, I went up to Nago for a short time. It is about 32 miles from here and a fairly good-sized village. The road runs along the west and is quite scenic.

Friday, I had to go down to Yonabaru for several hours. It too is a fairly large village. Leading the battle for Okinawa, the east anchor of the Japanese defensive line was in this area and while there are not many signs of the battle left, occasionally there are ruins of a cement building.

All along the coast are numerous wrecks of landing craft with a few larger ships; both as a result of warfare and typhoons. While there is a fairly deep bay here, Yonabaru is not the shipping port. Naha is. There are no wharves or piers at all.

Our intermediate Japanese class started last week (Tuesdays and Thursdays again). I had to work Thursday evening and didn't go. Saturday afternoon Willhelm and I went to Naha and bought a tent and looked around the market some. Earlier in the afternoon, Koza village had a ceremony marking the second anniversary of its business district (which consists of a wide, bumpy dirt road bordered with one- and two-story stores selling very little of anything of interest).

They had wrestling and dancing, both of which were quite interesting, especially the latter.

Sunday Major McCaffery and I went to Naha on business and I didn't have much of an opportunity to get a letter off.

Last night I was duty agent and outside of having to shake down three people around six, nothing happened, and I got a full night's sleep.

ANSWERS TO QUESTIONS

As far as the office personnel is concerned:

2 ADMINISTRATIVE OFFICERS:

a. District Commander—Major Jacobs

b. Operations Officer—Major McCaffery, direct supervisor of:

* 9 AGENTS (including myself)

* 3 CIVILIAN SECRETARIES

* 5 ADMINISTRATIVE ENLISTED MEN {1 M/Sgt, 1 Sgt, 2 Cpl, 1 Pfc}

* 1 OKINAWAN INTERPRETER AND TRANSLATOR

* 1 CIVIL SERVICE (NISEI)

* 1 MILITARY INTERPRETER (PFC-NISEI)

In addition, we got a new man this week—a 1st lieutenant to aid the Operations Officer

_____

23

In addition: four agents, one clerk, and a couple of interpreters at Naha AB.

In addition to some books I brought with me, there are several libraries. Also, the Pacific edition of *Time* and the Pacific edition of *Stars and Stripes* for current news in addition to the local radio.

I received the 1st can of cookies. While they are broken, they were very good. I had no idea postage was so much. I think we had better dispense with them in the future.

Pa, I'm ashamed that I forgot about your birthday until just now. But anyhow, I'll wish you a belated Happy Birthday.

About cables: RCA has a radio telephone station here, but I'm not sure exactly how they work. I imagine there are provisions for telegrams. If so, you can use the mailing address telephones:

Office: Kadena 43103
Quarters: Kadena 47275

Well, that's all for now. Again, a late Happy Birthday, Pa!
Love,
Peter

Law enforcement on the base

Sunday, June 1, 1952
Kadena Air Base; Okinawa

Dear Ma and Pa,

Well, no typewriter available this evening, hence the pen.

This last week has been a pretty busy one although there has been little of great interest. Somewhere along the line, I picked up a rather mild case of intestinal flu and as a result haven't been feeling too well.

Last Thursday morning from 2:00 till 5:00 the office [personnel]—most of them—went out and held an inspection of one of the Okinawan labor compounds, hunting for people who had no business on the base. Managed to get about a half-dozen. No telling how long they had been hiding over there as there is absolutely no supervision.

They are probably back over there now if anyone around here would look.

Payday yesterday, and as a result, several assaults were reported. One of the big troubles around here is a lack of supervision by the command. Some of the people on the actual combat crews get away with an awful lot. They seem to think that while they are not flying, anything goes and there is little they don't do—and often get away with.

Today, Willhelm, Masters, and I went to Ishikawa beach along with some other people. It is a pretty nice beach and I managed to get a good sunburn. This evening it is raining and quite bad.

Had a court-martial Thursday and we'll have to testify again tomorrow. Had a two-day delay so they could try to prove the defendant insane, I think. Well, will write again.

Love,

Peter

Details on the cement case

Tuesday, June 10, 1952
Kadena Air Base; Okinawa

Dear Ma and Pa,

Well, here it is Tuesday evening and I haven't gotten my weekly letter off yet. I had great plans of getting it written both Sunday and then yesterday evening, but the typewriter was in use. It is an old one they had down at the office and it was extra, so Drummond brought it up to the shack. It makes it nice for writing letters rather than having to write them out longhand.

About the only place I went to this week was down to Yonabaru again on my cement case. It seems that the native drivers trucking the cement to Kadena from Naha via Yonabaru were dumping it off in various villages and then going back for more. Then they would turn in the tally sheets at the end of a shift and pay the checker at the Kadena cement warehouse a little something to check in the cement.

If it hadn't been for some native policeman hearing gossip about it in Yonabaru, they would still be doing it. There was, and probably still is, a great lack of supervision on the part of the civilian contractors employed by the Air Force. The CP (Civil Police) station is looking more and more like a cement warehouse what with the cement they have recovered and are holding for evidence.

As long as there are only Okinawans involved, they are doing almost all of the questioning etc., and I just have to check with them occasionally and see what they have dug up and then put it in my case. In cases like this, they are pretty good. It really helps us as we don't have to cope with the language problem.

On the way back, I happened to stop at a native roof tile manufacturing place just to see how the tiles are made and I ran across fifty sacks of cement that the bird had no business possessing. I suppose that if I had time, it wouldn't be much trouble finding others around the area.

Friday afternoon, some little monster shot himself in the hand with a carbine and I had to go down to the hospital Saturday morning and talk to him about it, but he was still goofy. I shall have to go down again soon and try again. He was bordering on being a psycho, I believe.

Saturday afternoon, John and another agent in the office picked up a couple of civilians for stealing food from the mess hall and I helped take statements from them all afternoon and most of the evening, so last weekend went rather rapidly. I think that one of them was an alky [alcoholic] and by the time we got through with him, he had been off the stuff quite a while and could hardly sign the statement.

Sunday one of the agents had to go to Tokyo and Ernie, being duty agent, had to take him down to the plane at Naha (that is the base where all of the passenger transports leave from—Kadena is strictly an operational base) so I went along for the buggy ride.

On the way back, we stopped and went through the market at Naha and he wanted to get some material for seat covers. The market there is interesting and colorful. When I get a camera, I plan on taking some pictures of it. I think you will be interested in it.

They opened up a new PX over at Rycom the other day and Sunday evening Ernie and I went over there to look at it. It is quite nice, and they had a fairly good selection of things there. All of the PX merchandise for the Air Force PXs come through the Army PX system and as a result, our PX is often sadly lacking in some items. From what I understand, they had been saving all of the camera shipments for some time, so they could have a good selection when they opened up the store the other day.

I don't know how true it is, but it seems very believable that when they were constructing it, they left a cement mixer inside and couldn't get it out the doors and had to lift it through the roof with a crane. At least it is a good story and sounds very typical of something the military would do.

When we were over there, it was late and about the only ones left were these damn Filipinos buying up cigarettes and soap. They go right down to the villages and sell them to the natives. In the short time I have been over here, I have come to hate the Flips [i.e., Filipinos] with a passion.[1] They are responsible for most of the black-market activities and money-changing on the island.

Everyone is allowed a weekly ration of two cartons of cigarettes and then they can have an extra carton of Kools or Chesterfields to bring it up to three cartons in addition to a daily limit of two packages. And the Flips take them all. But the PX managers are more concerned with maintaining their sales than they are in the suppression of black-market activities. It certainly is disgusting.

Frankly, the Air Force general here on the base doesn't show me a thing. And I think that the Army general is lacking also.

The Army is responsible for the administration of the Ryukyus Command (Rycom) and as a result, the Air Force is forced to scratch for any- and everything

Most of last week it rained although the temperature didn't get much below 75 degrees. And then yesterday afternoon it rained harder than I have ever seen it rain. It came down in sheets for about five hours. As a result, there were quite a few washouts, and transportation is pretty well messed up. Luckily, the shack didn't leak but we had to close the windows, which makes it pretty hot. There was quite a wind with the rain.

I think that your trip up on the boat sounds like a lot of fun. I only hope that the weather is good for you. Won't you be going farther north this time than ever before?

Pearson is coming in this Saturday and Sunday if the boat is on schedule. I had originally been scheduled for duty agent on Sunday, but I traded with the person who has it for the following Sunday, so I will be off.[2]

In addition, the person with whom I share a jeep is the same one up in Tokyo and he probably won't be back by then, so everything is working out as far as that is concerned. But I'm just afraid that the

---

1. A derogatory and generally offensive term for Filipinos.

2. Donald C. Pearson: see p. 115, note 2.

weather is going to remain wet for a couple of more weeks. At least that is what the natives say.

Well, I can't think of anything else to report this time, so I shall close and go to bed. Will write later.

Love,

Peter

The conviction of a deserter—and another cement thief

Tuesday, June 17, 1952
Kadena Air Base; Okinawa

Dear Ma and Pa,

Well, here it is a couple of days over again for my weekly letter. And as usual, I'm not quite sure where the time has gone. Last Saturday, Pearson came in on the *Breckinridge* and I went down there. In the afternoon we drove around a little and then went over to the Rycom Officers Club for dinner.[1]

I stayed on the ship last night and then we drove around a little Sunday before the ship left again. Quite a few dependents onboard both ways. It certainly must be a strain on the crew with all of the wives and children on board ship getting in the way all of the time.

The weather cleared up Saturday afternoon, so everything worked out quite well. It has remained clear for the past few days, which is a relief after the rain for about two weeks. However, it has warmed up quite a bit.

Pearson has a few days when he gets back and is planning on going south, and he was desirous of getting Cooper's address. I was wondering if you would mind putting it on a postcard and airmailing it on down to him so it will be waiting there when he gets back? His address is 810 Granada Avenue, San Marino, California.[2]

I had planned on enclosing a card with his address, but it seems that I have none available this evening.

Had a small amount of excitement around here for about an hour Sunday evening. Last week they convicted the bird we picked up in the village who had been living on the northern part of the island for about eight months, of desertion, among other things.

---

1. Donald C. Pearson: see p. 115, note 2.

2. Martin Cooper: see p. 35, note 1.

Around eight o'clock in the evening, he broke out of the stockade (for the second time—the first time [was] about three weeks after he was apprehended for the first time) and managed to get to Kadena village before he was picked up.

Major Jacobs was the one who got him this time. He was sentenced to 18 years and was not too happy about it and managed to get a pair of pliers smuggled in by his girl. That makes the third time the office has picked him up and while it looks good on our reports, the Air Police in charge of the local stockade are getting a bit of trouble about it.

The other day, someone found a bunch of home-made bombs used by the natives for fishing in one of the old landing craft near the base but as it was off of the base, we had to turn it over to the Army CID for action.

I went along with the bird they sent over and when we got to the place there was a native fishing boat tied up to the bulk but when we waded out to it, he hopped in the boat and managed to get away with about ten feet to spare. I don't remember just when I have ever been so mad. The boat had a little inboard motor, and I do believe that it was the first time that I have ever seen a small boat motor start on the first crank. Neither of us had a gun and they managed to get clean away without a trace.

Saturday, I went tramping around a village on the way to Yonabaru to find a cement thief, but he wasn't home but the CP's picked him up that night so that is just something else for me to do. As soon as I get rid of my criminal cases, I am going to start taking over the counterintelligence activities of the office but at the rate I seem to fall into new criminal cases, I'm not sure just exactly when that will be. This bird had worked as a driver at Kadena about three months ago but had been laid off and then a week ago Sunday, he turned up at the Motor Pool and said that he was working on the cement haul and they issued him a truck. He went to Naha, picked up about 80 sacks of cement, and unloaded them in a village and then brought the truck back. They caught it Thursday. Another example of the good control they have around here.

Well, your trip in the Mother Lode country sounds like a good one. I hope that the weather is nice but not too hot for you. Mother, about your driving, I'm afraid that you are mistaken. Also, where is the dissertation on snuff that you mentioned last February? The flu is all over.

    Love,
    Peter

The annual rice harvest—and an airman drowns

Wednesday, June 25, 1952
Kadena Air Base; Okinawa

Dear Ma and Pa,

Well, late again. Somehow, I seem to be having a bit of trouble lately keeping up with my regular weekly schedule on Sundays. I had great plans for getting a few letters written last Sunday but we had a typhoon in the offing, and I spent most of the day helping board up our shack and the office and the duty agent's shack.

The typhoon hit here starting around seven in the evening but never did hit the island full force. It veered off and the center of it passed to the west. At that, we had about 50-mile winds around midnight, but it was bright and shining the next morning at eight, just in time for work.

The lights went off around 11:30 and there wasn't much to do but go to bed. A little bit of water came in under the door to our shack, but it didn't amount to much. About the only good thing about it was that I didn't have to sleep in the duty agent's shack. I traded last weekend, so I could see Pearson when he was here, and I got it a week late. I am on again tonight and now back on schedule.

About five Sunday afternoon, an airman fell in one of the creeks near here that was in a mild flood stage and drowned; and I was out until about ten o'clock on that. By that time, it was blowing quite hard and it was also raining. While actually not that much rain fell, the strong wind made the rainfall seem rather heavy.

While it missed the island for the most part, there was some damage to the north. I saved an article about it that I shall send. When it got to Tokyo, there was quite a bit of damage done, and several people were killed.

They are harvesting the rice around here now. It is really interesting. Last weekend, I saw several women with flails beating out the rice from the husks. I wish that I had had a camera along with me.*

The winds didn't seem to do too much damage to the rice around here, but I don't know about the northern part of the island that was hit the heaviest. However, the rice season up there is several weeks behind that in this area, so I don't imagine that any was shattered by the wind.

Yesterday, I spent the whole day down at Yonabaru and I shall have to go down there again tomorrow but for not as long, I hope. The civil police did not do a good job of taking statements and the thieves are out on bail and things are quite complicated. It will be a relief to get rid of that case and be able to spend all of my time on counterintelligence matters.

I sent Ann a telegram for her graduation. I only hope that it got there in time. I had planned on sending one to her just before the boat left but things started to gang up on me and I didn't have an opportunity to get over to the RCA station in time.

Last week I sent you some clippings that I had been saving that I thought might interest you and I think that I have about enough to send again this week. The news here in the papers isn't too interesting for the most part. About the main regular feature, in addition to baseball news and the three comic strips, is a picture of the latest colonel to be awarded the Bronze Star for conspicuous and meritorious action behind some dark desk in an air-conditioned office. I think they are awarded to every thousandth person that they manage to thoroughly confuse or for every tenth time they get drunk and make a spectacle of themselves in the club. Some of these people around here in responsible positions show me absolutely nothing.

Well, I can't think of anything else for this evening. I hope that you had a nice time on the way back from Ann's graduation.

Love,

Peter

---

* Flails are threshing tools.

Translation issues; factory life

Tuesday, July 1, 1952
Kadena Air Base; Okinawa

Dear Ma and Pa,
This last week has really gone by rapidly. It seems like only yesterday that I wrote the last letter.

Last Friday, I had to go down to Yonabaru again, but I didn't get anything accomplished as they had let the people out on bail—the ones I was interested in. But I made arrangements for them to be there Thursday and Friday, so I shall have to go down there again.

I have to get statements from them, and what with struggling with the interpreter, it is quite a job; believe me.

After working with him a couple of hours I feel like I have been through the ringer. The statements have to be taken in Kanji (Japanese) and then they have to be translated up here afterwards. And, I am never quite sure what has been put into the statements until I actually see the translations. The interpreter is not too good at times and periodically has to be straightened out.

Getting it translated back into English is just about as bad although I don't have to do anything about that except worry. The Okinawan interpreter who took the statement originally reads it to the Nisei interpreter who in turn writes it down to English. I find that after talking to the Okinawan interpreter all day, it takes me quite a while before I can do a proper job talking to anyone in English again.

Instead of giving an Okinawan (or Japanese) an oath, after finishing the statement, they affix their right thumbprint to the statement which is just as binding as an oath. This is referred to as a hand statement. Quite often, the more affluent Okinawans will have their own stamp which is nothing more than the symbols of their name carved in the end of a small piece of wood or ivory which serves in lieu of a thumbprint.

In addition, businessmen usually carry with them a small tin of orange dye for their signature stick or thumbprint. It is nothing more than a gauze pad with orange dye in it.

Last Sunday, Willhelm, Masters, Gosh, and I drove down to Itoman to look around. It is about ten miles below Naha on the coast. It is perhaps second to Naha as a seaport; most of the shipping, however, is extra-legal. Or at least a good percentage of it is. It is the home port for much of the native shipping that is capable of making extended sea voyages.

We went through the black-market there and it seemed better equipped with hardware than is the black-market area of Naha. Much of the stuff is brand new and obviously of doubtful origin but there is no way of determining true ownership. It makes a person pretty mad but there is nothing you can do about it.

Just before we got there, someone had brought in a large sea-going turtle and it was being cut up. Talk about a Roman holiday. Kids, dogs, and flies all over the place.

The meat markets are also quite interesting, although often rather repulsive. Outside of skinning the animals and hacking them up into chunks, there is absolutely no further preparation. Heads, feet, eyeballs, and all, complete with a goodly sized swarm of flies at no extra charge.

I took several pictures with Willhelm's camera that I hope will come out. Showing the type of native vessels and also some of the coral blocks used to make walls around some of the larger houses.

The coral blocks are about eight to ten inches square and up to six or eight feet in length. They make a nice-appearing building material when they are cut properly and put together in the right manner. For mortar, when they can't steal any cement or don't want to buy any on the legitimate market, they make a mortar using lime and clay mixed with straw. The lime is obtained by heating round chunks of coral gathered along the coast—about the size of a small watermelon. These chunks of coral are heated in large hive-like ovens burning charcoal usually, or less often, tar or asphalt. It is really interesting to observe the process.

There was also a noodle factory down there that we looked at. It was in a small building right along the main street where we could look in. The natives eat quite a fair amount of the noodles. They come out quite yellow—I imagine the color is a result of some type of vegetable dye rather than a result of the use of eggs.

There has been another typhoon in the offing the past couple of days. It is down around Guam but not heading this way. I wouldn't be surprised if it managed to get here about Saturday when I am duty agent again. But as long as I can't do a great deal anyhow, I suppose the typhoon had better come then than any other time.

Each typhoon of the season is given a woman's name according to the alphabet. Supposedly, they manage to go through the alphabet about twice a year. However, only a small portion of these ever have any great influence on the weather here.

The weather here the past couple of weeks has been quite warm—between 80 and 90 with high humidity. The fan I purchased certainly is coming in handy as it doesn't get much below 75 at night.

The oatmeal cookies arrived in good shape—no breakage—as did the candy from San Francisco. I was quite surprised at the candy as it showed little sign of melting. As yet, *The Saturday Evening Post*s have not arrived but coming by boat, it will take a little time, so I shall get them pretty soon. The magazine concession here recently was turned over by the PX system to a private supplier—as a result, we now have a wide assortment of aviation and movie magazines and a wider assortment of comic books. I only hope that they manage to maintain the service on *Time* magazine. That is about the only magazine worth the mention that we do get here.

I'm sorry the weather was so hot for you on your trip through California after Ann's graduation. I hope the weather will be better for you when you go north. Both of you have mentioned you are going but then go on to say that you imagine the other has written concerning the details.

I got a letter from Ann yesterday from South Hampton. It certainly made good time. I got it the same time as one from you postmarked a day earlier. She seemed to enjoy her trip over on the boat.

Well, that is about all that I can think of to report for the time being. I had a haircut today. The Flips do a fair job of cutting hair but they can't seem to realize that the clippings belong on the floor, not down a person's neck.

Love

Peter

Interrogating a cement thief—and cockfighting

Wednesday, July 9, 1952
Kadena Air Base; Okinawa

Dear Ma and Pa,

Well, late again but then as you will not be home when this arrives, I suppose that it doesn't make too much difference.

First of all, Mother, the magazines—*Saturday Evening Post*—arrived yesterday and I imagine that from now on, their arrival will be fairly steady, depending upon ship arrival; usually about every week to ten days.

This last week has been quite a busy one. Both Thursday and Friday I had to go to Yonabaru again on the cement business. Needless to say, it is becoming a little tiring, especially in view of all of the other things that should be attended to immediately.

In the course of interrogating the cement thieves, I ran across four of them who admitted to the theft of lumber sometime in April—each [took] a truckload and there is no record of any lumber missing so we can't open any kind of a case on it.

While the Army got the 4th off, we had to work. In fact, the Army even gets Wednesday afternoons off. They really have a deal here on the island and are certainly taking advantage of it.

Over the 4th, there was a carnival at one of the beaches near here. It consisted of different gambling devices whereby one could lose his money. Willhelm and I went up there Sunday. All of the Flips around the base have sponsored cockfights. Having never seen any before, it was interesting. I got quite a kick out of all the bickering and wagering before the fight, which usually lasted less than a minute.

All proceeds went for the beach fund, which is supposedly for the betterment of the recreational facilities at the beaches maintained by the military.

Monday, I again had to go down there about the cement but things [are] beginning to shape up and I shouldn't have to make many more trips.

I was sorry to hear that you missed the Krass collection when it was in Portland.* I'm sure you would have enjoyed it. Perhaps you will be able to see it again sometime.

Outside of the one cement case, I have no more criminal cases and am spending my time on counter-intelligence matters. It is quite a bit more interesting but there is a great deal to it. I have one sergeant working for me, which is a big help.

One of the big handicaps of the office is lack of transportation. Having to wait around for a jeep when something comes up is an inconvenience, to say the least. I like the work, but it is the little things like that which make things disagreeable.

Today, the jeep that I share was in the shop all day just getting a new spring. The other fellow I shared the jeep with abused the privilege and was shifted around so he would not exercise as much control over the jeep, which certainly was a break for me. Out of all the people in the office, we only have two ringers, a pretty good average considering everything. That one and a warrant officer who gets on everyone's nerves. He also acts as supply officer. He misspelled my name again today, so I gave him a calling card to put in his files for future reference.

Major Jacobs left Monday for Tokyo to attend a Far Eastern Air Forces skeet shoot. He may get back tomorrow. However, if by chance he gets hot and makes the team for the Far East Air Forces, he will go to Dallas for the main event. He was only up there last week. One of these days, he is going to go up to Tokyo and stick his head in the main office one too many times and he will get his head chopped off by the colonel, who doesn't go for all of this traveling around. When that happens, things will be a little grim around here as Jake is a little difficult to get along with when he figures the colonel is breathing down his neck. He is very likable as an individual, but he simply doesn't realize what is going on around here and it doesn't seem that he is just about to find out. Everyone around here takes him with a grain of salt and hence the office as a whole is oftentimes handicapped a bit.

---

* Peter may refer to the work of furniture designer Christian Krass, 1868–1957.

All the stuff that goes on around here is really amusing. Thank goodness I'm not planning on making a career out of this. I don't think I would get too far.

Major McCaffery, operations officer—who actually runs the office—is leaving here in less than a month and as yet we have had no replacement sent in. As the type of work that is expected of an operations officer—and especially here, where he has to do all of Jake's work—varies quite a bit with each district, if we don't get a replacement soon, things may very well become a bit confused soon. Quite a bit of his work depends upon his liaison with other offices here on the island. This is especially true when we have to beg for just about anything we need in the way of supplies and especially in the way of services.

Don't get me wrong, I'm not unhappy or complaining. It is a shame the way things are done most of the time around the island.

Will write later,

Peter

Club life

Wednesday, July 16, 1952
Kadena Air Base; Okinawa

Dear Ma and Pa,
Well, I seem to have slipped again but as the mail doesn't go out every day, it doesn't make much difference if I get the letters written on Monday or Wednesday. Usually, on Sundays, Willhelm and I go up to the club for Sunday dinner and often get delayed until rather late.

Instead of the usual 65 cents for the evening meal, they have a dollar dinner which is either steak or chicken; more often, it is steak. On the average, the steak one gets here—at any of the various messes and clubs—is good but not worth much more than a dollar.

However, we have been rather lucky the past couple of months in that our cuts have been better than most, judging from what other people have to say. All of the meat—whether it is served in regular messes, officers clubs, or the civilian club—comes through the Army quartermaster with the only possible difference being in the preparation which, for the most part, is pretty fair.

Of course, Sunday dinner is a bit of rat race what with everyone bringing their families up there, but it is a bit different. One of the main drawbacks—in addition to some of the drunks who manage to regularly make spectacles of themselves, including the Base Commander here (rumor has it that in a drunken stupor he hit an Okinawan last Saturday while driving with another drunken colonel), is the caliber of single civilian women who are hired here on the base (and island).

Below a certain civil service category, they are not supposed to have access to the officers clubs, but that rule, like so very many around here, is not enforced. I saw one this evening walking through the club in her bare feet—the same one who was at one short-time [i.e., briefly] employed in the Wing Provost Marshall's office. She didn't like it because he wouldn't let her take her shoes off around the office. (The one before that was canned because she was telling her "boyfriends"—

and I use that term charitably—all about our cases, which are classified a minimum of "confidential," and the only way we found out about that is that one of these friends was a bit too much on the "gay" side and we had to run a case on him and during the course of that investigation he was a bit worried about it getting out to his other friends).

Sounds a bit complicated now that I look it over, but it isn't that involved. There is also a group of women with the title of Special Service Workers who run the libraries, service clubs for the airmen, and act as Red Cross liaison workers. Several of these are performing "services" which very likely are not written up in their official job descriptions.

It is too bad in that there are those—even if they may be in the minority—who are honest and sincere in their efforts and do perform duties that are necessary. Sounds like the ramblings of a prude but I don't believe that I am being unfair.

There have been several showers here the past few days and as a result, the humidity has been rather oppressive.

Saturday Willhelm and I went through a couple of the local black markets and market areas which I always find quite interesting although often quite smelly.

Sunday, we took a jeep and drove around a bit near the base and along the beach. Came across a bunch of stolen cement in a local block factory but as yet I haven't had an opportunity to make arrangements for a truck to go out and pick it up.

This morning we had a weekly district meeting and then this noon, Major Jacobs and I went to the monthly CIC meeting and lunch which took a couple of hours. The whole day was shot what with the two meetings—that is, as far as my work was concerned. The man who is the American (civilian) head of the civil government of the Ryukyu Islands attends these meetings most of the time. If he showed me any less, there would be an empty chair in his place.

I was duty agent last night. Outside of a flat tire early in the evening, nothing happened, luckily, and I got a full night's sleep. I have been lucky lately as far as that is concerned. I'm just afraid that one of these nights when I'm duty agent, there is going to be a triple homicide or something. Next month at this time, unless we get some replacements pretty soon, we will be pulling duty every eight days instead of every ten as it now stands.

Two men are scheduled to leave sometime after the first of August. One of them is the operations officer. If they don't send a replacement down here before he leaves, I'm just afraid Jake is in for a rude awakening. He has no idea just what in the hell is going on. We could be baking bread in the office, and if it didn't smell, Jake wouldn't know about it for a week. The past couple of days he has suddenly decided to do a little investigative work (after it is a sure thing). Today he had a man that one of the agents had the goods on and started questioning him. The man claimed that he was being framed and wouldn't tell Jake the truth. It was really funny—Jake was all for throwing the man in the stockade right then and there. He took it as a personal affront that the man would lie to him.

Well, out of paper and it is getting late. Will write later.

Love,

Peter

A Republican looks at the other party

Wednesday, July 23, 1952
Kadena Air Base; Okinawa

Dear Ma and Pa,

Again, this last week has passed quite rapidly. I still manage to keep good and busy. In fact, I have too much to do if anything, but I suppose that is better than not having enough to do.

For the most part, this past week has been rather wet. Not too dissimilar from our May weather what with showers and then sunshine. Of course, when the sun comes out, it is much hotter and extremely humid. It rained most of last weekend and as a result, I didn't have much of a chance to get out anywhere.

Saturday night, I helped one of the other agents in the office with one of his cases and then did a little more Sunday morning and afternoon.

Am listening to the rebroadcast of the Democratic Convention.[1] They certainly have played up the 'common man' to the high heavens. That's the main trouble with them; they are too damn common. I struggled through them last night until one of the Roosevelts came on and started haranguing and I had to turn it off.

The caliber of their speeches certainly can't begin to be compared with that of the Republicans but then when you consider that most of the delegates—without the aid of Roosevelt and the New Deal— would under normal circumstances be pushing a broom in a warehouse someplace, they really do fairly well for themselves.

The woman speakers are especially poor. Talk about the exaggerated half-truths used by the Communists. I'm just afraid that we aren't too much advanced when it comes to these speeches. One of these women

---

1. The 1952 Democratic National Convention nominated Illinois Governor Adlai E. Stevenson, who would lose the Presidential race of that year to Dwight D. Eisenhower.

is talking about Ethiopia. I suppose that it is very important and all of that, but I fail to see what it has to do with the convention.

Had a little bad news this week. I had thought that I would be able to close up my cement case, but it seems that it still lacks quite a bit. I added another eight subjects to it today to bring up the grand total to 23 different persons. What with one to three subjects as being normal, you can see that the thing is turning out to be quite a mess.

What gripes me is that although the Air Force lost well over a thousand sacks of cement, there is no paperwork that reflects this loss. They claim they haven't enough personnel to check up on the native drivers etc., but I saw in the paper here about a week ago that they are sending about half a dozen men up to Tokyo for a week, so they can attend a school for football coaches.

So far, I've had two letters from Ann since she got off the boat—the last one arriving today. Took ten days which isn't too bad at all. It sounds like she is having a wonderful time. I hope that it continues as pleasant for her as it seems to have been so far.

Right now, they're cheering Eleanor and are making quite a production of it all. I suppose that considering what all her husband did for all the two-bit politicians in the country, it is the least they can do for her.[2]

I also received your postcard from Sullivan Bay today.[3] It took ten days which was pretty good I thought as I imagine that there isn't any airmail service from there. The letter written on the 12th of July also arrived. It sounds like you are having a good time and are getting to see a lot of new country. I hope that the weather has been good and that it hasn't been too hot for you.

Saw a lovely linen tablecloth the other day that was made in Hong Kong, but as it cost $250, I figured that it might not fit the table. They

---

2. Former First Lady Eleanor Roosevelt (1884–1962) was the widow of President Franklin D. Roosevelt. A public figure in her own right, she was U.S. Delegate to the United Nations from 1945 to 1952. From 1935 to 1962, she wrote a newspaper column, "My Day."

3. Possibly Sullivan, Quebec.

have quite a bit of Noritake china from Japan for sale around here. Several patterns are nice, but I don't know enough about it to know exactly how it compares with the china that one gets in the states.

Our headquarters in Tokyo still haven't sent down any replacements although the two men are due to leave here sometime next month, and the time is getting a little short to have to start training anyone else for their jobs. On top of that future problem, Jake has been especially trying this last week. We had our regular weekly meeting this morning at which he harangued us about being more careful in our investigations and then he went out and shot skeet for a couple of hours.

He is nothing more than a big dumb Texan. This has been a rather bad week for him. He has had to make a couple of decisions and whatnot. On top of that, there has been a little trouble with one of the three secretaries. Seems that she has her own ideas about the wording of the reports and one of the agents got mad and turned the case back to be rewritten. Two of the three have very definite minds of their own and it is funny when they start in about something. Too bad they are as good as they are, otherwise, it would be no trouble to fire them and get a couple of others. Working in that office is undoubtedly one of the funniest things that has ever happened to me. There is never a dull moment.

Outside of Jake, there is only one other ringer in the office which isn't too bad, considering everything. Really sort of funny although rather tragic when one considers all of the U.S. money in the project. It seems that the U.S. built a large ice plant at Naha mainly for the benefit of the fisheries. But it seems that most of the boats are too small or they don't have the facilities for ice, or they are out smuggling so they can't use all of the ice production.

The rest of the ice is sold to the bordellos about the island who use a lot of it. Not quite what was in mind for the ice when the plant was built but they figure that it might as well be sold than let it go to waste.

If you should ever have occasion to run across some person in the future by the name of Douglas Lamont around town stay clear of him. At least he claims that he is going to settle in Portland and practice law. A more completely obnoxious person I don't believe that I have ever come across. He is getting ready to be routed home from here after having been assigned to one of the bomber outfits for six months.

The maids had some sort of spring housecleaning today and had everything spread out on the grass to sun. I only hope that the rugs and cushions didn't pick up too many fleas. A little while ago, a portable sprayer came on by the shack and the next thing we knew, you couldn't see across the room because of the dense clouds of DDT. I'm not too sure how much good this spraying does, as there are several various insects flying about the room right now.

I'm duty agent again this Friday but as it is near the end of the month, I hope they won't have enough money to get into too much trouble in the villages. However, seeing as how they are broke, I suppose that might tend to produce some burglaries. Never a dull moment around here.

This next week is going to be a busy one what with the end of the month and the monthly reports to submit. While there does seem to be a lot of paperwork, most of it is necessary so it isn't too bad.

Really funny. A day or two ago the office received some sort of communication from a personnel management branch of some sort on the base informing us that we were not allocated any civilian stenographers and that we would have to justify the need for the three that we have in the office. I'll never be able to figure out what practical purpose there is in sending down such a communication when everyone knows there isn't going to be any change or action taken. It is merely a waste of time. But I suppose that if someone didn't keep making these surveys, he would be out counting cement as it is received (where he is really needed).

It's a shame that appropriations have to be increased for the military when such things are going on, but you know darn well that any cut in appropriations would not affect such operations but rather would affect some operation that is of importance.

Well, it is getting late and I have a lot to do tomorrow, so I had better close. I've forgotten if in my last letter I made any mention of receiving the shirt you sent us from California. It arrived about a week ago. Thank you very much. What with the weather such as it is, the shirt is the most practical one.

Well, by the time this arrives, I imagine you will be back on schedule from the vacation. Don't work too hard.

Love,
Peter

A padlock and some fishing hooks

Wednesday, July 30, 1952
Kadena Air Base; Okinawa

Dear Ma and Pa,

Well, I have managed to keep myself quite busy this last week but nothing of unusual interest has happened except for an armed assault Monday evening.

Last Saturday, Willhelm and I went down to Naha for a few minutes to buy a padlock and some fishhooks. We had planned to go fishing on Sunday, but it rained and didn't clear up until around four in the afternoon, so we decided to go some other time.

I received a postcard from you yesterday mailed in Canada on the 21st I believe, which is pretty good time. Sounds like you are having a nice time, but I imagine that by this time, you are back at home again.

I also received two letters from Ann in which she seems to be having a fine time. She certainly is taking advantage of every moment of time she has extra.

I still haven't gotten a camera yet although I have put my name in for one, so I imagine that it shouldn't be too long. I hope it comes in soon as there are many things I want to get pictures of. They are planting the second crop of rice these days. It seems that in some places, the rice more or less re-seeds itself, so they don't have to plant more small rice plants.

As yet we have no replacements. The two who are leaving got their orders the other day and they are to be transferred on out by the eighth of August. They probably will leave on the 12th from the island as that is the departure date of the next large ship. . . .

Well, can't think of much else to report this time. I guess that the last letter just about talked me out for a while. Will write later. Take it easy. (The weather here this last week has been pretty good with the exception of last Sunday).

Love,
Peter

"This is typical of the way our headquarters operates."

Tuesday, August 5, 1952
Kadena Air Base; Okinawa

Dear Ma and Pa,
Well, nothing of unusual interest this last week. Last Saturday I was
duty agent again and then on Sunday Ernie and I took a trip in the jeep
and went down to Shuri, the site of the main Ryukyu Government
buildings and the University of the Ryukyus. We went down the east
coast and from there to Naha and on back along the west coast.

It was warm and sunny and a nice day for a trip. The big strain of
taking a trip is the dust and also the bumpy roads. Riding around in a
jeep is not the most comfortable way to do it but with the roads the way
they are, a jeep is the most practical method of conveyance.

Shuri is up in the hills overlooking Naha and is really well-situated
as far as scenery is concerned. You can see across the island from many
places there. During the battle for Okinawa, it was one of the main
Japanese defense positions and was the headquarters area for some
time. It was completely flattened with only the remains of a couple of
concrete reinforced buildings remaining.

I went down there to buy a couple of wood carvings but the man who
carves them was not at home. Saw some of his carvings at the Ishikawa
carnival over the 4th and hope to get a couple sometime. We went to
Naha from there to buy you (Ma) a birthday present but they didn't
have what I wanted so I will have to wait until later.

Jake went to Tokyo Monday morning and is due back again
tomorrow sometime in the afternoon. Went by way of Korea—
exemption of income tax I believe but am not sure. The general had
planned the trip originally in his plane. In addition to the regular crew,
they were taking another crew up to Japan in order to ferry down
another plane.

What with the extra crew going along, there was not going to be
enough room for everyone, and Jake was due to be bumped, as he had
no official business to conduct in Tokyo. So, he comes up with the story

that he had to take the gun and bullet (on Willhelm's assault case) to the crime lab for a ballistics test.

Well, that got him on OK but then he decided that he had actually better take the gun up with him in case the general asked to see it. In the meantime, an order for Ernie's trip arrived from Tokyo. All of this changing around is making the paperwork that much more difficult as the chain of custody must be maintained all along the line.

Ernie is leaving tomorrow to go on up to pick up the evidence from the lab. Sounds complicated and it is.

That damn Jake is the most aggravating man I have ever seen. I [think] that it is a good thing that he is away from the office as much as he is; otherwise he would just be around underfoot, causing more confusion. He was fairly well-panicked that the colonel in charge of our headquarters would find out about the deal but with his luck, he will get out of it. Last month, he went on up to Tokyo for three days for a skeet meet without the colonel finding out. The colonel bothers him a lot but not enough to warrant him doing anything about it.

Got a new man on Sunday but not the one we were expecting. He had been assigned to Tokyo for a couple of months, but he was having some type of domestic troubles where it was necessary to get his wife over here as soon as possible. So, those people up there send him down here where the wait is even longer—now it is a year from the time of arrival on the island before a married man can get his dependents over here.

That is typical of the way our headquarters operates. They have no idea of what is going on down here and apparently don't seem to be worried about it. Jake won't do anything about clueing them in unless it is something that affects him personally.

The weather here this last week has been hot and humid. It rained the other afternoon for a couple of hours but has been nice since then. Still no typhoons but there have been a couple around Guam these past two weeks.

Will try to catch up on my back correspondence this next Sunday when I am duty agent again. In the meantime, say hello to everyone for me.

Love,
Peter

"A rather bloody week"

Monday, August 11, 1952
Kadena Air Base; Okinawa

Dear Ma and Pa,

Well, this last week has gone by about as rapidly as the previous ones and I remain plenty busy. I had duty agent again last night (and all day yesterday) and this time things weren't as quiet as they have been. A guard shot an Okinawan who supposedly jumped him, and I didn't get to bed until 2 a.m. Luckily, he didn't die but he was pretty badly injured. As he wasn't employed by the government, they wouldn't keep him at the Army hospital any longer than to put temporary patches over the holes and then they sent him off to the native hospital which, from what I gather, leaves a great deal to be desired.

It seems to me that the man should have been kept by the Army a couple of days at least but then they seem to think differently about it. They hustled him out of there, and the nurse explained that they didn't want to take the responsibility—which seems to be a stock answer to any problem that arises.

I made some remark to that and as a result, we didn't part friends.

Also, this last week, another Okinawan was shot and killed when he jumped another guard. Also, some airman committed suicide, so you can see that this has been a rather bloody week.

I still have that damn cement case. I haven't had an opportunity to do any work on it so far this month, but I do have great hopes of being able to close it out sometime before the end of the month.

Major McCaffery and John leave on the boat tomorrow afternoon. I hate to see them leave. Jake is going to be a big problem. Willhelm is going to take over as Operations Officer for a couple of months until we get the new man broken in as to the operations in the field (the other new man arrived this last week from Tokyo, so we have gained two for the two we are losing but just barely in time).

Jake does get credit for income tax suspension for his trip to Korea. Talk about a tax loophole; that is a prime example.

Spent six hours Saturday night and Sunday morning north of here a little way along the coast looking at a rock that was supposed to be a boat. These people around here certainly have no plans in case of an emergency. It is pitiful.

About the check, I shall send it on in my next letter. However, I was under the assumption that you were going to draw against my bank account in Portland in such matters. Thank you for going to the trouble of getting it for me.

Well, Ma, seeing as how this will probably go out in the mail tomorrow, this letter will just about get to you on your birthday so: Happy Birthday. I hope that you have a nice birthday and that you don't try to do too much.

I had to go to Naha today and on the way back I stopped so see if there was any lacquer that looked good, but I didn't see anything that especially appealed to me and as I was in a hurry, I didn't want to take the time to order anything at this time. There have been quite a few dependents arriving here on the island the past couple of months and also quite a few leaving and between the two groups, they have been checking around for things to buy.

Ever since before last Christmas, they have been working on a new four-lane road from Kadena to Naha—a distance of about fifteen miles. So far—and just within the last four weeks—they have managed to pave about three miles of it. And, at that, the new pavement seems to have quite a few waves in it, and I doubt if they will be able to complete it before they have to start making repairs on the part that was first completed. In one place, the pavement (macadam) hadn't been down two days when they had to dig up a little of it for a culvert or something.

The weather here this past week has remained just about the same— still with no typhoons which is just fine with me.

We will have about another six weeks of warm weather as near as I can find out before it is due to cool off a bit. August is supposed to be the hottest month.

Well, it is getting late and I still have to take a shower and do a little reading yet. Will write later.

Love,
Peter

"The burglaries have been pretty thick . . . "

Saturday, August 16, 1952
Kadena Air Base; Okinawa

Dear Ma and Pa,

Well, outside of the typhoon that we had this last week, there isn't too much to report. It started to blow Thursday evening and then increased all day Friday until about 9 p.m. Friday when it was over 80 mph with gusts up to 105 mph.

By Saturday morning, it was fairly calm, and we were able to go back to work. The electricity was turned off around 1:30 Friday afternoon and wasn't turned on again until Saturday morning. The shack stood up well. No leaks in the roof or walls but water was blown in under the front door and along the foundation on the south side of the building.

For the most part, the buildings here at Kadena held up pretty well but a couple of warehouses of the Army blew down. The native villages seemed to have held up pretty well from what I have seen with just a few houses with the thatch looking even ruffled. However, the paper said that some of the fishing villages were damaged.

It also said that quite a few of the native fishing boats were beached and some were sunk which will probably mean that the smuggling industry will be comparatively inactive for a few weeks. About the only signs of the typhoon in the villages near here are the battered banana trees.

Had a new man move in this last week—a major—who seems like a pretty nice person.

This last week has been another busy one. Things piled up what with not working on Friday. Today Jake wanted to know why one of my reports was a couple of days late. It sat on his desk for two days while he didn't read it, but I decided to blame it on the typhoon instead.

Poor Ernie is having his hands full trying to learn the job as operations officer and at the same time trying to learn Jake's duties. That man has absolutely no conception of what is going on around here and he thinks he knows it all. And what an apple polisher.

A couple of idiot colonels stationed here left their doors open and were robbed. Jake nearly broke his neck trying to get everyone out in the villages hunting up the stolen property. Luckily the things were found fairly soon, no thanks to him though. You would think that by the time a man got to be a full colonel, he would have been around enough to realize that not everyone is honest and that he would make a slight attempt to take care of his things, but it doesn't seem so around here.

It happened at night when one of them was flying and the other one was sleeping. They came in their shack and cleaned them out. The only thing one of them had left were the clothes he had on his back. The other one reported that he just lost some money and was rather surprised when a pair of his pants were recovered.

Last week—a week ago Sunday—an Okinawan was shot and seriously wounded by an Air Force guard. Just the previous Monday, another one was killed for being off-limits. The natives in the area are pretty unhappy about it and have been making complaints to the United States Civil Administration of the Ryukyus (USCAR) in Naha.

The burglaries have been pretty thick lately with at least an average of one a night. There is one construction camp supply warehouse that has been hit repeatedly during the past couple of months and the civilian supervisor wants permission to go down there with a shotgun at night and stand guard seeing as how the Air Force can't (or won't) supply guards. But both the wing and the 20th Air Force Provost Marshals are afraid that he will shoot another Okinawan and cause more trouble. I sometimes wonder just who is occupying whom.

Another big problem around here is large tires used on construction vehicles—mainly earthmovers and large trucks. According to the contracts let by the Air Force, the construction companies have to furnish their own equipment although they can buy it from the Air Force (or borrow it from the Air Force as long as they keep it up) .

It seems that some sizes are a bit short so some outfit (probably a Japanese construction company) has been stealing tires left on unattended vehicles during the night. There doesn't seem to be any pressure put upon the leasing companies to safeguard their equipment. A six-foot tire worth $800 would seem to be fairly hard to get away with but it seems to be fairly easy around here. The security around here is pathetic.

I am enclosing a check for the amount to cover the purchase price of the bond and the extra rights. I just received a statement of my bank account with the Bank of California and I see by it that you haven't been drawing any money out of there. If something like this should come up again, perhaps it would be easier if you were to draw on that account and then notify me later of the date, amount, and to whom the check was made out.

Well, I can't think of anything else to report this time. Will write later. Don't try to do too much work.

Love,

Peter

End of the cement case?

Wednesday, August 27, 1952
Kadena Air Base; Okinawa

Dear Ma and Pa,
Well, I ran over again this week. I forget what the reason was for not writing Monday evening. Last night I was duty agent again and didn't have an opportunity—although nothing happened. Sunday Willhelm and I went to the beach for a couple of hours and managed to pick up a sunburn, not as bad as the one a couple of months ago. In the evening we went to a civilian club for dinner. The last couple of weeks, the food around here has really deteriorated for some reason.

Please, for goodness sake, don't worry about my getting along with Jake. Give me a little credit for having some sense!

Sometime this coming week I am going to send my cribbage board home so you might expect it in about another six to eight weeks. It is a pretty good sample of the lacquer-wear you can get over here. I have been looking for a cigarette case and ashtray set but as yet haven't been able to find any. There are only two places here on the island where they manufacture the stuff and they are fairly well picked over. I haven't had an opportunity lately to get down there. Both of them are down at Naha. A couple of us had to go down there the other afternoon on business but we didn't have time to stop by and do any shopping.

The weather here this last week has been quite warm with a few clouds and on occasion a shower. Had a little excitement this last week. About 50 yards from the shack, they are grading for a new road, and in the process they uncovered a couple of 200-pound bombs that had been in the ground since the war. While they were fused, they didn't go off, which is a good thing, being so close to the BOQ area.

I'm enclosing a couple of newspaper articles that I have been meaning to send for some time. The one about the office is the case of the colonels who left their door open and the case where Jake damn near broke his neck getting everyone out of the office. A reasonably accurate account of the whole thing but in contrast to much of our work out here, it is quite inconsequential.

There is also the article about the typhoon. It seems to be a slight bit exaggerated if anything, but as I understand it, with every typhoon that occurs, the Air Force gets additional expenditures to patch up the damage and hence blames the wind for a lot of damage for which it was not directly responsible. Even almost all of the banana trees have grown new leaves since then.

The rice paddies seem to have gotten by OK, but we saw quite a few sugarcane fields—especially around Naha—that looked pretty badly hit. I don't know if they will come out of it or not.

Just today a supply officer from one of the bomber squadrons—one of the heroes—called up and reported the loss of several hundred sheets and pillowcases and a dozen or so Army folding cots, which were supposedly stolen during the typhoon. Upon further questioning, it became apparent that he was just trying to cover up a shortage.

Sort of gripes a person to see some bum trying to get away with that sort of thing, but there is nothing that will be done to him.

The hotel is finally open for business. When we were down at Naha last week, we got a warrant and searched the place for about 60 inner-spring mattresses that were stolen from here last Spring, but we didn't have much luck. In fact, none.

But it was interesting looking around the place. It is a good-looking building from the outside but the workmanship on the inside certainly isn't up to the standard of the native carpenters, who are very good when they put their minds to it. What with the conversion rate being 120 yen per dollar, you can see how expensive it is. There are about 37 rooms, of which five are set aside for transients and the rest rented by members of the military so they can get their wives over before they are eligible for government housing. As yet there are no telephones or radios in the rooms and the furniture is very shabby. As yet they have no mattresses, just two blankets folded over the springs.

Nor is the bar operating, which seems strange to me. The dining room is a nice room, but without a bar, they haven't been doing too well financially on that part of their operation.

The gardens are also some distance off. At the present time, there is a small rock quarry about 30 yards from the main entrance; and the view from the hotel is scarcely more attractive.

The past week has been about as busy as the rest. Tomorrow I have great hopes of getting finished with the cement case. At least I am going to close it out and hope that our headquarters in Tokyo doesn't think of anything else to do on it. It certainly has been a big pain in the neck.

Jake was driving today and saw a couple of people go into some heavy grass, and, thinking them to be burglars, sent me in after them. It turned out, after I had nearly broken my neck, that they were merely visiting the family grave and were scrubbing off a pile of bones in preparation for a Ryukyuan holiday coming up next week. I felt quite embarrassed intruding on them that way.

Jake hasn't caught anyone without a pass for a couple of weeks now and he is beginning to panic a little bit these days. It is really an experience driving around with him. About every third person he sees is a burglar and whoever is riding with him has to shake the person down for contraband of various sorts. I probably shouldn't mention this to you for fear you will become upset, but he is always good for a couple of paragraphs anyhow.

That certainly was too bad about Ann and her passport. It is a pretty tough way to find out that many people cannot be relied upon.

The two new men were added to this week's duty agent list, which helps out a little bit, but another man was dropped as he is being returned home so the net gain was one.

Drummond's family is getting over here in another week or so, which means that I will be getting a new roommate. I think that he is going to have a pretty good chance of drawing one of the nicer homes as he is fairly high up on the list; just the way things worked out.

The new man in the shack is planning on building a house off the base. Seems that some landed native near here leases out lots for a dollar a year on a 12-year lease. A person can get a small but fairly adequate cement block house built for about $3600 which according to the contract, must be depreciated at the rate of one twelfth of the total amount a year. At the end of the 12 years, the houses revert to the landowner. When the person leaves for the States, he can sell the house to anyone he wants to at the depreciated value (or less). And what with the terrific demand for housing, he can always get rid of it anytime he wants. So, his housing is going to cost him around $360 plus utilities and upkeep. A pretty good deal for say, a major who gets quarters allowance of about $117 /month, as long he is not living in government-provided quarters.

Well, I can't think of much else to report this time. Take good care of yourselves.

Love,
Peter

"The colonel made a deal with her . . ."

Saturday, August 30, 1952
Kadena Air Base; Okinawa

[No salutation]
Heard a pretty good one yesterday and thought I would get it down
before it slipped my mind.

Yesterday afternoon some new lieutenant-colonel who is the CO of
the Rycom Military Police came into the office with a problem. Seems
that upon his recent departure from the States he was not eligible to
have his automobile shipped over right away. But he did want it with
him in spite of the rules and regulations that are set up for shipment
of privately-owned automobiles.

While at Stoneman, the day before he left, he met the wife of an
Air Force captain who was traveling to Japan, who did not have an
automobile but who was eligible to have an automobile (if it was hers or
her husband's) shipped over right away with her.

The colonel made a deal with her whereby he transferred the title to
her to have the automobile shipped to Japan on her orders. She was to
have use of the automobile until he got settled here and then he was
going to write her, have her transfer the title back to him, and arrange
for immediate transportation of the car from Japan to the Ryukyus.

Everything went according to schedule until it came time for her
to transfer the title back to the colonel. The husband (the Air Force
captain) said that the automobile was the property of his wife and that
she had the title to prove it and that she would not transfer it back to
the colonel.

The colonel checked around his command and it turned out there
wasn't a hell of a lot he could do about it, so he came over to OSI in
hopes that we might be able to do something about getting the Air
Force captain to turn the car back to him.

Jake wasn't here (as usual) so he talked to Willhelm, who stalled
him. The colonel was especially unhappy because the captain had
written and offered to sell the car back to him for $900. Insult to
injury. The last time we saw the colonel—leaving the office—he was

muttering about getting the captain tried for conduct unbecoming of an officer!

I thought that the whole thing was a tremendous gag—just two common chiselers working on each other. Actually, I don't think that either of them is a bit better than a common wallet thief. They should cashier the two of them out of the service but probably won't. It would be interesting to see how the whole thing comes out, but we probably won't hear anything about it.

PK

"I finally closed that cement case . . ."

Sunday, August 31, 1952
Kadena Air Base; Okinawa

Dear Ma and Pa,

Well, outside of the enclosed story that I typed up the other day, there really isn't a great deal to report about this week.

I finally closed that cement case and it goes out tomorrow. All I have to worry about now is that our headquarters in Tokyo might decide they want something else done with it. Unless something completely unexpected comes up this next week, and it probably will, I may have a chance to get rid of a few odds and ends that have been about for some time now.

Friday or Saturday a bunch of Congressmen arrived on the island, supposedly for the purpose of inspecting various installations. So far, they seem to have managed to hit all of the clubs and to have wined and dined quite well. They arrived from Hong Kong via Formosa where, supposedly, they had been checking up on our military commitments in that area.

We sure have a lot going on in Hong Kong these days for them to see. And then they have the nerve to go back and say that everything is in good order and that no one is wasting any money. They are having an open discussion period here on base tomorrow morning. For two cents I'd go over there and ask them what in the hell there was over in Hong Kong that needed 11 Congressmen to inspect. Really gripes me.

Saturday morning, I had to give a short talk at one of the troop information and education programs that they have every Saturday morning. It was really Jake's job to do it, but he managed to pass it off, but I didn't mind too much.

Saturday afternoon Ernie and I worked down at the office for a couple of hours, working on the monthly report. It is quite a job, and what with all the daily things to take care of, a person almost has to work nights to get it out of the way.

Drummond drew one of the better houses [in the housing lottery] last Friday and this afternoon we went out there and moved furniture around a bit and generally straightened it up a little. The people who had it before weren't too careful with it but even at that the house isn't in bad shape. His family arrives here Thursday sometime. He has arranged for a couple of maids to clean it up before they arrive. He was just out there again this evening and said that there were an awful lot of cockroaches running around.

I only hope that the PX has some kind of poison that will get rid of them.

Last week the weather was clear and warm but both yesterday and today we have had showers.

Well, can't seem to think of anything else to report this week. Will write later. Don't work too hard.

Love,
Peter

An old grenade

Tuesday, September 9, 1952
Kadena Air Base; Okinawa

Dear Ma and Pa,
Well, not too much has happened of interest this last week. About the only thing unusual is a cold that I managed to pick up about last Friday, but I am over it now, for the most part; however, yesterday I certainly sneezed a lot. I think that all the dust in the air was responsible for most of it.

Drummond's family got here last Friday, and he is fairly well settled down now.

Got a new man in the shack this afternoon—a captain.

It was really funny. Seems that when Drummond moved into the room—after Jake got his family here and moved out of the BOQ—Jake had left an old disarmed land grenade in the room, which Drummond never bothered to throw out. Drummond, in turn, left it behind and when the new man moved in, he took one look at it and called the Air Police and Ordinance. Caused all kinds of excitement around here this afternoon. None of the maids could figure out what all the fuss was about.

Can't seem to remember just what we did last Saturday but Sunday Willhelm and I went to the beach for several hours in the afternoon. It was a lovely day. The water was very warm but quite dirty still—probably from the typhoon although that was about a month ago. A lot of seaweed ashore and still in the water.

Too bad that none of you caught any fish but it sounds like you had a good time anyhow. I suppose that by this time Ann will be home and will be quite busy trying to tell you everything and at the same time trying to get caught up on her rest. I hope that her ankle didn't give her a bad time and that she was able to see all of Paris without having to hobble around on crutches or anything.

Really funny. Seems that last week down at Naha, the detachment commander—who is sometimes a bit of an apple-polisher and had decided to operate like Jake when it comes to shaking people down—happened to stop an Okinawan to see what he was carrying and found a camera that the fellow had stolen from the PX. It still had the price tag on it. Well, that put this guy one ahead of Jake, which rankles, to say the least. The last couple of days Jake has been herding about everyone he comes across into the office to see what they are doing on the base. Today he caught a couple of native boys who didn't have a pass and didn't work on the base which helped things a little, but Jake is still behind. He will be stopping people for the next six months.

Got a letter down from headquarters today complimenting a survey I wrote up last month which made Jake feel pretty good. About the first one they have had in some time. Most of the letters coming down from Tokyo are pretty nasty.

Starting this month, I get about a $1 raise for longevity. Hope the Air Force can afford it. A single person in the Air Force certainly does operate at a disadvantage, especially an officer. A single enlisted man getting separate rations gets about $75/month for food while an officer gets only $42. In addition, an enlisted man in OSI gets a civilian clothing allowance and a civilian clothing maintenance allowance. Sort of gripes me at times.

The water went off again today. I guess while they were fixing some of the faulty pipes they have been having trouble with.

Well, can't think of much else to report about. Will write again. Don't work too hard.

Love,
Peter

"... the Army colonel and his car ... "

Wednesday, September 17, 1952
Kadena Air Base; Okinawa

Dear Ma and Pa,

I certainly did manage to slip somehow this last week! Here it is Wednesday already, and I haven't gotten to writing. Well, I suppose that Ann is safely home and unpacked. I hope that the trip home was pleasant and that she didn't arrive too tired.

This last week has been quite busy as usual. I had quite a bit of trouble getting the jeep to run. Spent the better part of two days fussing around with the motor pool trying to get someone to do a little something to it. I sometimes think that a well-run livery stable would furnish more efficient and effective transportation than the motor pool here on the base.

I finally broke down and bought a camera last week. I think it is a pretty good one. Or at least it had better be, seeing as how I paid $90 for the damn thing. Even at that, it is quite a bit cheaper than if I were to buy it in the States someplace. It is a Zeiss Ikon Contessa with an F2.8 lens, if that means something to you. It is a German camera.

The office has film that Jake wants people to use to practice on so there won't be that expense to worry about for some time to come. Now, if I can work some deal with the base photo lab to get the developing done, everything will be all right.

Saw Pearson last Thursday.* His boat arrived Thursday morning and left Friday morning for Yokohama. Went on down to see him and then back here and went to dinner at the other club that Willhelm and I belong to (we split the membership costs of $2/month, so it is fairly cheap). Then took him back to the boat and got back here around 2:00 a.m.

Two round trips over that beat-up road in the jeep sure played hell with my back and kidneys for a day or so.

----

* Donald C. Pearson: see p. 115, note 2.

Got in a new man this last week to replace one that left on the Friday boat. He was transferred up from Guam with his wife and two children. He came over on the same plane that I did last March. Seems that the delay for dependents down at Guam is about two months while it is around twelve up here now.

However, concurrent intra-theater travel is authorized so he has his family here with him, which is a break for him.

Last Sunday Willhelm, some of the other new men, and myself were invited over to Jake's house for Sunday dinner, which I thought was very nice. Mrs. Jacobs is a very good cook, and everyone seemed to have a good time.

Well, can't seem to think of a great deal else to report this time. Haven't heard any more about the Army colonel and his car. I rather imagine that he has decided it would be best not to make too big a fuss about it.

I still haven't got around to mailing off the cribbage board, but I do have great hopes of getting around to it one of these days.

Haven't heard from you for several days now but I imagine that there will be mail tomorrow when the regular mail plane comes in.

My knife broke (the spring) so you might get me another one for Christmas if you want a suggestion.

Love,
Peter

Reassigned to counterintelligence cases

Sunday, September 21, 1952
Kadena Air Base; Okinawa

Dear Ma and Pa,

Well, again not too much to report this week, except that as usual, I have been quite busy. I no longer have any criminal work as such.

As far as the set-up of the organizations is concerned, on paper all of the investigations are roughly grouped into criminal (such as one would expect to find in civilian law, i.e., burglary, arson, murder, rape, robbery, misconduct, narcotic violations, thefts of various sorts and similar crimes) and counterintelligence investigations including such things as Communist matters, subversive activities, disaffection, sabotage, espionage and treason. Along with this type, I also get quite a few security violation investigations most of which involve incompetent supervision and control of classified material (documents). It seems that few people around here having access to classified information have any idea about the necessity of keeping it secure.

This is especially applicable to the heroes. I shall never understand how they manage to fly their airplanes when they have so much trouble when they do anything on the ground. I have just about come to the conclusion that the planes fly in spite of the heroes and not because of them, and that in reality, the planes are little more than remote-controlled guided missiles.

In addition to this, anything dealing with possible racial troubles comes my way as do all matters dealing with records checks of indigenous personnel. All of this in addition to occasional letters that Jake should be taking care of but isn't.

At the present time I have a couple of main cases, one a security violation and the other a disaffection case. Neither of which will prove to be very serious, but they nevertheless do necessitate action on the part of local organizations.

I think that the weather here is beginning to change. This last week there have been quite a few showers and it has been overcast quite a bit of the time. The wind changed from the southwest to the northeast this last week which redirected the minimum temperature to around 77 degrees.

It won't be long until we will be having to wear long-sleeved shirts and then, a little later, neckties. I am going to have to get a couple of pairs of slacks. I have been planning on writing away to Hong Kong for samples. The prices are quite reasonable, and the material very good, as is the tailoring.

Rained Saturday and didn't have a chance to do much of anything except go out for a few drinks in the evening. Today it is quite nice, and we took a trip north on this side of the island up to Nago and then around Motobu Peninsula and back down the other side of the island.

The roads are in pretty good shape though a bit dusty. I have never been out on the Peninsula before and it was quite interesting. It is very hilly and rugged for the most part but quite pretty. Took a few pictures with the camera. I hope they turn out OK. I imagine that it will be a little while yet before I figure out how to take good pictures with it.

Well, can't seem to think of much else to report this time. I'll write later.

Love,
Peter

"No one around here seems to have any sense of responsibility."

Monday, September 29, 1952
Kadena Air Base; Okinawa

Dear Ma and Pa, and Ann,
Well, another week and again not a great deal to report. I have
managed to keep busy with always several things to do all of the time.

This last weekend was a rather uneventful one. Saturday afternoon I
rode around near the base for an hour or so.

The weather this last weekend was very nice, with the exception
of the wind. About two weeks ago, it shifted around to the northeast
and right over the hill from where we live and from the office there is a
large rock quarry (coral) and asphalt plant that belches dust and smoke
24 hours a day. Things get very dusty in a very short time.

Got down to 73 degrees this last week one night so you can see that
it is definitely getting cooler. Rained a couple of days. The yearly total is
now about 80 inches.

I certainly was sorry to hear about Ann's ear trouble. I hope that
she is all over it by this time. Also about her ankle. It certainly was a
strenuous trip.

Ann: about the camera situation. They are getting pretty touchy
about selling cameras to people who are not going to use them for their
personal use, but I shall see what I can do for you. Was there any special
model that you were interested in? Also, about the ties. You had better
keep them. I really haven't any need for any more over here and I would
be afraid that something would happen to them. I also got the picture
that you sent from Rome.

About Christmas presents: I haven't had an opportunity to go to
Naha on the weekend for a couple of months, so I have no idea just
what is down there that would be suitable for presents.

I can't seem to think of a great many suggestions of things that
I would like. I seem to have just about everything I need. All of my
clothing is holding up pretty well. I am planning on getting some slacks
and a couple of suits from Hong Kong, but I don't know just when I will
get around to sending away for them.

Buying the camera this month was a major expense. In addition to that, I seem to have gone over my allotted budget, so I shall have to try and slacken off this next month.

McCord is stationed in San Francisco as Harbor Security Patrol, which is a pretty good deal.[1]

Pearson is just about due in San Francisco and it will probably be his last trip before he gets out. That is just about all of the gossip that I have picked up.

That certainly was something about Kurt. You would think that a person his age would have had a little more sense than that. If it had been a six-year-old child, I could possibly see some excuse but for anyone 19 years-old, it is positively disgraceful.[2]

Speaking of explosives, a couple of local fishermen near here managed to get hold of some old ammunition and were taking it apart for the powder to use for fishing when it went off and killed the two of them. Don't know why they bothered with old ammunition when it is so easy to steal new stuff around here. A week ago, some people managed to get away with a couple of truckloads of the stuff. Seems that one of the magazines wasn't even locked. The captain-in-charge ought to be busted down to the recruiting office, but they will probably give him a promotion.

No one around here seems to have any sense of responsibility. One of these days they are going to wake up to the fact that guns and explosives can cause a lot of trouble but by then it is going to be a bit too late.

Well, that's about all this time.

Love,

Peter

---

1. Frank McCord: see p. 114, note 1.

2. Peter's cousin Kurt George (b. 1933) had inadvertently touched an electric blasting cap, causing him to lose a finger.

". . . a bullet had hit a bicycle. . . "

Monday, October 6, 1952
Kadena Air Base; Okinawa

Dear Ma and Pa,

Well, I certainly have had a busy week. Got a couple of new cases toward the end of last week in addition to a couple of preliminary investigations.

Wednesday was the monthly CI meeting down at CIC. The staff car was broken, so Jake and I had to take the jeep, which recently has been getting along on about two- or three cylinders 90 percent of the time. In addition to that, the steering wheel sticks.

It was really funny to hear Jake complain about the trip down there, especially on the rough road.

One of the cases was a security violation, which I should be able to get rid of tomorrow, and the other one is a Communist matters case, which will undoubtedly linger several months.

Saturday afternoon I didn't do too much. Puttered around the shack for a while. Read a while in the evening and then Nielsen got a call to go out to find a housemaid who was suspected of stealing fifty dollars.

I went along just for the heck of it and didn't get back until around two in the morning.

I traded with another fellow for duty agent and had it Sunday and we went back up there again to find the maid. Found her and most of the money and took her to jail back here.

When we got back to the base we got a report that there had been a homicide up the island, and we took off up there only to find that a bullet had hit a bicycle someone was riding. Tried to track that down but didn't have much luck and got back here about five in the evening.

Had dinner and then after dinner got another call and didn't get to bed until 1:30 a.m. And that was my weekend. And I had such plans for getting caught up on all types of little odds and ends that have been piling up for some time.

The reason that I changed duty agent is that next weekend Willhelm, Nielsen, and I are planning on going up to Okuma for the weekend. We plan on leaving here Friday afternoon and coming back Sunday evening. I hope that the weather continues to be as nice as it has been this last week or so.

It got down to 69 the other night and has been good sleeping weather. The wind is still from the north and we are still getting all kinds of smoke and dust from the rock crusher and the asphalt plant, but it is a lot less uncomfortable than the hot humid weather.

The mail leaves here about three times a week and arrives about three times a week. I think that the incoming mail is often carried by commercial lines while some of the outgoing mail is carried on military lines which would tend to explain the delay.

The club that Willhelm and I belong to is one run by the District Engineers, who are mainly engineers. It is a little more expensive—the food and whiskey—but not a great deal more so than the officers clubs around here.

As a person has to submit a regular application for membership and as it takes a little time and effort to join, you don't see too many of the obnoxious heroes over there as you find in the club here. The other night up at the local club, a full colonel was making quite a spectacle of himself by whistling through his teeth. However, there are also just about as many of the civilian engineers who are pretty disgusting.

I think that the food is quite a bit better over there even though they do get their food from the same places that the local messes do. Willhelm and I are going over there tonight for dinner.

Well, it is now 7:30 and I had better clean up. Don't work too hard.

Love,

Peter

Driving a crooked road

[Undated letter postmarked Friday, October 17, 1952]
Kadena Air Base; Okinawa

Dear Ma and Pa, and Ann,
I certainly am sorry that I haven't written sooner—somehow or other I just haven't seemed to be able to get around to it. In addition, the typewriter—which I have out on a hand-receipt (from an extra one at the office) had to be turned in for about a week for a periodic overhaul. It is quite a chore writing letters in longhand.

Friday afternoon we left work about three and drove on up to Okuma. The weather was beautiful, and the water was extremely colorful. During Friday night, it clouded up and a wind came up, so Saturday was quite cool and pleasant even if it didn't sunshine.

We drove about twelve to fourteen miles up north of Okuma. While the road north of Nago is quite narrow and windy, it is much smoother and easier on the car than most of the roads around the base.

The island north of Okuma rises quite abruptly from the shore—it doesn't look too dissimilar from the Californian coastline near the Big Sur area—quite a rugged coastline.

The villages up north are much cleaner and neater than those around here and to the south. North of Nago (and outside of Okuma), there are no military installations, so the villages are more or less in their natural state.

Tuesday and Wednesday of this last week were quite warm again and uncomfortable. Today was cool and cloudy and this evening it has sprinkled a couple of times. The wind is again from the north.

Well, I will write again as soon as I get the machine back.
Love,
Peter

CHECKLIST FROM MA AND PA

Do you want   Yes   No

Food
Candy ✓
Cookies ✓
Nuts ✓
Canned fish of any kind
Fruit cake

Clothes
Shirts, white dress ✓
Shirts, colored gabardine type with long sleeves ✓
    Maroon
    Green
    Blue, Navy
    Beige
    Grey
    Tan
    Brown

Socks
Nylon ✓
Hand knit woolen and nylon ✓
House shoes of any kind ✓

Anything else you can think of, give details

A book of the comic strip "POGO." * Paperbound—maroonish in color, I think.

Did you receive the cookies I mailed you in August? ✓

Plus—one of my electric razors if you can find it. (I have faith in Mother's ability to find wherever I might have left them.)

---

* *Pogo was a popular comic strip that ran in newspapers from 1948 to 1975.*

A suicide—and questions about ballot measures (U.S. election)

Sunday, October 19, 1952
Kadena Air Base; Okinawa

Dear Ma, Pa, and Ann,

Seems like yesterday that I wrote you last but then it was rather late in the week when I wrote the last letter. Not too much of interest has happened this last few days since I wrote on Thursday; however, I will try to remember what I left out. Seem to forget a lot of things when I write longhand. The typewriter still hasn't come back from the shop, so I came on down to the office to write this.

I don't remember if I mentioned it or not but last Monday one of the airmen around here stole a gun and went AWOL Monday night. Nielson and I prowled the village hunting for him but weren't able to find him.

Yesterday afternoon they found him by a tomb near the office. He had evidently committed suicide about as soon as he took off. Being hidden by the bushes and wall of a tomb, it took some time before he attracted any attention and then he was found by an Okinawan cutting grass for a new road right-of-way. Was really a mess. Good thing that I didn't happen to receive the call originally last Monday when he was reported missing for the first time.

The squadron from which he left and from which he stole the gun reported the serial number of the weapon; however, the weapon that was found by the body had an entirely different number. Just goes to show the type of control that these people keep on the weapons that they are responsible for.

Had to bring the boy's wallet back to the office to check on his identification; as a result the office is rather strange this morning.

These past couple of weeks have been very busy. Get one case closed and a couple of more come up.

Speaking of good control over things, it seems that for some months 90 percent of the employees of the main PX here on the base have been keeping their own set of books—just exactly what they have been borrowing from the till and just exactly when they have returned the money!

A really involved case turned up by accident just this last week. As long as the PX inventories don't show a loss of over one percent per month, everything is considered to be running along very well and there is nothing thought of the matter. Certainly wish I owned a business that could afford a one percent loss per month and think nothing about it.

Most of the employees would borrow things and then return the money when they had it. However, a few of them were taking stuff and just not returning it. Really complicated but they certainly kept an elaborate set of books. Each cash register had a set of books that was very methodically kept.

The weather here the past few days has varied from the hot moist weather of the summer to the relatively cool and pleasant weather we have had off and on for the past couple of weeks. However, the mosquitos lately have been very bad.

I certainly would like to know how they manage to get into my room, also where they are coming from as we have had no rain for the past couple or three weeks. I think that they may be coming from the shower which is dark and damp, but I always thought that there had to be water standing in puddles before they could lay their eggs.

I received my ballot yesterday along with Pa's letter and suggestions. There were several things that I was wondering about a couple of the amendments.[1]

First, what advantages would be gained by changing the two years when the legislature is officially in office? I had always thought that a lame duck session was not as desirable as having the men take office immediately upon election.

Another: #318 and #331—taxing trucks and motor vehicles, etc.? Also, advantages about the veterans bonds. Seems to me that that is an

---

1. These would be amendments to Oregon's state constitution. And being an "initiative and referendum" state, Oregon periodically asks its citizens to vote on legislation—a form of direct democracy that effectively bypasses the state legislature. The ballot measures Peter refers to were the questions to be decided in the 1952 election.

expense the state could do without, especially in light of all the other advantages that a veteran is afforded by the federal government.

Of course, I realize it is nice to keep taxes down but the bill making a majority of legal voters approve a tax seems to me would hamper any bill that is absolutely necessary—as would the bills limiting the tax base. (#306 and #318).

Also, just what was the bill having to do with an emergency committee concerned with parking? The description certainly left much to be desired. I hope that the purpose of that bill is a lot clearer and better defined than the brief description that was on the ballot.

Also, just what kind of blighted areas were they talking about in another one of the bills? Seems to me that the state would do well to hire someone to clearly write out the purpose of the bills they are trying to get enacted. (However, in this last case I guess that it was the county that was at fault).

Well, so much for the election. I was beginning to panic a little bit when I didn't receive the ballot when just about everyone else that I know had long since received theirs and had mailed it in. The ballot for the primary elections just barely got back in time. Just what is all of the confusion with those people?

Haven't as yet ordered any clothing from Hong Kong. Haven't even sent for the samples. I haven't lost any weight—in fact, during the past couple of weeks, I believe that I have put some on. However, the food around here oftentimes leaves much to be desired. The food itself isn't bad; it is just the cooking. Simple lack of supervision on the part of the responsible officers, but inasmuch as that seems to be the modus operandi in this area, I guess that I shouldn't be too critical.

Dental care is available but like so many of the things around here, it doesn't pay a person to take advantage of it unless it is absolutely necessary.

I'm glad that you enjoyed Groucho Marx over at the Monroes' television.[2] I find that television will occasionally have some good

_____

2. Actor and comedian Groucho Marx (1890–1977) was the host of the popular television program "You Bet Your Life," which was broadcast on NBC affiliates from 1950 to 1960.

programs on it and that after you get the schedule down as to what programs you like, it is a pretty good form of entertainment. The big strain is sorting through the average, run-of-the-mill program, which isn't worth the time it takes to watch it.

I suppose that with the new station being constructed, it won't be long before there will be much conversation concerning various different programs. When I was at Travis, the conversation of all the office help—stenographers—seemed to revolve around and concentrate on the television programs that came on the evening before. I oftentimes wondered what in the hell they talked about before they had their television sets.

As far as living from my various allowances, it is not possible, unless a person has absolutely no expenses other than food. Even then, it is not possible if a person eats three meals a day during a 31-day month.

We never receive our quarters allowance. As long as we live in government-provided quarters, we are not eligible for it. That always has been a rather sore spot for Willhelm and myself.

Here, a married man with his family is afforded a nice $20- to $30,000 home complete with furniture and floor wax and a fairly good system of maintenance and all it costs him (if a 2nd lieutenant) is his allowance, which is about fifteen dollars more than we get (not being married). While for our allowance, we get a room-and-a-half with one bed, one desk, one chair (some have another lounge chair, but I had to scrounge for one), and a dresser with a mirror, plus the absolute minimum of maintenance. Willhelm has been trying to get a window fixed since last May but still has had no satisfaction.

Pa's story about the Brigadier General from the Air Force was quite amusing. Being a PIO (Public Information Officer) would certainly be a tough job. Of course, the way most of them do it, the job amounts to nothing at all because they don't do a damn thing. However, for a person interested in doing a good job, I would think that it would be an extremely thankless position at best what with in the first place trying to defend the absolutely ridiculous policies the Air Force has, and trying to cover up for the gross mistakes and terrific mismanagement all along the line.

They broadcast the World Series here twice a day—once in the middle of the night and then in the middle of the afternoon. I certainly was glad when they were over because I think there are a few things less interesting than hearing a baseball game over the radio. Especially when they are rebroadcast and when you know the outcome of the original game.

I'm sorry that the letters haven't been coming through to you regularly. Occasionally, as I did last week, I do not get around to writing regularly on Sundays but not as often as you seem to be getting the mail late.

I checked up the other day when I was over at the Post Office; they said that the outgoing mail is taken out of here mostly by MATS (Military Air Transport Service) although occasionally a commercial line will fly some out. Even then, it is flown out of here on a space-available plan.

They also said that if a letter is mailed through one of the Ryukyuan Post Offices, it goes out right away and there is seldom any delay.

There are a couple of cleaning plants here in the area. One is a privately-operated concern that isn't too good and the other is the Quartermaster Laundry and Cleaning which, while better, isn't too good either.

Got interrupted—will write again,

Love,

Peter

A new notebook and a knife

Tuesday, October 28, 1952
Kadena Air Base; Okinawa

Dear Ma and Pa, and Ann,

I seemed to have slipped up a couple of days again. Saturday, I was duty agent. I traded with the person who has it Saturday as he had something planned. A pretty good deal as next Saturday is payday.

Did get a call early Sunday morning. And then something else came up around noon so there wasn't a great deal of opportunity to go anywhere or to do anything special.

Saturday, it was overcast and sprinkled a couple times with Sunday being just about the same, so it turned out just as well.

This last week has been just about as busy as the rest. Did manage to get a couple of things out of the way but have gotten a couple of additional things to look into so I am just as busy as before.

The supply man for the outfit is leaving and I have been appointed to take over. I'm afraid that it may turn out to be a bit of a headache as we have three different supply accounts.

I am enclosing a piece of paper from my notebook. The notebook fell completely apart this last week and isn't much good anymore. Would you please check with Gill's and get me another one the same size? * Since it doesn't weigh too much and since I need another one badly, would you mind airmailing it to me?

Outside of that, and another knife, I can't seem to think of anything else that I need at the present time.

Pearson was in last week for the last time. There was a last-minute change in the shipping schedule. He hadn't planned on coming back again before he gets out. It was quite nice that he was able to get over here again.

---

* J. K. Gill was a Portland, Oregon stationery and office-supplies store.

I got some more pictures back the other day but gave a couple of them away, so I won't send you them until I get some reprints made. Most turned out pretty good although there were a couple that weren't well-exposed. All in all, I am very satisfied with the pictures that the camera takes.

Every Sunday there is one of the major football games broadcast over the local radio station. Last week's was the Cal-USC game which was a pretty good one to listen to. Stanford certainly shouldn't have lost their game. That was too bad.

Still haven't gotten my typewriter back from the repair shop yet and am down this evening, after work, typing this. However, having the additional duty as Supply Officer pretty soon, I certainly don't anticipate having any trouble having a typewriter to use in my shack as long as I am the Supply Officer.

This has been a busy month for the office. Crime seems to be on the upswing around here. Haven't been duty agent for a couple of months now that I didn't get a call.

Well, can't seem to think of anything else to report this time. If there are any questions, just let me know. Don't try and do too much.

Love,

Peter

Giving the Democrats "the better deal"?

Sunday, November 2, 1952
Kadena Air Base; Okinawa

Dear Ma, Pa, and Ann,
This past week certainly has gone rapidly again. Still have managed to keep good and busy although there has been nothing of unusual interest come up.

The weather this past week has remained very nice although this dust and smoke from the rock crusher has been quite obnoxious, as usual. Right now, there is a typhoon about 500 miles southeast of here that had been heading this way for the past two days. However, around noon today, it altered its course and if it doesn't veer off again, it will pass about 400 miles from here. It is a good thing, what with the rice harvest just getting underway for the second time this year.

The winds were reported up to 170 miles per hour. It certainly would have leveled the island with winds that strong; everyone is keeping their fingers crossed because it certainly could change at any moment's notice.

Really haven't done a great deal this weekend.

Yesterday afternoon I did manage to do a little shopping, which was quite a chore considering that Friday was payday.

Didn't get up until late this morning and then went around and looked at a couple of PXs early this afternoon but didn't buy anything except a magazine. Now all I have to do is get a box made and the things mailed.

There certainly isn't any selection at all for men's gifts of any manner.

Wrote away this afternoon for swatches from Hong Kong and for a catalog for a couple of filters for my camera and that has been just about all that I have managed to do. Didn't want to wander away too far just in case the typhoon should change.

In that event, I would have many little chores like taking the top down on the jeep, getting kerosene for the lanterns, nailing down the shutters, and filling up pails with water. All kinds of various little chores.

My watch has been giving me a lot of trouble lately, so I finally broke down and put it into the shop to have it overhauled. Probably cost at least $5 to get it out again this next week.

It's a good thing that I traded with one of the other agents last week because they have had quite a bit of business this weekend what with fights and wallet thefts. The local crime wave seems to be on the upswing lately. Maybe what with the cooler weather, it isn't too hot to get into trouble.

Friday night there were a couple of BOQ burglaries right here in the area. People just can't seem to learn that it is not a good idea to sleep with their doors unlocked and with all of their money lying in open sight on the table.

The local paper (*Stars and Stripes*) and the local radio station seem to be giving the Democrats the better deal as far as space and time are concerned. Judging from what we are aware of through the papers and the radio, the Democrats are giving about three speeches to every one of the Republicans.

This evening in the paper they had a picture of one of the McClatchys, who was formerly on the *Stars and Stripes* staff but who is going back pretty soon.* Perhaps that accounts for the apparent bias. But then again, someone else could say that I am biased.

Well, can't seem to think of much more to relay. Don't work too hard.

Love,

Peter

---

* The McClatchy family owned the McClatchy newspaper chain, which included *The Sacramento Bee, The Modesto Bee,* and the *Anchorage Daily News.* Peter probably refers to C. K. McClatchy (1927–1989). Lieutenant C. K. McClatchy worked for *Stars and Stripes* during the Korean War.

Tokyo—and a payroll heist

Thursday, November 13, 1952
Kadena Air Base; Okinawa

Dear Ma, Pa, and Ann,
Really late this week but for once I do have some sort of excuse. What
with another suicide last week and a rather serious assault in one of the
villages, there was need of a laboratory analysis of some blood, hairs,
etc., and I got to take the stuff on up there.

I left in a rather big hurry without a great deal of forewarning. I left
here Friday afternoon and got into Tokyo about 2:00 a.m. Saturday.

Saturday, I went to the lab and got them squared away and then went
over to headquarters and spent most of the rest of the day getting quite
a few odd chores done.

Sunday was very nice and clear and cool, and I managed to get in
quite a bit of sight-seeing—mostly just walking around.

Monday was the investiture of Crown Prince Akihito and I went out
and saw him pass in his carriage.[1] What with all of the crowds, it was
really interesting.

Tuesday the Royal Family appeared on the balcony of the palace and
waved to everyone which was also interesting. We got to go within the
Palace Grounds—a privilege that comes very rarely.

In all, it was a very good time to have been in Tokyo. I took quite
a few pictures which I hope will turn out well as they should be quite
interesting. Looked up quite a few people I knew and outside of that,
there wasn't much time left.

The weather was cool and clear all of the time—quite a contrast to
the weather when I arrived back here yesterday afternoon.

Turned warm and sticky here and was raining when I landed. During
my absence, there was a native payroll that was lifted—safe and all—
and one of the burglars that the office has been looking for during the
past several months was shot and killed (by one of the roving guards)

---

1. Crown Prince Akihito (1933–) would become the emperor of Japan from
   1989 to 2019.

as he was leaving the base with a whole load of property that he had just stolen. All kinds of activity.

I received both the notebook and the razor today—both arrived in good shape and thanks a lot. I was beginning to panic a little about what I was going to use for a notebook. Tomorrow morning, we are going to get up at 4:30 a.m. and shake down 150 men in hopes of finding the payroll robbers. They walked off with a field safe.

Good chance that we won't be able to do much good.

The Inspector General of the Air Force was on the base today and everyone in the office was dressed up in case he should appear, but he never did come in the office, so all the trouble was for naught.

I was interested in hearing about the outcome of the local elections. I was quite surprised about the drink-by-the-glass bill passing.

Your trip to the islands sounds like it would be a lot of fun. I hope that everything works out OK and that you will be able to make the trip. Is it on one of the Waterman ships again? I saw one of their ships in Naha yesterday—seemed to be a very nice vessel.

Well, the Presidential election turned out OK. Certainly, judging from the word that we received from the local paper and radio station, the Democrats seemed to be running away with the campaign. The only worry I have is about Eisenhower's career as a military man. I only hope that he can rise above it.

A prime example of the way they think: they are planning on constructing a new housing area around here (Naha actually)—on land presently occupied by about 200 Okinawan houses, the values of which vary from $25,000 to $120,000.

They plan on letting them build more houses in another area but are only planning on paying a maximum of $10,000 for each house. No wonder we are often disliked by other peoples.

Well, can't seem to think of anything else to report. Nice that Lee got defeated but too bad about the truck tax, cigarette tax, and the others.[2]

Love,

Peter

---

2. Dorothy McCollough Lee (1901–1981) was the mayor of Portland, Oregon from 1949 to 1953.

The payroll heist (cont'd)

Sunday, November 16, 1952
Kadena Air Base; Okinawa

Dear Ma and Pa, and Ann,
Well, seeing that I wrote last just a couple of days ago, there really isn't a great deal new to report, but I did want to get a letter off tomorrow morning. The past several days have been warm and cloudy.

Wednesday, Thursday, and Friday, it rained hard around here. What with all of the road construction, things are muddy all over the base. Really a mess. Today, it dried out some, but only in the less muddy stretches of the roads.

This afternoon, I drove around through some of the villages near the base here for a couple of hours and took a few pictures. Outside of that and wrapping some packages for mailing, I haven't done a great deal except some reading.

The transportation problem around here is beginning to get a little tight. The general decided last week that too many government vehicles were seen at the PX, movies, etc., and sent a letter around advising everyone of his displeasure.

The office still has all of its jeeps, but we may have to be a little more careful about going to the PX. Outside of that, there really isn't much to bother about.

Still haven't solved the safe robbery yet. The other morning everyone in the office got up at 4:30 and shook down about 150 men without any results. The money was for payment of the maids hired on the base.

More money was borrowed from the bank and the maids were paid off but now they are wondering how they are going to get more money to pay off the bank plus the interest that is accumulating. Really is quite a problem as everything that is paid into the Labor Office is immediately paid out and there is no method of accumulating extra funds.

I suppose that they will be asking us to make up the difference. When that happens, I am going to start writing letters since the loss was the direct result of very negligent practices on the part of the Foreign Labor Office. Seems that for some months now, the Comptroller for the 20th

Air Force has been recommending that all of the payroll money be deposited in the bank which is just a half a block away. But nothing was ever done about it. Further, all small field-type safes are supposed to be chained down to the floor, but as is typical of so many rules and regulations and common-sense business practices around here, this one regulation was not complied with. I have never seen or even heard of such a place where common sense seems to be so completely foreign to the majority of all persons who are in positions of responsibility. For example, one of the NCO clubs, which handles over a million dollars a year, does not even have a cash register—money goes into and is paid out from cigar boxes. The officers club here on Kadena doesn't run a tape in any of its cash registers. Someone could be milking both clubs of thousands of dollars without anyone ever knowing it. There is absolutely no control on any of the slot machines, which certainly seems strange. Whenever they run out of slugs during an evening, they open up one of the machines and take out a couple of handfuls. It really is something to wonder about, the way things are done around here.

Jake went over to Hong Kong Friday afternoon and should be back tonight or tomorrow. The safe robbery certainly has caused him a lot of concern and he has actually done a lot of work on it.

Well, it is getting late and I don't have much else to report this time. Don't work too hard.

Love,
Peter

PS: The packages have no inner-wrappings so they aren't to be opened until Christmas.

Wasted bombs and out of nails

Monday, November 24, 1952
Kadena Air Base; Okinawa

Dear Ma and Pa, and Ann,
Got some new stationery and managed to find a new ribbon so I am all
set, even though there actually isn't a great deal to report this week.

Friday night I was duty agent but luckily there wasn't any business
so there wasn't much strain about that.

Saturday a bunch of magazines arrived so that took care of Saturday
afternoon. Saturday night we went to the movies.

Sunday, I went driving for about four hours and after riding in the
jeep over these roads for that long, I was quite weary when I returned.
Luckily, my back didn't bother me today. It usually is a bit stiff after
riding for any length of time in the jeep.

Saw another movie Sunday evening. That just about takes care of
the weekend.

The weather here the past couple of days has been very nice. This
evening, however, it started to rain a bit. The fringe of another typhoon
hit here the beginning of last week, but the winds never did get much
above 35 mph and there was no damage.

However, for a while, they thought that it was going to hit here so
we nailed down the shutters again which is quite an inconvenience, to
say the least; also had to take the top down from the jeep. I hope that
is the last one of the season; I'm all out of nails and the wooden shutter
on one of the windows is about ready to rot off the hinges.

I don't know which McClatchy it was, Pa, but it did say that he was
going to work for *The Sacramento Bee* when he got discharged. Probably
the brother of the bird who was a Beta at school about the same time I
was there.*

---

* Beta Theta Pi is a college fraternity.

I got my watch out of the shop OK and after a couple of minor adjustments I made, it is running fine. It is a good watch and should last quite some time yet.

I was sorry to hear about your lumbago and hope that you are not trying to do too much. I suppose that by this time, it is completely gone. Do they have any idea just what causes it?

I think that if Ann got a job with the CIA, she would enjoy it as the type of work they do is interesting, although Ma might not like it too much as Ann probably wouldn't be able to talk much about the work.

Jake went over to Hong Kong for a few days and got back Wednesday evening. We went over there to see some of the things he had brought back. Mrs. Jacobs had gone over earlier and came back about the same time. He bought three suits—hand-tailored—that were undoubtedly the finest suits that I have ever seen.

Mrs. Jacobs brought back some lovely linen, one tablecloth in particular that was especially nice. I hope that I shall be able to get over there sometime.

Inasmuch as I will be wearing civilian clothing over and back, I may need a passport so would you mind sending me a photostatic copy of my birth certificate? I think that you had better have it notarized, as I believe that without it, some of those people down at the American Consul Office in Naha will give me a little trouble about it.

Last night, about 20 minutes to 12, one of the local bombers had some difficulty and had to turn back before it landed. It jettisoned its load of bombs into the sea right off the island. It certainly did shake things up around here. I sort of thought that the powder magazine for the quarry behind the shack had gone up. Ten tons of high explosive bombs certainly can cause a lot of noise even this far away.

Well, I can't seem to think of anything else to report this time. Don't try and do too much.

Love,

Peter

A stolen bus; a sea of mud

Wednesday, December 3, 1952
Kadena Air Base; Okinawa

Dear Ma and Pa, and Ann,

Well, I really slipped up this last week by not writing you before this, but I really have been busy. I should have written Sunday night but never seemed to have gotten around to it.

Monday night I was duty agent. A rather bad night, Monday being payday. Got called out in the middle of the night. One of the heroes stole a bus to get back to Kadena from Rycom and then a soldier got cut and blamed it on an airman—which might have happened, but I rather doubt it.

Anyhow, I didn't lose too much sleep, so it certainly could have been considerably worse.

Worked last night until about 11:00 p.m. and have been doing a little work this evening so far. Things seem to come in surges around here.

I worked almost all day on Thanksgiving. Originally had planned on working only half a day but something came up that had to be attended to. I was also duty agent last Wednesday night—making up for the time I missed when I was in Japan.

The weather was miserable, windy, and blowing. The duty shack leaked like a sieve but fortunately not over the bed.

The weather over the weekend was beautiful—clear and cool but it started raining yesterday and as a result, things are quite muddy and messy. One of these days when all of the construction has been completed, it won't be quite so bad when it rains but what with all of the dirt roads around here now, everything is a sea of mud once it rains. However, it doesn't take long for it to dry off.

Jake went on up to Tokyo last Tuesday for a couple of days—had a meeting and then will be going on up again next week for another meeting. The colonel up in headquarters just got back from a conference in Washington and has all manner of information to pass on.

When Jake was up there last week, he found out that we are getting a new man by the name of Vietch who was in our flight at OCS.[1] He should be down here in a week or two.

Last Friday night, Willhelm and I went over to Castle Terrace[2] for dinner. They now have a GI band instead of the Flips. While the Flips were pretty good musicians they were crooked as hell and the Army decided to get rid of them once and for all. Seems that they got the goods on the band members for black-market activities.

It turned quite cold yesterday and last night we turned on the oil burner in the shack and while it is now quite warm in the shack, it smells like a garage what with the diesel oil.

If you should have the time, I wish that you would send me some white iodine as I am getting a little dandruff again. Also, you might send me a bottle of Anahist as I am due for another cold sometime this winter and it does seem to help me.[2]

From your letters, it sounds like you had a nice trip to San Francisco even though Stanford lost the game. I only hope that you didn't try to do too much in too a short time.

If you and the Wilcoxes are not able to get reservations to go to Hawaii this winter, I think that you should consider waiting—and then flying to Japan this next spring sometime. I am certain that you both would be extremely interested in it and, actually, there isn't any really good reason why you shouldn't make the trip. Japan is a fascinating place; outside of the transportation, the costs wouldn't be too bad. Certainly not as expensive as Hawaii would be. Will write later.

Love,
Peter

---

1. Peter's OCS class book has no record of a Veitch in Peter's Flight B.

2. Castle Terrace was an officers club.

3. Anahist was a non-prescription antihistamine. Magazine ads called it "America's Number One Antihistamine" (LIFE, Nov. 20, 1950, p. 136).

"... haven't found the safe yet ..."

Monday, December 8, 1952
Kadena Air Base; Okinawa

Dear Ma and Pa, and Ann,

Well, late again this week but not as bad as last week. I am still very busy with all manner of new things coming up every week. All of last week's nightwork was sitting around just in case Eisenhower's plane should stop here on the way to Korea and then Friday night we did the same thing for the return flight. Luckily, he didn't stop but we had to stay up and wait until he arrived at the next stop both to and fro for fear that the plane might have to turn back for some reason or another.

Now, this week, it seems that I will be spending most of my time talking to those persons who did not have any official access to the information that he might stop but who nevertheless were intelligent enough to put two and two together and as a result get themselves in a little hot water. It just doesn't pay to do too much independent thinking in the service. It really is a laugh.

The weather this last week has been pretty wet for the most part. I noticed in the paper today that the yearly total is now over 92 inches and it is still raining. Rather inconvenient but I guess that I'm lucky that the jeep hasn't been flooded out by all of this water. It leaks like a sieve unless I park it uphill.

I'm glad that the packages all (should have been three) arrived in good shape. What with all of the volume, etc., I wouldn't have been surprised had they been delayed or even failed to arrive.

By the way, I received the box of candy for Thanksgiving in good shape. It was very good and thanks a lot.

I'm just sorry that I couldn't find anything that I thought Pa would be interested in but there just isn't any selection at all of presents suitable for a man. I guess that they figure, and rightly so, that most of the money spent is for women's presents.

When you have the time, I wish that you would send me that typing book that you have around the house. I think it would be a good thing if I spent a little [time] typing to improve my typing.

Still haven't found the safe yet and from the way things look, it probably won't be found. It really was a pretty good job. Jake is still quite unhappy about the whole thing and I can't say that I blame him as it doesn't look too good.

Jake went up to Tokyo this morning for a meeting and will probably be gone for three or four days. The colonel has called a meeting of all the district commanders so I rather imagine that there may be some changes when Jake gets back here. Probably won't affect us too much as we have a pretty smooth-running district compared to most of the rest of them.

Bought a pair of shoes Sunday as my other two pairs are beginning to wear out what with all of this coral gravel around here. I got another pair similar to the ones I bought just before I left home. They certainly don't look too good but are far more practical than leather-soled shoes.

Well, I can't think of a great deal else to report, so I guess I shall close and do a little reading. A couple of magazines came in today and I had better get at them before some more come in and I get behind in my reading. Don't try to do too much.

Love,

Peter

Black sugar

Sunday, December 14, 1952
Kadena Air Base; Okinawa

Dear Ma, Pa, and Ann,
This last week certainly has gone by rapidly. It seems just like yesterday that I wrote last. I have been about as busy as usual and have gotten quite a little bit done.

With any luck, this week I will be able to spend some time on the various supply accounts that I will be taking over either this week or next.

Right now, we have three different supply accounts and I'm afraid that we will have to consolidate two of them which will make it a little more complicated to get various items. While several accounts are a little more work, it is a lot easier to draw certain items when there are several different channels a person can go through.

In addition, they are reviewing all of the various items of supply that we are authorized so I am going to have to make out issue slips for about everything I can think of that we will be needing for the next year or so. Really a mess.

The weather here this last week really has been rather nice for the most part; even though there have been intermittent showers. It has been fairly clear and quite cool. Seems to have gotten rid of most of the mosquitos, which certainly is a break.

Today, one of the attorneys in the legal department and I went for a ride around the south end of the island, which was quite interesting. On the way, we stopped at a local bullfight in one of the villages, which was interesting; much more so than the one I saw last summer.

On the south part of the island, they raise quite a bit of sugarcane and are presently beginning to harvest it and render it down to raw sugar.

We stopped at one of the small refineries and watched. They utilize rather crude methods and a minimum of machinery. Outside of a crusher, which squeezes all of the juice from the canes, they don't have machinery. The sugar is obtained by a series of heatings in large open pans, which drives off all excess water. When they finish, they have what they call black sugar, which is actually brown.

Before the war, this black sugar was the main cash crop and export crop raised by the Ryukyuans. They had several large refineries in addition to quite a few of the smaller ones we saw today.

At the present time, they have just completed building a large refinery near Naha which will be able to completely refine the sugar and thus will be able to offer better competition with imported sugar. Much of the sugar is exported to Japan where there is a good market for the brown sugar; however, the price is quite a bit higher than sugar received from other sources and in the event of any general depression or recession in Japan, the local farmers will probably take quite a beating.

Jake is still in Tokyo although he will probably return tomorrow sometime. I guess that the colonel had a lot to report from his recent trip to Washington.

I heard the other day that Colonel Smith—my CO when I was at Travis—was lost in one of those big planes that went down last month in Japan. I certainly was sorry to hear about it. He was one of the fair-haired boys in the outfit.

Well, I can't seem to think of much else to report. I think that I will go to bed. I am quite tired after riding around in a jeep over those rough roads today for about five hours.

Love,

Peter

The under-regulated economy

Monday, December 22, 1952
Kadena Air Base; Okinawa

Dear Ma and Pa, and Ann,
Well, all of the packages arrived this last week and all were in good
shape. The big package containing the nuts, cookies, and presents,
the package from Pearl (the filberts are very good), the nuts from the
Monroes and the packages of pine nuts and the Anahist.

In all, I really received a lot of mail this last week. Thank you all
very much.

Please tell Pearl and the Monroes that I shall write soon and thank
them, but I don't know just when.

The weather here this last week has been very nice and cool
and clear to rainy and muddy.

Saturday and today were very pleasant but yesterday was really
miserable. However, as I was duty agent anyway, it really didn't matter
a great deal.

Not a great deal happened of interest but a Negro beat up a white
airman while he was sleeping. Seems that the Negroes are beginning to
assert themselves in one of the local villages; nothing especially new,
but it does crop up occasionally.

Along these lines, it is going to be rather interesting to see just
exactly what the authorities do about the construction of a new red-
light district near the base, not that they forbid any of these districts
but this in particular is only accessible through a nearby area that
has, by tacit consent, been frequented exclusively by Negroes. I rather
imagine that within a couple of weeks there will probably be quite a bit
of trouble down there.

I am a little surprised that the Okinawan owners did not think of
the problem before they built the houses, but I guess that they figured
that things would eventually take care of themselves.

The past week, in addition to fussing around with my three supply
accounts, I have been going around to some of the local Japanese

construction companies becoming acquainted with the labor foremen. What with a lack of any type of labor practices laws, or ordinances, it has been the practice of some of the companies to dismiss employees upon a moment's notice, which creates an ideal situation for the local agitators to toss around. You would think that as long as the military has been on the island, they would have formulated some type of fair-practices laws for dealing with the Okinawan workers employed at the base.

It is very interesting visiting the various construction camps, what with all of the bowing and scraping, and all of the little formalities that always seem to accompany the visits.

We are having an office party over at Jake's house tomorrow night which should prove to be interesting if nothing else. Jake's wife is a very good cook and a quite interesting person, so I think that everything will be a rather nice evening. Of course, there are a couple of agents that I would just as soon not see there but then that is the way it goes. Even two of the three secretaries are planning on attending, which is rather unusual as most of the time they are at each other's throats. The newest one (she is 32, looks like 42, and acts like 22), fell down about two weeks ago and cut herself over the eye and got a good shiner. We never have been able to figure out how or where it happened, but rumor had it that it happened in the BOQ area.

One of the agents left last week so we now have only nine people pulling duty agent which is certainly a break as I won't have it on New Year's Eve which is bound to be a bad night to have to work.

Well, can't think of anything else and I have quite a bit to do yet.
Love,
Peter

Christmas in Okinawa

Monday, December 29, 1952
Kadena Air Base; Okinawa

Dear Ma and Pa,

Well, I suppose that by this time Ann is in San Francisco getting all squared away before she starts her new job. It sounds like it might prove to be an interesting job. Just who sponsors the Committee and just what are the various schemes that it advocates?

You might write and ask her to send me some of their literature once she gets settled.

I want to thank you for the Christmas presents. Since I do not know just when I shall be writing Ann, will you please pass on my thanks to her when you write?

I had quite a nice Christmas even though I didn't do a great deal or go anyplace. Puttered around and did a little work in the morning and then drove around a little in the afternoon. They served a very nice meal up at the Mess Hall in the evening, which I thought was a little better than the one we had up there on Thanksgiving.

Supposedly, the Air Force personnel on the island were to work on Christmas but there was nothing much we could do since all civilian personnel got off and most of the offices only had one or two people present to answer the telephones. In fact, from Wednesday on, there wasn't a great deal done by anyone.

Saturday, Nielsen's car arrived at Naha, so I took him on down to pick up his car and then I walked around the market area for an hour or so. It had been since August that I had been down there to look around and even in that time, there had been quite a few new buildings constructed.

The weather was quite nice in the morning and part of the afternoon but by three in the afternoon, it had clouded up and started to rain. The weather here certainly can change in a big hurry. The weather here has remained cool with rain about every day or so

The road to Naha is completely paved—four lanes—so it is no trouble at all to go on down there to look around. But it certainly was a chore driving the fifteen or so miles on the old dirt road before they got it finished.

When these people put their minds to it they can build something fairly rapidly, but it seems that it is only in the last couple of weeks before the contract runs out that they manage to work up much speed or interest in the project.

However, things are really beginning to shape up around here as far as the construction work is concerned and it shouldn't be long before they have almost all of the roads on the base completed, which will certainly be a break.

I received a Christmas card from someone living at 2714 Sherwood Drive who didn't sign it, so if you should happen to know who lives there you might let me know, as I am rather curious.

Really a bit unhappy about the bird who takes care of our supply account in Tokyo. Around the first of the month, he sent down a camera without any case or instructions, so I wrote and asked for both and today he writes me that the camera is to be turned in because it is surplus or something. If only people could make up their minds once and for all.

Nielsen's family arrives here Saturday and I think that I shall move over across the street into his room. This shack has entirely too many mosquitoes in the summer. Last summer they got so bad, I thought that I was going to have to have a blood transfusion.

We are trading maids since his maid has to go home to take care of her family and he wanted a maid that would live in once he got his quarters.

Sounds rather confusing but it really isn't.

Well, that's about all that I can think of to report this time. Will write later. Don't work too hard.

Love,

Peter

"Still haven't found the safe . . . "

Sunday, January 4, 1953
Kadena Air Base; Okinawa

Dear Ma and Pa,

This last week also passed very quickly what with the holiday again on Thursday.

I was duty agent Wednesday evening but luckily, nothing happened.

New Year's, we decided that it would be better to get away from the base so Nielsen, Willhelm, our Nisei interpreter, and I went down to Naha and ate in a local restaurant which was quite interesting. Seems that we spent all evening eating. We had sukiyaki, which was very good.

Finally got a new jeep to replace the old one which was on its last legs. It is actually just a rebuilt jeep but it is in good shape which is a good thing as the last one was just about to stop permanently. It had rusted through around the window and the floor and would flood every time it rained at all.

Two new agents and a new secretary arrive on the first from Japan, so we will be in pretty good shape as far as personnel.

In addition, headquarters is going to send down an administrative officer this next week sometime. Just what they were thinking about I don't know. There certainly isn't enough for an administrative officer to do around here and then we are going to have to find someplace to put him which will be difficult as we are crowded right now.

I certainly hope that the new secretary turns out better than the last one we got or the one who is leaving. We certainly seem to have a lot of trouble with them.

New Year's Eve was rather quiet as far as work was concerned but New Year's Day turned out to be quite a busy one. Several bad assaults and burglaries. Never a dull moment. The new base commander, a colonel, caught an Okinawan boy going through his refrigerator at about 3:00 a.m. Nielsen was duty agent and after he arrived and had the boy taken off to jail, the colonel asked him how to work the carbine he captured him with. Seems that the boy had just broken out of jail the day before where he was awaiting trial for housebreaking last Spring. The boy had sneaked by a guard who was sleeping and as a result, the base provost marshal is in a rather uncomfortable position.

Jake is really on pretty good terms with the new base commander. Saturday just before noon, the colonel called Jake up and wanted to know if he was still planning on playing golf since it was overcast and a little windy. Jake told him yes, and then went on to suggest that the wind might improve the colonel's slice a little bit. It certainly was funny just the way he said it.

Still haven't found the safe yet and it is beginning to look like we never will. Jake is still unhappy about it but will get over it in time, I suppose.

Nielsen's family arrived yesterday, and he took them up to Okuma for a week.

Jake is going to draw Nielson's house for him sometime this week and I am going to see about getting some of the furniture arranged for him.*

The weather here this past week has been just about the same. We ended up the year with about 99 inches of rain. I managed to catch a cold this past week, but it isn't a very bad one.

Thanks for the money, Ma. So far, I have managed to save about a thousand dollars since I have been stationed here and if my promotion comes through, I should be able to do a little better.

I'm glad that your trip to Hawaii seems to be coming through on schedule. I'm sure you will have a good time. I hope that the weather will be nice for you, without any rain.

Still haven't received the candy from Gertrude Strowbridge that you mentioned in your letter of 15 Dec 1952. But it will probably come one of these days. Perhaps you had better send me her address, so I can write and thank her.

I filled out the Power of Attorney, Pa, and mailed them this last week. The person I had witness them is the staff Judge Advocate for the

---

* "Drawing" presumably refers to a housing lottery.

20th Air Force so there shouldn't be any doubt about his being able to administer oaths.

Just exactly what is Couch doing with the airlines?

Didn't do a great deal today. Got up late and ate breakfast and then this afternoon, Pat (the interpreter) and I drove around for a couple of hours in the jeep.

Visited the ruins of an old castle a little to the north of the base and took a few pictures, which I hope come out, even though it was rather overcast today. . . .

I think that I have just about got my supply business down to a point where it will start taking care of itself. I have turned in just about everything that we don't need and have requisitioned just about everything that we need and all I have to wait for is the paper mill to grind out the whole business.

I hope that you got all of your business wound up all right before the end of the year and that you are not too tired because of it, Pa.

Had a typhoon scare here this last week. There was a bad one south of here about 700 miles, but it veered away. Winds up to 180 knots, which would have really flattened the island, had it come this way.

Well, I can't think of a great deal to report so I shall close. Don't try and do too much work.

Love,
Peter

A hog's life

Monday, January 12, 1953
Kadena Air Base; Okinawa

Dear Ma and Pa,

Well, again not a great deal to report. Although I didn't do anything yesterday, I still didn't seem to manage to get around to writing a letter.

The weather here this last week certainly has been varied. Most of last week we had a strong wind from the north and the temperature got down to around 51 degrees, which coupled with the cold wind, really makes you feel a lot cooler.

Wednesday was an especially cold windy day although there wasn't any rain to speak of. Friday noon, the wind changed around to the south and it cleared off and turned fairly warm. Saturday was as nice a day you could possibly ask for. However, the wind changed again. Saturday night and Sunday and today were cold with a little rain.

Saturday morning, they had a formal parade for the general who is supposed to leave sometime this week. There were all kinds of visiting generals around the base over the weekend. Certainly will be glad to see him leave, as he didn't show me a great deal. He is going to retire and was coasting downhill all of the time he was here. Pretty good parade though.

The new man is only going to be a brigadier-general but he has been in grade for some time, so he will undoubtedly be bucking for a promotion, so he might help in shaping things up a little bit around here.

Saturday afternoon, I drove around a bit. Went down to Naha Air Base and looked around. At Naha port, they were unloading a bunch of hogs from some of the small native boats. They would manage to get a sling under the hog and get it lifted off the deck and over to the pier but then the winches would seem to stick and the hog would be hanging up in the air while they repaired the machinery.

It certainly was a field-day. All kinds of noise. I think that the boats must have come on up from one of the southern islands as they had quite a bit of raw sugar as cargo along with some bananas.

I don't know if there are any additional pictures around like the one I sent but I shall look around and see what I can do. I may have another one someplace or another.

The typing book arrived in good shape Saturday. I practiced a little Sunday and may even get around to a little more this evening. Eventually, I hope that it will do a little good, so I won't have to look at the keys all of the time.

Jake has two children, a boy and a girl. Both of them are pretty well behaved. Especially in comparison to some of the other children you see around here from time to time.

I received my W-2 form this last week, so I don't have to worry about that. However, they still haven't received the federal income tax forms here on the base, but I imagine that they will come in pretty soon. I imagine that I shall be able to send the form in before the end of the month.

Let me know when you receive the Power of Attorney that I sent last week. I sent them to the office.

I've spent most of this week trying to get some type of duplicating machine for the office that will work. The last one finally broke down and the first two new ones we drew didn't work. No broken parts. Just improperly designed and manufactured. They had parts in them that could not possibly have been made to function properly. May have to order one from our headquarters in Tokyo. Also ran out of mailing envelopes and there are none to be had on the base. All kinds of minor problems with the supply account.

Well, can't seem to think of a great deal else to report this time. . . .

Love,

Peter

Robbery, car theft, and lax discipline

Monday, January 19, 1953
Kadena Air Base; Okinawa

Dear Ma and Pa,

Well, there isn't a great deal to report again this last week.

The weather here for the most part has remained quite cool and overcast with rain about every other day. There has also been quite a bit of wind, which is rather uncomfortable. The roads around here have been quite bad the past few weeks.

They managed to tear up just about all of the old remaining roads with the result that there are about two inches of mud all over everything on days that it rains and about the same amount of dust when there has been no rain for a couple of days. The soil just doesn't hold the moisture for any length of time.

On a couple of stretches of road here on the base that have been completed for only two or three months, there are a great many broken places already. It is really a crime, the methods of construction utilized around here.

Supposedly, the Army Corps of Engineers are supervising and approving all construction work being done for the Air Force but there certainly is no indication that they are doing their jobs, judging from some of the results.

I received the candy from Gertrude Strowbridge. Please thank her for me. I shall try to write later but at the present time, I am very far behind on my correspondence. This last week I was busy all of the time but there really didn't occur anything that was especially interesting.

Friday night I was duty agent and had to do a little work in the evening. Then about 4:00 a.m. I got called out on a robbery. Seems that four airmen rolled a cab driver and stole his cab but by the time I got there, there really wasn't a great deal to be done. It certainly would help if they had something like bed-check around here. It is one of those practical traditions of the military that is not observed around here. There supposedly is a curfew around the island for all members of the military at 11:00 p.m. each evening. It doesn't have a great deal of meaning except that almost all of the MPs go off duty a short time afterward. I think that perhaps one reason there is no bed check is that there is no one around the base to do the counting. Those that are around either can't count or are in no position to do any counting.

I was talking to the first-sergeant of one of the bomb squadrons the other night in his barracks while he had a glass of whiskey in his hand. More discipline in a Boy Scout camp.

Nielsen finally got his family safely settled down here on the base. He got a good house in one of the better areas and seems to be quite satisfied with it. Concrete, three-bedroom house with central heating, about three years old.

If he could have waited another week or so he would have been able to draw one of the new houses they are just completing. They are a little nicer, but they have no central heating which is a bit inconvenient this time of year. They have two small wall heaters, one for the bathroom and one for the living room. The heaters are not supposed to be any good—of Japanese manufacture with no spare parts.

On top of that, they are blasting near the new area and some of the new houses are cracking quite badly; not so that it structurally weakens them but so that they look rather poor. On top of that, they painted some of them while the cement was still wet and as a result the paint is peeling. Some of the older houses, three to five years old, were painted with Japanese paint with a fish oil base that oozes fish oil. Speaking of paint, I got some and have great plans to repaint the room but I don't know just exactly when I am going to get around to it.

My new maid is quite a bit smaller than the old one, so I had to lower the ironing board several inches yesterday. She seems quite happy about it, so I guess everything will be all right.

All for now.

Love,

Peter

"Four homicides since yesterday afternoon."

Monday, January 26, 1953
Kadena Air Base; Okinawa

Dear Ma and Pa,

Well, this past week was another rapid one, although again nothing spectacular to report. The weather this past weekend was very nice. Fairly clear and warm but then at about ten minutes to five this evening it clouded up and started to rain and has been raining intermittently ever since although it is still pretty warm.

I rather imagine that so far this year—as little as there is of it so far—it has been rather dry; less than an inch of rain so far. Actually got very dusty the past couple of days. Here this past week or so, the lengthening of the days has become quite noticeable, it being light now until nearly 6:30 p.m.

I suddenly got ambitious last night and painted the room. Turned out to be quite a job and didn't get to bed until 2:00 a.m. The room really looks pretty good now, but I shall have to get new curtains as I painted the room sort of turquoise blue and the old curtains were green and orange.

The ceiling is a light grey. Occasionally they have some raw silk for sale that is an off-white, which may go fairly well. I certainly had a time getting the paint off of places it shouldn't have been.

The office had a rather busy day today. Four homicides since yesterday afternoon. One was a plain and simple accident so there won't be any type of an investigation.

This last weekend was a rather quiet one. Somehow, I didn't manage to get out to do any riding around. Saturday night Pat and I went down to Naha and ate in one of the native restaurants, which was nice. The food is pretty good.

I still haven't been able to get any federal income tax forms, but these people say that they will be available pretty soon now. They know damn well that the forms will be needed each year and at what time, but they still can't seem to plan for them.

I hope you have finished all of the necessary preparations for the trip.

I'm just afraid that both of you have been trying to do too much lately. You should start taking it easy.

I certainly think it was rather inconsiderate of Mr. Fields, on the surface of things, to be in such a hurry and then suddenly decide that he was going on a vacation and that he would conduct business when he returned. I certainly believe that I would put myself out again on the same business. Goodness knows there are plenty of other people around who need advice and aren't in such a rush for it. It isn't as if he were the only person around town with any business.

I hope, Ma and Pa, that you both start taking it easy for a change. All of your running around and all of your various and sundry activities are beginning to concern me.

Last week they put in six towel racks, three soap dishes, and a toilet-paper holder in the shack, and then today they come around and put doorknobs on the front door and replace the night latch.

I'm becoming a little concerned that they might be thinking of tearing down the shack. Here last summer they had just finished putting new storm shutters on a couple of BOQ's in the area and hadn't even finished painting them when they tore down both buildings.

They have been paving the road here near the shack this past week. They work when it rains and then lay off when it is nice and dry. They laid one stretch one evening, and by noon the next day the pavement had cracked and had broken up.

Well, can't seem to find any other letters from you asking any more questions, so I guess that I shall close. Perhaps I shall have more to report next week.

Nielsen and his wife have one little girl, nine-years-old. I believe that someone asked me about that. I received a letter from Ann wherein she finally came to the conclusion that Mary might be lazy.* I had just about given up hope by this time that she would ever arrive at that conclusion. It certainly does seem strange about her not looking for a job.

Love,
Peter

---

* Family legend has it that Peter's cousin, Mary Koerner (1929–2019), stopped working after receiving a large settlement in compensation for her injuries in an automobile accident.

"The whole island is crawling with incompetents."

Sunday, February 1, 1953
Kadena Air Base; Okinawa

Dear Ma and Pa,

I just happened to think today that you wouldn't be home to receive this letter and very probably did not receive last week's letter what with the mail service seeming to be slowing down a little these days.

But at least there will be some mail for you when you return from your trip. I hope that the weather is nice for you, both to and fro and during the time you are in the islands.

The weather here this last week has remained about the same. A day of rain and then a couple of days of cool wind with a little bit of sunshine. Actually, there hasn't been a great deal of rain so far this year. I think that January ended up with about an inch of rain.

However, I have no doubt that it will manage to catch up here before too long. A lack of rain is, however, quite beneficial as far as the construction work is concerned.

This last week I have managed to keep busy without any trouble although not a great deal has happened of unusual interest, with the exception of Monday, that is. I can't remember exactly when I wrote you whether it was Sunday or Monday. If it was Monday, I must have mentioned what a bad day we had as far as the four homicides were concerned.

I had duty agent one night last week but luckily nothing happened, and I got a good night's sleep. As good as is possible, having to sleep in the duty shack.

Looking over your letters of the last week I came across an interesting phrase that I'm afraid I am going to have to have explained to me: "Bea Grout Ann's Fielding." I'm with you for the first three-fourths of the phrase but after that, all is a blank. Sounds like a book but just what kind I have absolutely no idea.

Did Wallace Caulfield get married or have I been away too long and am confusing him with some other person? I hope that I am right. Otherwise, I am going to be quite embarrassed about the whole thing.

Today, Pat and I went on up to Nago. Up one side and down the other. The weather was rather cold and windy, but it managed to hold off raining. The roads were really in pretty good shape for the most part. They are doing quite a bit of construction work along the road on this side (China Sea side) on up north where the road is carved out of the rocks along the coast. They are putting in new sea walls in places where it has washed out. The few cherry trees there are around there are starting to bloom and they are beautiful.

A new and more powerful Ryukyuan radio station started broadcasting this last week, which is a relief. Now I don't have to put up with the usual line of drivel they broadcast over the Armed Forces Network. I don't believe they know the meaning of a good radio program. Occasionally, they will let one slip by but for the most part, they are pretty sad.

Saturday afternoon Pat and I were sent by Jake on down to one of the native theatres to review a movie he had been informed was a bit prejudicial to the military's interest on the island. It was the story of the senior class of one of the girls' high schools here on the island, who were nurses during the war here, up until the time the survivors were burned and buried alive in a cave on the southern end of the island where they were hiding.

It certainly depicted all of the suffering, bloodshed, etc. Although it never showed any American troops or planes, it certainly did show non-combatants being machine-gunned and bombed when they were hiding. Not that these things didn't probably happen, but I can see absolutely no use in bringing it to everyone's attention. It certainly went further than to merely portray the horrors of war. (Too many, certainly). Supposedly, someone down in USCAR approved the movie before it was allowed to be shown on the local market. I don't see how anyone in his right mind would ever have approved the movie; even not being able to understand Japanese would [not] make any difference.

Saturday night, we went down to Naha to eat and we were discussing the movie with one of the operators of the restaurant who stated that she thought the movie shouldn't have been allowed to be shown, especially to the younger generation, who would get the wrong idea about the actual conditions. Her contention was that the suffering was actually much more severe than that portrayed but the movie did not go on to fully show the part the Japanese occupation troops played in the actual circumstances.

She had been captured later and had been well-treated by American doctors. The older people would still realize the sufferings of the war and hence the picture would afford no practical end while the younger generation would gain the impression that all was well and rosy under the Japanese and that the only troubles were those brought about by the American troops.

I suppose that tomorrow I shall try to find out who approved the movie, find out his reasons and then write up a report. If his reasons aren't any better than I think they will be, there is going to be a rather uncomplimentary report forwarded. At the present time, I am still quite displeased with the whole thing.

As I said, we went down to a restaurant in Naha Saturday night for dinner. The food there is very good, and the method of preparation is far superior to that in the local mess halls. Of course, it is quite a bit more expensive, but it is a relief to get some diversion in the food department.

I had some fried eel last week that was excellent. It has a very delicate taste. About the only thing I do not care for is ginger, but it is not offered a great deal and you can always tell them to leave it out.

What really makes things expensive is the import tax on all Japanese beer. It brings the cost up to about a dollar a bottle. There is no beer manufactured locally and they can't use American beer as it is just about as expensive if they get it through legal channels—and the tax people keep pretty close track on the restaurants, so they can't take a chance on using untaxed beer.

Sake is also quite expensive and rather heavily taxed. The local sake isn't as good as the Japanese, although it is a little cheaper and much more available. There are quite a few small sake factories scattered throughout the island.

Occasionally, we have rice at the mess hall, but GI's do the cooking when they should be doing the looking while the Okinawans cook the rice. It seems rather strange the rice we have comes out so poorly when there are so many people working in the mess halls who could do a good job of it.

We are having an inspection this next weekend sometime by a couple of generals from the front office in Washington along with that 'nasty old colonel' (Jake's expression) from Tokyo.

And then sometime in the next week or so we are having a more detailed inspection by some people from our headquarters. Going to be quite a bit of work getting everything in order for these people. Not that we are doing things improperly, but it seems that certain local modifications are necessary for operations around here that are not easily discerned by transients.

I believe that I mentioned before that one of the men in the shack is building a house of his own near the base in order to bring his wife over earlier than the normal dependent-housing situation would allow. He is having a local contractor build him a house—two bedrooms— for a little over $4000. The house is certainly very adequate although there isn't a great deal of room and a minimum of fancy trimmings. He has a wonderful view. He has had several of the Air Force engineering inspectors look at the house during various stages of the construction and they have all told him that he is getting a better-built house for around $4000 than the Air Force is getting for an average of $23,000. Hardly speaks well for the Air Force housing program even if the Air Force houses are little larger.

I seem to have been carried away with myself this evening. This same man, a major, is assigned to the local AIO (Air Installations Office) which has the responsibility for all small construction and all maintenance and repair on the base. He was telling me that he heard that on the new houses they have what they call a "roof jack' which is nothing more than a hole in the ceiling for a stove pipe. On the top of the roof is supposed to be a cement box arrangement with holes in the sides to let the smoke out but to keep the rain from going on down the pipe. So far so good, but on some of the newer houses, the hole and the rain-shelter arrangement were about 3 feet apart. Seems that the houses were built and finished, and they didn't discover the error until they started getting rainwater in the stoves.

I suppose that you might place partial blame on the Japanese contractors, but it seems to me that almost all blame should fall on the people who have the responsibility of checking the construction work as it is being done. I don't care where you are having construction done or by whom, you are asking for trouble as soon as you start leaving the contractors alone and not checking on them. In this case, as with all Air Force construction, the Army Corps of Engineers has the responsibility on Okinawa to inspect all construction work being done for the Air Force. However, I don't imagine that in this case the man who was actually supposed to do the inspecting will be made to explain the error but rather he will be promoted and sent home with a letter of commendation. It is really a great life.

Saturday afternoon near the shack here, an oil truck tried to get a little nearer an oil drum that had to be filled so he drove over a water valve but didn't quite make it and broke the pipe. A mess. The driver told me that he saw the valve but that he thought he could straddle it—and so he drove right over it. The whole island is crawling with incompetents.

In preparation for the temporary closing of the Naha Airstrip for resurfacing, the Navy moved its patrol planes up here to Kadena this last week.

Eventually they are planning on moving the commercial air travel here also, along with some fighter planes. When they all get up here, Kadena is going to be a busy place. At the present time, they are only using the new runway and they are resurfacing the old one but should be through shortly.

If and when they ever finish all the construction here on the base, Kadena is going to be about the biggest base in the Far East. As it is, Okinawa in general—and Kadena in particular—must be becoming more and more desirable because they have been building several new VIP quarters near our mess hall.

Well, I can't go on forever and I seem to have just about run out. Just don't expect such a lengthy letter from me all of the time because there simply isn't this much to report every week.

Love,
Peter

On the waterfront

Monday, February 9, 1953
Kadena Air Base; Okinawa

Dear Ma and Pa,
I'm a bit late again this week.

Yesterday, I went to Naha and it was rather late when I returned and didn't seem to get around to writing. And then this evening, Willhelm and I were invited over to Nielsen's house for dinner and we stayed until fairly late. But I did want to try and get one off to you, so you would hear from me while you are on your trip.

The weather here this last week has been pretty good. Almost all of last week it was overcast with comparatively little rain. Friday, it cleared off and has remained quite clear and nice since then; however, it has gotten a little cooler.

Things are quite dusty around here at the present time and I doubt whether we will have any rain tomorrow as it is quite clear now.

The generals and the colonels from Washington and Tokyo arrived on Saturday morning very early and left early this morning. Coming during the weekend as they did, they weren't too interested in the office but rather looking around a bit and getting a little rest.

As a result, about the only person to come through the office was some colonel from Washington who arrived about 5:00 p.m. Saturday.

It was a waste of time since he was a rather pompous idiot. They had a couple of parties for them while they were here and from what I hear, Jake and Nielsen managed to shape the colonel up a little with the generals and the colonel from Tokyo, so I guess everything is in pretty good order.

However, in another couple of weeks, we are due to have an inspection from some team they are sending on down here from Tokyo. This is supposed to last several days so we will have to go through all of that again.

I was duty agent Saturday and outside of having to sit around the office all afternoon in case someone should come by and want to look at it, nothing of interest happened. Last week, we lost one agent—

transferred to Guam, and then got a new man in about the same time. What with dropping one man and waiting until the new man is familiar with the area, I will get it again on the 28th, which isn't too good being payday and Saturday at the same time.

Sunday afternoon I went down to Naha and watched them unload a couple of Japanese boats, which was quite interesting. Cement, flour, lumber, sheet metal (corrugated for building), and tile were the main things they were unloading.

For the return trip, they were taking on bales of tin cans. Scrap metal of various sorts is one of the main exports around here. Interesting to watch them.

At first glance, everything looks hopelessly confused and you wonder how they are ever going to get anything down on the dock. But they are surprisingly fast when it comes to unloading and hauling it away; trucks all over the dock all going in different directions. There was one boat—by far the largest of the Japanese vessels—which weighed about 2200 tons or so, one of the stewards aboard the ship told us.

There was a smaller one that came in that was unloading various types of fish paste, canned goods, and dry goods. There was also a converted landing craft, a pretty good-sized one that was Chinese-owned, from Formosa, that was unloading tea and canned pineapple.

Finally got the federal income tax forms today. Glanced through everything and I think that I shall have to pay about $29 extra. Didn't think that they would ever arrive, but they finally did.

Have been really busy this last week but should be through with the current business tomorrow morning. These heroes think nothing of making an appointment and then forgetting about it. Should get a little action, since I called the CO of the outfit this afternoon and complained.

Love,

Peter

The Organization Men

Sunday, February 15, 1953
Kadena Air Base; Okinawa

Dear Ma and Pa,

Well, by the time you get this letter, you will have returned from your trip. I hope that you both had a good time and that you managed to do and see everything of interest and still get some rest.

While I have been busy this last week, I can't think of a great deal to report.

Wednesday, Thursday, and Friday were very nice. Clear and warm. Just like summer only not as warm.

However, Saturday it rained and today it was fairly nice in the morning but started to cloud up around noon. Went out to dinner Saturday evening and have stayed around here today reading and doing my income tax.

Heard a couple of good ones this week. We got the new general in this last week. I heard this evening that from here on no one will be permitted to use a red pencil on any business—that the red pencil will be used only by him—and when someone sees a red pencil mark on anything, they will know the general means business.

Just hearsay so far but it makes a good story.

They have just built a new stockade for the 20th Air Force. A nice administration-office building out of concrete and an expensive double-cyclone fence, complete with a guard tower. The only trouble: the enclosed area is about the size of two tennis courts, and there is no place for the prisoners to be housed. The confinement officer saw what was going on and he called up the installations people and asked them to stop construction until the plans could be modified and he was told that it would cost more to delay construction than to complete it. So now, the 20th Air Force has a nice new stockade but no place to put the prisoners.

I suppose that they can always use it to keep the guard dogs they have around here. Might just as well; there are just as many things being stolen as ever before.

As I mentioned, I filled out the income tax forms. I had to pay the federal government an extra $23. The $3,000 state exemption covered me so I didn't owe anything.

Nielsen took some evidence to Tokyo this week and arrived back last night. From what he was able to pick up—from several reliable sources—our office is considered the best in the theater, which is certainly something to be thankful for.

From what everyone has been able to gather, the main office, and all of Japan for that matter, are quite a mess. It seems that everyone in Headquarters is trying to get someone, and that anyone who hasn't got about three people out to get him is a non-entity.

So far, we have managed to stay out of it all and I hope that we remain clear of all the mess. Right now, there is quite a bit of fast footwork going on up in Tokyo to see who will be sent down here to replace Jake when he leaves in another couple of months.

The two main contenders so far are rather poor ones. One of them being generally disliked and the other generally hated by everyone else in Japan. It will be quite interesting to see just how everything turns out. Actually, whoever does get it will have to conform to the local ground rules. The system here on Okinawa can't be bucked; the big problem will be how long the new man takes to find it out.

Saturday was Okinawan New Year's which they stretch out to about two days of celebrating and a day or two of recovering. Not a great deal of business being done. It is their main holiday of the year, similar to our Christmas what with the giving of gifts.

My ex-maid sent over a couple of presents which made me feel rather badly as she must have spent a week's wages on them. These people are generous to the point of being over-generous. They simply can't afford to give expensive presents.

Well, I can't seem to think of a great deal else to report. The captain is moving out Tuesday and has already arranged to move a friend into his old room. I told him this evening that I didn't like his choice of friends and that I was quite unhappy over the whole thing. He didn't like it too well but didn't say anything.

Will write later.

Love,

Peter

Crime wave?

Dear Ma and Pa,
Well, not a great deal to report again this week. I think that it must be
the weather; poor weather and not much to report. Rain all this last
week. Sunday, it started to clear off, but it was windy and cold, so I
stayed in inside.

Today, it was fairly clear and a little warmer. The wind changed
around to the south and if it holds there for another day or so, things
will have a chance to dry out and warm up.

I received a couple of your letters today that were mailed from
Hawaii. From what both of you report, you seem to be having a nice
trip. I'm glad that you have been able to see as much as you have
and that the weather seems to have been nice for you. I hope that it
remained the same for the rest of your trip.

Having access to a car I imagine was a big help. Traveling the way
you did on the passenger-cargo type of vessel seems to have enabled
you to see a great deal more than those who take the usual tour offered
to the typical tourist.

Outside of the weather, there isn't much to report of interest this
week. I have been busy all of the time but there has been nothing out
of the ordinary that is interesting.

Someone knocked over another safe around here this last week.
Didn't take the safe this time—just the contents. Poor Jake is about
to have a fit. Two unsolved safe cases. Doesn't look like we will be able
to do any good on this one either.

The past month or so there seems to have been a rather large
upswing of crime around the base. Much of it is theft of government
property. Most of it being removed in trucks. What with the lack of
guards who are reliable, it is not too much trouble to remove stuff.
Coupled with the fact that there is no effective check at the gates, there
is an inviting field for anyone who wants to make a few fast bucks.
Much of the stuff is building materials, although recently someone

got away with a bale of mosquito nets worth several thousand dollars. Much of the trouble is the result of improper storage and supervision. Often several days pass before a large loss is discovered by the responsible person. Quite a life.

I'm sort of glad that I'm not working with the criminal cases. It must be rather irritating to be working on several cases at the same time, which could have been partially prevented if the responsible persons had taken some precautions. But I suppose that has always been the way things have been run in areas considered to be within combat zones.

Went down to Naha last week to do a little coordinating with the Ryukyuan Police system. We have always gone out of our way to cooperate with them and as a result, I think that we are better liked and get better results than do the Army CID and CIC. A great deal of our success can be attributed to our Nisei civil service interpreter. He knows about all of the wheels in the local police system and is well-liked by them and as a result, they are happy to cooperate with him. I shall probably have to go down there again sometime this week.

Occasionally, we have to deliver lectures to some of the various organizations here on the base and last week it was my turn again and I had to give a couple of talks on the organizations. Doesn't seem to have done a great deal of good as we are still in business this week as before with no noticeable decrease in crime.

Unfortunately, I am duty agent next Saturday evening, which is doubly poor as it is also payday. However, I haven't had it on payday for some time now and, I guess that it is just unfortunate that it comes on a Saturday night. However, typically Saturdays aren't as bad as Sundays as it is often some time before we get notified of the Saturday evening deeds and by that time the Sunday agent is on. However, I don't imagine that I shall be getting much sleep this time. A good thing that it is Saturday, I suppose, as I can always sleep the next day.

Well, all for now.

Love,

Peter

Okinawa's cops

Tuesday, March 3, 1953
Kadena Air Base; Okinawa

Dear Ma and Pa,

Well, again there isn't a great deal of interest to report.

To begin with, however, enclosed are a couple of pictures of myself that were taken last Saturday morning when a couple of us didn't have a great deal to do. Saturdays are rather difficult in that it is difficult to find anyone to do any business with.

Last Saturday was especially bad what with payday.

Actually, the exposures aren't too good—I believe that because I do not have the suntan that appears. The other picture is one of our two native interpreters, by the name of Higa. He is a very good interpreter. He taught himself English and is quite proficient at it. On top of that, he is aggressive and very quick-witted. He just returned last week from a rather prolonged two-week trip to Japan. In all, he was gone about five weeks. It was the first time that he had seen his mother in about eleven years, and it was quite a big event in his life. The Okinawan on the left is a CP (Civil Policeman) who had helped nab the bird in the back seat of the jeep. Notice the handcuffs—I didn't happen to notice them until just now.

The CP's are a pretty good bunch of policemen. All of their organization is handled down in Naha and is quite similar to the organization of the Japanese police system. Considering their tremendous lack of all kinds of equipment and facilities, they do a remarkable job.

On top of that, they have to deal with the Civil Administration (USCAR), which is just an additional burden, rather than a help as it should be.

Almost all of last week was pretty nice and fairly warm. I was duty agent Saturday and the weather was lovely but Sunday it rained hard all day.

Quite a bit of business Saturday but nothing of any great importance.

Sunday, the man who relieved me managed to skid the staff car into a ditch and bang it up some. A bad way to start the week—especially as far as Jake is concerned. He was, and is, really unhappy.

I managed to shake up a little trouble on my trip to Naha a couple of weeks ago and for the last two days, Jake has been going around shaping up several Army colonels. It is really a laugh.

Tomorrow, we have the regular monthly meeting with them, and it ought to be quite interesting how I am received by a couple of majors from G-2 and CIC. One thing about this place, there is never a dull moment. To me, with my perverted sense of humor, it is good for quite a few laughs.

Last Saturday, the new British jet transport landed at Kadena and I managed to get down to see it for a while. It is a strange looking plane. From what I hear, it is going to start making a regular weekly run through here. They have finished building the new operations-and-terminal building on the flight line and they have moved up all of the air travel from Naha, so there is a lot more activity going on around here.

Sunday evening, a friend of mine who is stationed in Japan arrived on Okinawa en route to the Philippines so yesterday I took the day off and we drove around sightseeing. It was a lovely day but today it turned cold and it started to rain this evening.

Well, I can't seem to think of anything else of interest. If you should happen to see some pine nuts, I would appreciate them. Also, some good cheese if it isn't too much trouble. Both should ship by regular mail in good shape.

I shall try to think of more to write next time.

Love,

Peter

"Heard a pretty good one last week"

Monday, March 9, 1953
Kadena Air Base; Okinawa

Dear Ma and Pa,
Well, I received a letter from both of you and from the sound of
everything, the trip was a success with the exception of no grass huts
for mother. Too bad.

I have some pictures of grass-thatched houses that I shall try to get
sent off one of these days; just when, I have no idea, but I am planning
on it sometime in the future.

Too bad about the rough weather and getting bruised up on the way
back. However, I guess a few bruises are a lot better than being seasick.

The meeting I mentioned last week came off very nicely and
everyone was pleasant and cooperative. Things seem to be straightened
out in pretty good shape. At least for a while.

At any rate, the work certainly has piled up these past few days.
Worked a little Saturday afternoon and then a little Sunday evening.

Heard a pretty good one last week. Seems the Army has some POL
(petroleum, oil, and lubricants) pipelines that they are supposed to be
patrolling but the path doesn't always follow the lines so parts of them
don't get inspected once a week as they are supposed to be.

In one place, an Okinawan built a house over the line and then dug
down through the floor (and a little ground) and tapped into the line.
Everything would have been fine, and he would have continued to have
a nice oil-well-and-distributing-business if he hadn't gotten sloppy and
spilled a bunch of oil around his house. A CP got suspicious and found
him out. The lieutenant in charge of the POL Division was certainly
made to look foolish.

The weather this past week, for the most part, was pretty wet but
getting a little warmer. Sunday about noon it cleared off and today
was very nice and fairly warm but rather hazy and dusty from the rock
crusher and asphalt plant over on the other side of the hill.

I certainly do feel sorry for the Monroes, what with all of their
troubles with Bill. He always did want to do something a little bit

different or in a grander manner than everyone else but marrying a widow with five children seems to be going a bit too far in asserting himself. I'm just afraid that he is going to have a terrible time supporting all of his various dependents. Too bad he didn't do it before the first of the year. What with nine dependents, the government would end up owing him money. Actually, he would be getting a much better deal in the Army than just about anyplace else.

Where did Pat and Vinnie get the name Post? It is a new one on me. Too bad about Ann's tooth. I have great hopes that one of these days she will wise up and arrive at the (right) conclusion that she simply isn't coordinated and that she has no business engaging in anything more active than slowly climbing stairs—if there isn't an elevator handy.

What is this bird "Don" like that Ann has been going out with? She wrote and said that he had been 'affiliated' with the SAE at some university back East?* I assume that by this she meant he was a member; however, I am still not quite sure.

I hope that the next trip you people take will be to Japan. From the comparatively little of it I have seen and heard about, it has a great deal to offer, and I think that it will increasingly become more of a tourist attraction. Especially now with the establishment of 17-hour air travel to Tokyo from Seattle.

I got a letter from Ann today in which she mentioned she is moving again. I hope that the new apartment is a good one. Should be for what they have to pay for it. I hope that if Mary doesn't shape up, she will decide to go back to Phoenix, so the rest of the girls can get things settled and not have to worry about getting food when they come home in the evenings.

From what Ann said, she seems to be enjoying her job, but it doesn't look like it will last past summer.

Will write again,

Love,

Peter

---

* SAE is a college fraternity.

Hoping for rain

Monday, March 16, 1953
Kadena Air Base; Okinawa

Dear Ma and Pa,

Well, I'm a day off schedule again this week. Yesterday afternoon it cleared off a little bit, so we drove around a few hours in the afternoon and then in the evening we went on up to the club for dinner and by the time we got back it was rather late and I somehow didn't get around to writing.

This past week has been rather wet and cloudy although it seems to be a little bit warmer all of the time. The temperature range now is from around 60 to 70 degrees. In another month or two, we will be able to shed neckties for the summer. I hope that it comes pretty soon as the few I've been wearing are getting a bit old.

I don't know if I mentioned it earlier but supposedly this summer the uniformed troops will be able to wear short sleeves and short pants. All of the heat rash last summer finally wised them up.

This evening we have an inspection team arriving from Tokyo for a stay of about 10 days. What they are planning on doing here for 10 days is beyond me, but they must think there will be something for them around here.

Actually, Okinawa is getting more and more developed and desirable than before and there are more and more colonels, etc., coming on down here on longer and longer inspection visits. I guess that is a sign of the arrival of an area as a desirable place to hold an inspection.

I hope it rains all of the time they are here. Maybe they will leave earlier if they can't get in any golf.

Saturday afternoon we had training for a couple of hours which seemed to shorten the weekend considerably. This time, it was on the preservation and handling of evidence. The next one will be on the use of the camera—that is, if the person who is giving the lecture doesn't ruin it as he did with the other one. He wasn't familiar with the workings of the camera and broke a couple of little parts. The Air Force supply catalog doesn't list the parts and I will have to write away to the factory. Never a dull moment with those damn supplies. It wouldn't be so bad if the people who use the equipment would take care of it and put it back, but they never seem to learn.

We got a couple of new men in last week and once they start pulling duty agent, we will get it a little less often than we are now. One of the agents is leaving this next week. Good riddance as he wasn't at all reliable. Why Jake didn't court-martial him I'll never know, and Jake has said the same thing. Actually, he is a pretty good-natured person when it comes to stepping on one of his men.

One of the new men has been assigned to help me, which will be nice as I have certainly been rushed lately. Give me a chance to do things that I haven't had an opportunity to do previously.

Well, I have to go down to the office and do a little work this evening, so I shall close short of the two full pages. Will try to think of more to report next time.

Love,
Peter

An inspection, a new man, and a problematic colonel

Monday, March 23, 1953
Kadena Air Base; Okinawa

Dear Ma and Pa,
Well, what with the inspectors here all of this last week, things have been rather upset as you can well imagine. The three of them arrived Monday. One of them, the one for supply matters, left Saturday noon and returned to Tokyo while the other two aren't due to leave until sometime Wednesday.

From what I have heard, there is nothing special that they have found that we are not doing properly. However, they certainly have gone through just about everything imaginable.

Tuesday evening, we took them down to a tea house in Naha for dinner. They went with some misgivings but seemed to have a good time. Had a good meal.

Friday evening, we took them over to Castle Terrace and they seemed to like that also.

Saturday afternoon I took the two of them riding about the base and then yesterday we went for a drive up around Motobu Peninsula.

Outside of Saturday and today, when it has been overcast and rather cool, the weather has remained very nice for them. This has been the first trip for any of them to Okinawa and they all seem to be favorably impressed by everything here.

However, it has been a little difficult to get a great deal done. They have to ask questions as they come to them; as a result, I have to more or less stay around the office. On top of that, space is at a premium what with extra people in the office.

One of the new men who arrived here this past couple of weeks has been helping me out, which is a break. While he has had no experience at all, he seems to be capable and intelligent and will probably get along pretty well.

I'm sorry that I forgot to mention seeing Alex Chilton when he was here a couple of weeks ago. He looked fine. I believe that he will be coming back through in about another month and will probably be here for a couple of months before he moves on again. He seems to have a pretty interesting job, but I imagine that all the traveling around will get a little dull eventually.

Jake is due to be leaving here sometime in May and as yet there is no word of his replacement. Headquarters in Tokyo isn't getting anyone in from the States who will be able to act as his replacement and there is no one up there presently who is available to transfer down here.

On top of that, there are about five other field-grade officers in the theater who will be leaving in the next couple of months, and there are no replacements for them, either. That headquarters of ours, both in Washington and in Tokyo, shows me nothing.

The colonel in Tokyo, while seemingly competent, has an obnoxious personality and is doing quite a little bit in getting the other people up there completely disaffected with him and the organization. Interesting to hear all of the gossip and all of the politicking that goes on up in the headquarters.

Enclosed are some pictures that Pearson took when he was here last summer.

#1 and #2 are taken out at White Beach where the large passenger ships dock. The buildings in the background of #1 are the clubs for the Navy personnel off of the ships when they arrive. Off to the far right of picture #2 is the general direction of Kadena.

#3 is a typical native village.

#4 are the wrecks of some of the wartime shipping. Mainly beached by typhoons.

#5 is a typical native store.

#6 is a florist shop of sorts.

#7 (a poor picture) is a horse cart with cement tile.

#8 is one of the busier intersections near the base with a couple of bordellos painted as restaurants.

Enclosed is an article concerning the manufacture of clay roof tile. Makes roofs like those in picture #8. Very good looking. Makes a good roof. However, quite expensive and heavy. An average-sized roof costs around $500, which is about half the cost of one of the better houses. It weighs about 1300 pounds per 36 feet (1000 kin per tsubo by Japanese measure). Heavy roofs help keep the houses together during the typhoons. All of the joints are mortised together. No nails except for the sideboards.

Well, that is all for now. Will write later.

Love,

Peter

The local elections: a Cold War skirmish

Tuesday, March 31, 1953
Kadena Air Base; Okinawa

Dear Ma and Pa,

Well, I seem to be late again this week. Don't know just where the time has gone. Sunday evening, we went to the club for dinner and I didn't have much time after I returned. Then last night Nielsen was duty agent, and he and I drove Jake around the villages a little while and then came back; by that time it was late, so I went to bed.

This evening, Pat and I went to the movies. Busy but nothing of unusual interest.

I filed a state tax return at the time of the federal one. I meant to mention it last week, but I forgot about it.

I have been reviewing some of your latest letters but there doesn't seem to be a great deal you have been asking me so there isn't a great amount of material that I can comment on. I suppose that with the new uniform regulations, we will be permitted to wear short pants. However, I don't know just how Jake feels about it. However, the way the weather has been, it will be sometime before we have to cross that bridge.

This last Saturday we had a very heavy rainstorm in the morning. I imagine that it must have rained a couple of inches in a couple of hours.

Sunday, yesterday, and today have been fairly clear but windy and cold. Supposed to remain that way for a couple more days. I wish that it would warm up. Come the 15th of this month we can take off neckties, which will be a welcome relief.

I also want to thank you for sending me the cheese; I shall let you know its condition when it arrives. This time of the year there shouldn't be much danger about it getting too hot in transit.

One of the other people in the shack went to the hospital yesterday after having an attack of ulcer trouble. He should be getting back tomorrow. One drip left today for one of the other islands for about a month, which will be a welcome relief. Hope he stays there indefinitely.

I was duty agent Friday night but luckily nothing happened. Didn't even get a call, which is quite unusual. This past week has been rather quiet as far as crime is concerned.

The big news of the week was the putting of all villages off-limits last Sunday night from sunset to sunrise, to be continued until further notice. I believe that I mentioned the inspection trip of the generals a month or so ago when the local provost marshal and the PM from FEAF gave them a guided tour through one of the red-light areas.

As a result of that trip, there was quite a bit of correspondence and comment. Now there are a couple of generals, Army and AF chiefs of the Chaplain Corps, who are arriving tomorrow along with a bunch of rather prominent church leaders from the States.

Although I imagine that this off-limits business is strictly for their benefit, so far there is nothing official concerning the reasons for placing the whole island off-limits other than a couple of rather feeble excuses.

Good thing they aren't staying more than a couple days. I hope that this time the conducted tours of this island are a little better planned. Going to be a lot of trouble with the troops if they are kept on the base for any length of time. Needless to say, the local economy is going to suffer quite a bit.

A rather important election tomorrow. One seat of the Ryukyuan legislature is to be filled. The Socialists have teamed up with the Peoples Party (Commie) against the Democratic Party (pro-American) and are very likely to defeat them, which would mean quite a blow to the present government of the Ryukyus.

What sort of burns me is that the American Civil Administration doesn't seem to be doing a great deal to discredit the left-wing and the socialist parties around here. Perhaps the big bone of contention is the uncertain status of the Ryukyus. At the present time, they are neither fish nor fowl but hope that they will be returned to Japan. That is very improbable but they have not been told so and are still hoping.

Well, will write more about it later.

Love,

Peter

The local elections: a left-wing victory

Monday, April 6, 1953
Kadena Air Base; Okinawa

Dear Ma and Pa,

Well, this week certainly has gone by in a hurry. I've been quite busy and from the looks of things, I shall be very busy for a couple of days to come. Seems that many things happen at the same time. I think that Jake is going to Japan tomorrow which will be a break as every time I see him he gives me something else to do. Don't get me wrong, though; I certainly am not complaining.

Alex Chilton arrived on Okinawa Friday afternoon and will be here about six weeks before he moves on again. Had lunch with him Saturday and drove around a little in the afternoon. Yesterday, we drove down to the southern part of the island where he looked over the area he had been stationed during the war. It was quite interesting. Went a few places that I haven't been before.

In the evening, we went over to the Air Force club for their regular Sunday dinner which was pretty good. The heroes were only mildly obnoxious.

The villages are still off-limits during all hours of darkness. Sort of expected them to remain off-limits until after Easter and after the visiting chaplains had left the theater—which I believe was today.

They [the chaplains] were supposed to remain in Korea over Easter. However, I wouldn't be a bit surprised if they [the base leadership] didn't put the villages on-limits again for a week or so. In the meantime, the local economy is taking a terrible blow. Some of the local punks (whether it is the same ones or not we don't have any idea) are still beating up on the cab drivers.

I'm duty agent tomorrow night so I suppose there will be another robbery and assault along those same lines. More order and discipline in an anthill than there is on this base, sometimes.

As was more or less expected, the left-wing coalition won the election here last week for the one seat in the legislature. However, there is an ordinance or ruling on the books that anyone convicted of a felony cannot run for public office.

It seems that the Socialist-Peoples Party candidate had been given 45 days back in 1946 for some minor act of fraud. And it was known by USCAR all of the time, but they didn't see fit to disqualify the candidate until after he had been elected.

Now there is quite a bit of controversy about the whole thing and needless to say nothing is being said that reflects favorably on the American occupation of the Ryukyus. Seems to me that all of those high-powered, high-paid civilians they have down in USCAR could make up their damn minds before it is too late.

Whatever the outcome, it seems that both leftist parties will become more and more firmly consolidated as a result of the whole thing. Sounds impossible that a person in a position of authority could be responsible for such a stupid move but it certainly doesn't seem much out of line around here.

Would be sort of funny if we weren't made to look so foolish by the mistakes of some of the fools they have running around here in positions of responsibility. Just couldn't seem to make up their damn minds until it was too late and then they made the wrong decision.

Got a letter from Ann today. She seems to be pretty well settled down in her new apartment but didn't give me any kind of rundown concerning just who she is sharing the apartment with, how her job is progressing, and what she is doing. Or what the present status of Mary is nowadays.

The weather Saturday was beautiful and fairly warm but on Sunday it was cloudy and then it started to rain later this afternoon. I imagine that it will turn nice around tomorrow afternoon. Seems that it is nice for a day or two and then clouds up for two or three days and then turns nice again.

The roommate who went to the hospital got out of there Saturday and then moved into a two-man shack. This evening, a new man moved in. He seemed worried about paying his maid too much and thereby upsetting the native economy. Must be a big spender.

Well, that is about all that I can think of to report for the time being.

Love,

Peter

The local elections: and the winner gets his seat

Monday, April 13, 1953
Kadena Air Base; Okinawa

Dear Ma and Pa,

Well, not a great deal to report this week. I wrapped up a few pictures and will send them off in the morning when I mail this.

Just one comment on your letters. Why, of all cars, did you happen to choose an Olds 88? A nice car all right but it certainly has a lot more power than the two of you will ever use.

Saturday afternoon we had training class for a couple of hours which turned out to be pretty dull. In the evening, I took Alex Chilton over to Castle Terrace for dinner.

Sunday, it was raining and quite cold. Originally, we had planned on going up to Motobu but what with the weather, we drove around Shuri and Naha instead and had dinner at the Rycom officers club, which was pretty good. It was the first time that I had eaten there since last August and the food was good, but I still don't especially care for the club itself. Speaking of clubs, the Air Force officers club here on the base made a net profit last month of over $13,000, which certainly seems completely out of line to me.

Jake went to Tokyo for a couple of days last week but came back without knowing just who is going to replace him or when. Those people in Tokyo certainly are disorganized. He still hasn't sold his car and is beginning to worry about it now.

Of course, he wants a couple hundred more than he paid for it a year and a half ago. Really is sort of funny.

The villages are still off-limits and no word when they are going to go back on-limits. Supposedly, it was just for the chaplains. However, now I wouldn't be a bit surprised if the general (Odgen, the army general) will try and keep them off-limits indefinitely. Be interesting to see what happens.

A couple of days ago they decided that the elected candidate would be allowed to take his seat in the legislature after all. I wish to hell those people would make up their minds. They certainly make the military, etc., look like a terrific bunch of fools.

The weather here this past week has been rather wet and cold for the most part. We are getting a fair amount of rain, which we were lacking, around the first part of the year.

Down around Naha, the District Engineers dredged out a small boat harbor for the local vessels and made a deep harbor out of it, complete with steel pilings and cement quays. They had finished the piling and cement work and were just about through with all of the dredging when two sides of the harbor fell in—steel pilings and cement and all. Quite a mess. Still haven't heard their explanation for the whole mess yet but I am sure that it will be a good one.

They pretty nearly have the road through the base paved with four lanes of asphalt now. Of course, there are several places where the pavement has broken through already but that doesn't seem to bother them at all. These engineers of the Army certainly don't show me a great deal.

Got a letter from Ann today in which she mentioned that she was transferred to the 'Operations' division of some sort. I've written her a couple of times asking more about her job, but she doesn't seem to pay much attention. Nothing but vague answers and detailed accounts of her evening activities. You might mention that I am interested in hearing a little more about her job, as I am through asking her about it.

Well, I can't seem to think of a great deal else to report this time, so I shall close and go to bed.

Love,

Peter

"Looks like the left-wing coalition is going to win this one again."

Monday, April 20, 1953
Kadena Air Base; Okinawa

Dear Ma and Pa,

Well, not a great deal to report this week. Things were comparatively slow as far as I was concerned, and I had an opportunity to get caught up on a lot of little things that had been hanging around for some time.

The weather this last week was quite miserable, especially over the weekend. However, almost all day today there wasn't a cloud in the sky and it managed to warm up quite a little bit. Just like a summer day. This evening it started to cloud up and undoubtedly tomorrow it will be raining again. However, the rain should be just about finishing up here one of these days.

Saturday, I was duty agent and worked from about 3:00 p.m. until around 11:00 p.m. and then had an uneventful evening.

Sunday was especially nasty and I stayed in all day. Saturday, I managed to put a small dent in the staff car. Hope we can get it in the shop before Jake gets back from Hong Kong. He left in a big hurry last week. Got as far as Formosa or the Philippines and must have been weathered in, because he got word back to get a three-day extension of his leave.

Actually, he will have quite a bit on his mind when he gets back and won't have much of an opportunity to get all shaken up over the dent in the fender.

Jake, and the rest of the office, for that matter, still haven't been able to sell his car. Had a couple of good leads, but so far they have all fallen through. He wants too much for it and then takes it as a personal affront when no one wants to buy the car or even shows any interest in it.

A four-door car is easy to sell to the taxi companies but a two-door cab is just not wanted; especially since they can get all the four-door cars they want.

Last Thursday (Jake left around Wednesday) the powers that be around here decided that we didn't need three of the jeeps we are assigned from the base motor pool. Needless to say, it came as quite a blow.

Without transportation, we might just as well close up shop. But seems that there was some major down from FEAF with instructions from Air Force headquarters to survey all vehicle utilization and he must have been trying to make a name for himself by cutting transportation. Just about every organization was hit by his findings.

Anyhow, Nielsen managed to get the final action delayed for a while. At least until Jake gets back and can shape things up. I hope that he can iron things out, but I am just a little afraid that he won't be able to do too much. Too bad he is leaving before the new man comes in.

He spends most of his time around here (when he is around) shaping people up and without his shaping, things may get a little tight. It would be just like our headquarters to send some ringer down here as a replacement. Goodness knows there are plenty of them around in the outfit that they could send down here.

The villages are still off-limits, and the local press is beginning to remark how the local economy is hurting.

They are having another election here in about a month. Looks like the left-wing coalition is going to win this one again. It will be interesting to see just what USCAR will do about this one. They are going to have to realize pretty soon that if you are going to let people hold free elections, you can't disqualify the victorious candidate and get away with it very often. Bunch of idiots.

Got a letter from Ann. Long and very informative. However, I was quite distressed to hear that her organization is instrumental in sending things to the Flips. Big mistake not to let them starve. Nothing but a country of thieves and brigands. Ought to send them thistle seeds if you are bothering to send them seeds.

Well, can't seem to think of a great deal else to report this time.

Love,

Peter

"$330 completely down the drain."

Monday, April 27, 1953
Kadena Air Base; Okinawa

Dear Ma and Pa,

Well, I seem to be a day late again in putting my letter off to you. Yesterday (as is going to occur once a month in order to use aging supplies) all the mess halls here on the base served C Rations and I went out to dinner and by the time I returned, it was getting pretty late to start writing any letters.

Again, this last week has been comparatively quiet and I've been doing a lot of things that had been gradually piling up.

Tuesday, and Wednesday it rained and was comparatively cool. Since then, it has warmed up and has been quite nice.

Sunday was lovely, and Alex Chilton and I drove up around Motobu. Nice trip but the jeep got a little uncomfortable by the time we returned to the base.

The villages are still off-limits, and I haven't heard a great deal from any official sources concerning the duration of the ban—or anything more about the reasons for the ban. Might be a political move on the part of the military in an effort to discredit the coalition parties— which by the way won another rather important election in the northern part of the island last week.

Actually, the ban is putting a severe strain on parts of the local economy.

On the day after payday here on the base, less than 50 percent of the normal amount of MPC has been converted into yen. Doesn't seem to me that the ban is doing anything for the morals of the troops. Those who don't have any are not going to get any and those who have them and haven't lost them by this time aren't going to be affected by anything that goes on. It's going to be interesting to see the long-range result of the whole affair. Any way it turns out, I don't think that the military is going to benefit.

Jake got back from Hong Kong. After having much trouble finally getting there. That landing field is one of the toughest ones in the Far

East. Only got to spend two days of his leave there. The rest of the time, he spent trying to land.

Jake finally sold his car. Didn't get as much as he wanted for it but still got about as much as be paid for it. The bird he sold it to, gave him a $100 down-payment and then when Jake went to cash it, the check bounced. Jake nearly had a stroke but finally managed to contact the buyer who immediately made it good. He certainly has had a hard time getting rid of that car. Yesterday he came to work wearing short pants which turned out to be quite a spectacle. Got a sunburn the day before out on the golf course.

Wednesday afternoon, a couple of us took off and went down to Naha to see *The Tales of Hoffman* in one of the movie theaters. It was very good. I had seen the same movie up in Tokyo last year just about this time.

Today was quite warm. The radio announced that the low tonight would be around 70 degrees, with a high of around 80 degrees tomorrow. However, the weather reports around here are notoriously poor. Wouldn't be at all surprised if it snowed tomorrow.

Received another radio-transmitter-receiver sent from supply last week. Brand new; never out of the packaging. When I went to open it, I found that it was soaking wet and completely ruined. $330 completely down the drain. Went to the base supply officer and told him that I wanted to write an unsatisfactory report on it and he said no, but to turn it in and to forget about it. He is the one who was just recently brought up here from Naha AB and who is supposed to be such a hot-shot supply man. Couldn't get the time of day from that organization without having to wait six weeks for the paperwork to go through.

Rumor has it that the replacement for Jake is going to be one of Nielsen's pet peeves from Headquarters in Tokyo. Another major. One with little practical experience and less common sense from what I hear.

Jake really got a bum deal from the colonel as far as his rating was concerned.

Will write later,

Love,

Peter

May Day—and the marching band refused to yield

Monday, May 4, 1953
Kadena Air Base; Okinawa

Dear Ma and Pa,
Well, this last week has been a rather busy one and the next couple of days should be quite busy also.

May Day was uneventful; just a rather small, orderly meeting at Naha and another smaller meeting up at Nago.

The Army, for once, played it rather smooth and on the other side of the vacant lot holding the May Day demonstration, the Army had a band, a fancy drill team and a couple of pieces of artillery—and had what might be considered an open house.

However, the Army workday was over before the Communists' and they left before it got dark. But it was a step in the right direction and did show a bit of common sense that seems to have been lacking in most of their policies.

The Army general put one small, isolated village on-limits this past week. It will be interesting if that is only a beginning of a gradual movement to put the villages on-limits or whether he is merely going to use that as an example that not all villages are off-limits and let it go at that. He also got a promotion to major-general this last week.

It will be interesting now to see just what the Air Force is going to do about their general. Supposedly, I have heard, there was an agreement whereby both the Army and the Air Force commanding generals would be the same rank. Either the Army pulled a double-cross or the local general is also due for a promotion soon. In any event, the Air Force general is going to be outranked.

The weather here this last week has been rainy about half of the time, although it has on average been a little bit warmer than a month ago.

On Sunday, Alex Chilton and I drove around by White Beach and then over to the other side of the island. The weather was pretty nice but not as warm as it was the previous Sunday.

Went down to the dock at White Beach and watched them unload ammunition from a couple of ships. Sort of interesting. They hire native trucks and drivers to haul the bombs from the ships to the storage dumps. Seems sort of strange but they must figure that it is cheaper. Also, the natives will work longer than eight hours a day without going to see the chaplain.

In the evening, we went to the local club for dinner, which was pretty good.

Saturday evening the office had a going-away party for Jake over at Nielsen's house. Nielsen didn't get back from his leave in Japan until today, but we had the party anyway and everyone seemed to enjoy it.

I am planning on going over to Hong Kong around the end of the month. As yet, I don't know exactly how I am going to get over there. I would like to be able to get a hop but there isn't much going over there from here that I can get a ride on. I would hate to pay for the ride but may have to. There are a couple of tentative deals that I am working on but the big trouble with all of that is that I wouldn't know until the last minute just what was going to work out.

I believe that I wrote and thanked you for the cheese. But in case I didn't, thanks a lot. It arrived in good shape and is very good. Ann's pine nuts also arrived in good shape. I am going to try and get a letter off to her sometime this week but may not have an opportunity.

Eight magazines arrived here last week, and I am quite far behind on my reading.

Some meathead . . . put some classified material in a safe last week and then left the door open. As a result, I have been trying to get in touch with various people about it today without much luck. One of them, a major, spends most of his time playing softball with the outfit's team!!!

Well, that is about all that I can think of to report this time.

Love,

Peter

Crimes and punishments

Monday, May 11, 1953
Kadena Air Base; Okinawa

Dear Ma and Pa,
Well, while this last week has been a rather busy one, there isn't too much of interest to report.

Saturday afternoon we had training and then in the evening, Alex Chilton and I went to Castle Terrace and had dinner.

Sunday, I had the duty and didn't manage to do anything constructive all day long. Luckily, there was no business.

The weather here this past week—except for today when it has been warm and rainy—has been lovely. Still not so hot that it doesn't cool down in the evenings. However, it won't be long before it is really hot.

Jake will be leaving this Friday. He has more than been hustling around, doing various little chores. Today he went on a flight up to Korea for the day—also for the flight time and for the income tax exemption. Goodness knows what he will be doing tomorrow and the next day. Play golf more than likely. Outside of getting special permission (I have no idea how) to take his golf clubs on board the ship with him and going down to the baggage warehouse to put in some more stuff he forgot that his wife packed, Jake hasn't knocked himself out. Really amusing.

The villages are still off-limits. The burglaries are definitely on the upswing. Had one last week where a couple of burglars (Okinawans) entered a tent and removed a footlocker while everyone was sleeping and took it outside and went through it right beside the tent. One of them found some underwear he liked and so changed underwear right there on the spot. Pretty good, I thought.

On Wednesday, we had the regular monthly meeting. Heard a pretty good one. Seems that in accordance with a new directive from FEAF, any of the cons around here who gets sentenced to 20 days or more in the guardhouse is flown down to the Philippines to a "Correction Center" the AF set up down there. First, of course, the sentence must be approved by the local reviewing authorities which usually takes a couple of days. Then space must be arranged for him on the flights down to the Philippines. However, all of these flights originate in Japan, so nothing is ever definite until the plane leaves here. This reservation also takes a couple of days, usually—perhaps more. Then after he has served his time out in the Philippines, which may be no more than a couple of weeks by this time, he is returned to Okinawa. However, they won't send the man back until the sentence has been fully served.

After the sentence is completed, the wheels start turning until transportation back can be arranged. Again, some more delay because they return on a "space available" basis. However, as soon as the sentence is completed, the ex-prisoner is placed on a TDY (Temporary duty) status complete with per diem and nothing to do but sight-see. What a waste! Hardly pays to keep on the straight and narrow these days with deals like that floating around.

Quite a bit of activity this last week repairing the new four-lane road through the base. Patches all along it; like a quilt, only not as sturdy.

Right now, it is the middle of the wild Easter lily season. Quite a few of them have been planted around various places—especially around the clubs, and they are really pretty.

Had the lottery drawing this last week. I managed to get back 160 of my 600 yen which isn't too good. Maybe I'll do better next month.

Lots of mosquitos and flies out lately. Sure sign of summer.

Well, seem to have a hard time thinking of anything today. So I shall close.

Love,
Peter

The end of Jake—and getting ready for Hong Kong

Wednesday, May 20, 1953
Kadena Air Base; Okinawa

Dear Ma and Pa,

Boy, I am far behind on the letter-writing schedule this week for some reason or other. I should have done it Sunday but never seemed to get around to it.

Sunday afternoon Pat and I went to Naha and had a couple of beers and ate and then came back and I went to bed early.

Monday night Nielsen came over for a while and it was late when he left and then last night I had some work to do.

Today I am duty agent and am writing this during lunch—or rather what passes for lunch. I have to stay around the office while everyone else is eating and get a sandwich at the local coffee shop.

Alex Chilton left Sunday for Japan. I had dinner with him Saturday evening before he left. I guess that he will be up in Japan for several weeks.

The weather here this past week and so far this week has been pretty poor. We had about ten inches of rain last week with no sunshine and so far this week it has been rainy and quite windy. While it is generally getting a bit warmer, the temperature is still quite reasonable and it is quite comfortable both during the daytime and the nighttime.

Well, Jake got off, finally, last week. Certainly was confusing, to say the least. He put about everything off to the last minute or completely forgot altogether. He took just about everything that he managed to accumulate during this lifetime—or so it seemed, judging from the large amount of baggage he had.

Somehow he managed to work a deal and get his and his wife's golf bags on the boat with them. A practice strictly frowned upon—golf clubs are supposed to be sent in with the hold baggage or the household goods. Working deals up until the last minute.

As yet, not any word about the actual time of arrival of the new CO. Still sometime in July. However, in the meantime, he is trying to get out of OSI, so he may not be arriving at all. For all the noise the organization puts out about the Management and Procedures branch of the organization, they still seem to have a lot of confusion about some simple matter of getting bodies in the right place at the right time. Sort of funny to see all the maneuvering that goes on and still no results.

I leave tomorrow bright and early and will return on the 31st. I have just about everything done but there is always a lot of last-minute running around. Especially packing. I certainly have a hard time doing any packing. I don't want to take too much with me in the way of clothing, as I plan on buying clothes down there. Also, there is the weight limitation which will have to be considered when I return. Afraid that the trip is going to be rather expensive, but there isn't a great deal that I can do about it now.

Got a radio installed on a jeep yesterday, all except the microphone, and I have to try to scare one up this afternoon. Don't know how much success I am going to have. No one seems to have any around or at least they don't want to part with them.

Well, it's getting late and I have a lot to do this afternoon before I go. I have to travel down there in uniform although once I am there I shall be wearing civilian clothing. Seems rather ridiculous but that is the way the orders read.

Will write later,

Love,

Peter

CHAPTER SEVEN

Hong Kong

"Hong Kong is really a very beautiful city . . . "

Monday, May 25, 1953
Hong Kong (British Empire)

Dear Ma and Pa,

Well, I arrived here in good shape at about 1420 hours on the afternoon of May 21 after an uneventful flight and one stop at Taipei, Taiwan. It rained here that one afternoon but since then has been dry (no rain but humid) and warm. Very muggy.

I have a nice room here that while rather expensive by local standards ($40HK at $6HK/1 USD), is well worth it—being air-conditioned.

It is fairly well located on the Kowloon side, about a five-minute walk from the ferry to the HK side—which, by the way—is 20 cents HK, which is quite reasonable.

Hong Kong is really a very beautiful city, and colorful—as is the island on which it is located. Very mountainous with lots of scenic viewpoints. Tremendous amount of shipping.

Certainly, much more than would normally be necessary for an area with 2½ million; certainly very picturesque seeing all the ships and the harbor but at the same time rather discouraging when one thinks of all the money, favors and privileges we are squandering on the British, supposedly in return for their cooperation and our efforts against the Communists. But of course, there is really little cause in getting all disturbed over the entire situation.

[Peter does not sign this letter. He continues his thought on the next airmail letter].

Cold War Geopolitics

Monday, May 25, 1953
Hong Kong (British Empire)

[Continuation of last letter.]

. . . While I realize that I am undoubtedly not cognizant of all the various diplomatic, economic, and political forces at play in this area (Japan included), the more time I spend over here the more I am convinced that any effective aid the U.S. will ever receive along these three lines will only be gained through assistance and cooperation with the Japanese.

A lot of American greenbacks floating around. I fail to realize how the presence of greenbacks (or traveler's checks, as I have) is doing a great deal either to hinder the development of the Chinese Communists or to aid the U.S. efforts in combating Communism. A sop to the British, more than likely. However, don't worry for fear that I am becoming unduly discouraged or pessimistic; these are just some casual observances and thoughts on my part.

Well, it is getting late in the afternoon and I am having dinner with some people off the carrier *Princeton*. One of whom is a person by the name of Fletcher who used to work for Emerald Investment.

Will write later.

Love,

Peter

CHAPTER EIGHT

Back to Okinawa

The election that failed

Monday, June 1, 1953
Kadena Air Base; Okinawa

Dear Ma and Pa,

Well, I returned from Hong Kong yesterday afternoon after an uneventful trip—with one refueling stop at Taipei. It was raining when we left and slightly bumpy for about the first ten minutes out but then it cleared up and remained nice and calm all of the way.

Even pleasant here when we landed, although in the time I was gone, it warmed up and the weather here is just about the typical summer weather: hot, uncomfortable, and a little cloudy.

During the days, the snakes and snails came out. Lots of snails around. Don't know where they hide in the winter, but they are very abundant now.

Haven't seen any snakes but have heard several reports. One Okinawan schoolboy was bitten on the head while he was sleeping, and it killed him but that is the exception rather than the rule. Very seldom do we see the snakes or the snails during the daytime—too hot for them.

The Air Force here is on a modified daylight savings time—working hours advanced 30 minutes. Longer daylight hours in the evenings but actually it doesn't make too much difference what with losing an extra half-hour of sleep every day.

In all, the leave in Hong Kong was very pleasant. It rained three of the days I was there (including the two last days) but in all the weather was pretty good though quite warm and sticky. Actually, the warm weather doesn't bother me too much outside of sweating and as a result, my glasses are inclined to slip a bit. I have to go over one of these days and have them adjusted.

While I was over there bought myself a couple of suits, a sports coat and a couple of pairs of slacks and an overcoat—dress variety—of dark blue cashmere. Really a very good-looking coat. Perhaps a bit extravagant but no more than an ordinary overcoat in the states and certainly much less than a coat made of comparable material—normally over $200.

I also bought a tablecloth for you, Ma. I wish that I knew a little more about it than I do. While it looks very nice I have no idea as to what you would like or what is considered to be presentable. I hope that it helps make up for all the birthday, Christmas, and Mother's Day presents that I have been neglecting. I really feel very badly about it and shall try to do better in the future. Also, while on leave, I forgot all about Pa's birthday for which I feel very badly but I'll wish you a belated Happy Birthday now, Pa.

I had a notice that you renewed my subscription to *The New Yorker*. Thank you very much. I really enjoy it very much.

The British in Hong Kong were really working up a big sweat about the Coronation. All kinds of various lighting displays, programs, commercial tie-ins, etc. I only hope that the tablecloth doesn't have the Queen's picture woven into it.*

Read an article in one of their papers, which said there is a daily average of 40 ships, over 2000 tons in weight, at the harbor in Hong Kong.

Then they claim that they are doing their best to fight the Communists. The papers there went into lengthy explanations as to the circumstances of the British ship that carried Communist troops. Claimed that they were forced to do it and had no choice.

They are also quite alarmed over the increasing volume of Japanese trade in Southeast Asia. While they claim that they have not been hurt yet, they do admit they have had to improve the quality of some of their manufactured goods to maintain their edge in various markets for some goods.

Received a wire from Headquarters in FE Air Force today appointing Pullen the District Commander in place of Nielsen. Which probably means that there won't be a replacement coming on down here.

Pullen is a captain who has been head of the Naha detachment,

---

* Queen Elizabeth II—who would eventually become the longest-serving British monarch—was coronated on June 2, 1953.

while Nielsen is just a 1st lieutenant—really too bad as they need more rank than that here.

On top of that, Pullen is strictly a hillbilly, which is rather poor as the CO here spends half of his time shaping up other people and Pullen simply isn't capable of doing that. Those people up in Tokyo don't know the time of day.

You will remember me telling you about the election here last month and the disqualified candidate. Well, yesterday was the day for the re-election but none of the parties put up a candidate—not even the conservative Democratic Party, which is quite unusual considering that they are in a rather poor political position. Actually, quite a slap in the face to the military—and as much as I hate to say it, a deserved slap in the face.

Villages are still off-limits; there is a hot rumor that they will go on again this week.

Well, that's about all on my mind this time,

Love,

Peter

"... they can't treat these people like animals ..."

Sunday, June 7, 1953
Kadena Air Base; Okinawa

Dear Ma and Pa,

Well, not really a great deal to report this week, with the exception of a typhoon scare we had yesterday. They even went to the point of declaring 'Condition I,' which means everything closes down and no more travel.

However, the wind supposedly reached only 52 mph, which seems a little high. About an inch of rain fell late yesterday afternoon and today it has sprinkled off and on. The main winds of it were somewhat dissipated when it hit the Philippines a couple of days ago. It is supposed to hit Japan this evening. The lights didn't even go off here, so you couldn't really classify it as a typhoon. This one came a little earlier than the first one we had last year—which came on the 22nd of the month. Last year I was duty agent when we had the first one and a guy fell in the river near here and drowned the same evening.

I have been pretty busy this last week what with getting caught up on lots of little things. On top of that, we have been waiting for a truck to move some [furniture] of the office into the duty agent shack. From here on, we can pull the duty in our shacks, which is a big help. That was one thing that we were never able to convince Jake on.

Also, we are not going to be called in (supposedly) on minor offenses which will mean less nightwork. I hope that it works out all right and the Air Police manage to do a good job on the matters referred to them. However, I'm a little bit dubious about the whole thing, judging from past events in which they managed to completely confuse things. It will be interesting to see how things work out in the long run.

Had the regular monthly meeting last week which turned out to be just about the same as all of them—no one having a great deal of interest to report. Also had a meeting Friday afternoon with all the Chiefs of Police from Okinawa and a representative from USCAR. Really interesting to see how the bird from USCAR conducted the meeting. While it was all conducted through an interpreter, I'm just afraid that the Chiefs understand more English than the USCAR man gives them credit for. Certainly, they are a great deal more intelligent than he is. Knowing what he does about police work, he would be lucky to be a traffic cop back in the States but here the government has him in an important, responsible position supervising people who have forgotten more about the business than this bird will ever know.

As much as I disagree with the British and their methods and policies, I do believe that their civil servants overseas are a great deal more competent and respectable than are the Americans. Another thing, they still use the cane for the punishment of felons. A bit primitive, perhaps, but certainly quite appropriate and effective when it comes to dealing with some of the little monsters that the military seems to be composed of.

The military is getting ready to evacuate some more land around here again. This time about 316 acres of farmland and houses—about 800 people. Some of the people have been moved four and five times so far, and needless to say, they are becoming quite unhappy about the whole thing. As yet the rabble-rousers haven't started in on this one yet, but once they do, there undoubtedly will be quite an ado about the entire matter.

The big trouble is that almost all of their criticisms are entirely justified. One of these days I'm afraid that relations with the Okinawans will become very serious. The military is simply going to have to realize that they can't treat these people like animals and that they are going to have to use some common sense—a commodity that unfortunately seems to be completely lacking in a majority of the undertakings on this island. It makes a person damn uncomfortable when some Okinawan comes up and inquires about the whole thing and you have to try to defend the actions of the powers-that-be.

Well, I can't think of a great deal else to report on at this time, so I shall close.

Love,

Peter

Out to Sea

Friday, June 12, 1953
Kadena Air Base; Okinawa

Dear Ma and Pa,

Well, seeing as how it is Friday and I am duty agent tonight, I sort of thought this would be a good time to get a letter off to you both—also, getting it off a couple of days earlier, it should arrive just about in time to wish Pa a Happy Father's Day.

With the exception of last Monday when it rained hard all day, it has been quite warm this week but with clouds and an occasional rain—especially in the evenings and during the night. As yet, the temperature has not reached the usual summer high, but it has been up around 87 during the daytime and 78 or 79 in the evenings. The humidity is high so even this temperature is a bit uncomfortable.

While the typhoon did no damage here, from what we hear over the radio quite a bit of damage was done in Japan—mostly from rains and floods. Actually, the rain from the storm didn't reach here until a day later.

Tuesday morning early, I took a boat out to one of the off-island Air Force installations. The island is approximately 51 miles west of Okinawa. I had made arrangements for a small boat to take me out—a 63-foot boat run by the Army Transportation Corps. The trip took five hours out and a little longer coming back, as it was dark by the time we reached Naha—and the radar scope went out just as we picked up the first harbor marker.

The sea was calm and the weather was very nice although we did hit a rain squall on the way back.

Passed quite a few islands—small ones mostly—to and from the island which were very picturesque; very green with grass and small shrubs and quite ragged—rising straight out of the sea. The island I went to, Kume-Shima, has a population of about 15- to 20,000 and is really a very beautiful little island.[1] Almost entirely agricultural with little trade and no manufacture.

The island was bypassed by the war and there is no sign of any foreign influence other than the few people the Air Force has stationed there, and they are away from all the towns and farmlands. However, I didn't have much of a chance to do any sightseeing as we had to get back before dark.

On the return trip, we brought back a couple of people who were being transferred and they had all kinds of baggage and had to say goodbye to everyone. Got all the people aboard and all the baggage except one large box when the dinghy swamped and dumped the box in the water. It took quite a bit of trouble to get the box into the boat, and the dinghy aboard, and when they went to pull up the anchor, they found that it had fouled a rusty old oil barrel—which delayed us even more. Really a comedy of errors, but we finally got underway, but quite later than originally planned.

Except for a few isolated areas, the villages are back on limits again much to the relief of just about everyone—until 11:00 p.m. That was the time limit previously. However, during the time they were off-limits, the Okinawan economy was seriously affected. Fewer burglaries now that the villages are on limits but also a corresponding increase in assaults—but not an especially serious increase.

Went down to the tea house last night after dinner for a while and had a pleasant time. Didn't have much to eat though. It is named after the tea house of the book you mentioned last week, Ma. It is really a very nice place. Half Western-style restaurant, which doesn't get much play—and half Japanese-style tea house, which is quite popular.[2]

---

1. Later renamed Kume, the island is about 66 miles from Okinawa. It is part of the Kumejima Prefecture. As of 2010, it had a population of approximately 9000.

2. Peter likely refers to a restaurant named after the tea house featured in Vern Sneider's 1951 novel *The Teahouse of the August Moon*, later adapted into a film of the same name. The address of the real Teahouse of the August Moon: 3-17-1 Maejima, Naha 900-0016, Okinawa Prefecture, Japan.

The latest periodic economy drive around here has resulted in the abolishment of free transportation for Okinawan employees on the base. Many of them live five and ten miles from the base so there will be quite a bit of inconvenience and in many cases, hardship, as bus fare can run about a third of some of the monthly salaries. My maid, for instance, would have to pay about Y30 (25¢) just for bus fare since she lives about ten miles from the base. While it is undoubtedly going to save the Air Force some money, I doubt if the saving is going to offset the hardships caused by it.

I think that starting this next month, I'll give my maid an extra 1200. She is really a very good-natured person and a good, reliable worker.

Well, that is about all for this time.

Happy Father's Day, Pa.

Love,

Peter

Reflections on Hong Kong

Sunday, June 21, 1953
Kadena Air Base; Okinawa

Dear Ma and Pa,
Well, I had great plans today to get some letters written and to do some cleaning up down at the office, seeing as how I was duty agent. But I got a call around 1:00 p.m. and didn't manage to get through until about eight, so I am a little behind schedule today.

Actually, not a great deal to report on this last week's activities. I have been quite busy but nothing of unusual interest. As far as the strictly criminal end of the business is concerned, things have been quiet now for a couple of months. but this is only probably the lull before the storm.

The new CO is due in here Tuesday, by boat from Japan where he has been in headquarters for about a year now. He has been trying to get out of OSI—especially since he heard that he was coming to Okinawa, but he didn't make it. Probably will be quite disgruntled once he gets here.

He will be bringing his family down with him, so I imagine that he won't be much trouble for a week or so until he gets his family settled down and squared away. He is a major by the name of Reese. A man with criminal investigation experience, which is too bad as we really need much more emphasis on the counterintelligence end of the activities around here. It shall be interesting to see how he turns out.

The captain we have now doesn't like the job, hates to make any decisions, and has been putting off just about everything he can, which isn't too good but in a way you can't blame him since he knows there will be a new man in a couple of weeks—and he isn't going to be able to set things up the way he wants them for more than a couple of weeks.

Our headquarters doesn't show me a hell of a lot when it comes to personnel changes.

Pretty good example of the caliber of some of the officers the Air Force has around here: the major who is temporarily the Director of Intelligence for the 20th Air Force called the maids in his shack a bunch of 'dumb bastards' in their presence. Good thing I wasn't around, as I would likely have made some remark and have had a lot of trouble for it.

I'll try to go over some of your last letters and answer what questions I can.

About Hong Kong: I went both ways on commercial airplane. Northwest to Taiwan and Hong Kong Airways on in. Same plane but it seems that Hong Kong Airways has a monopoly or something like it on American flights into Hong Kong from Taiwan.

Possibly could have gotten military hops but they would have been very uncertain, and I would have had to spend too much time checking around getting there and then start in getting a hop for the return trip. It would be virtually impossible to meet any schedules that way.

I took a couple of trips around the island of Hong Kong and spent the rest of the time just walking around the main part of the city (both on the Hong Kong and the Kowloon sides) and also shopping and getting fittings on my clothes.

Managed to walk a blister on the bottom of my foot one day and had to take it easy the next day which rained so it didn't make a great deal of difference. I believe that that is the first time that I have ever walked a blister on the bottom of my foot—on the sides and heels yes, but never on the bottom.

Kowloon is on the China mainland and is, for the most part, quite flat. The majority of the Chinese lives on the Kowloon side because it is large and flatter than the island of Hong Kong, which is quite mountainous and rather small. I believe that the island of Hong Kong is about three by five miles and most of that is up one hill and down the other. However, there are quite a few buildings (apartment-type of various ages and categories). The main business enterprises—financial and trade—are on the Hong Kong side. Many of the buildings are quite old with a few new ones—the main one being the Communist Bank of China which was just completed a couple of years ago and is about 15 floors.

The more the desirable apartment buildings and large private homes are stuck on the hillsides on the island. Almost reminds a person of parts of San Francisco only the hills are higher, the highest one being over 2000 feet.

The main business center of Kowloon consists of many small shops and various small business enterprises. Many of the tailors and some of the shopkeepers are Indians who really don't have too good a reputation for workmanship as far as tailoring is concerned. On top of that, they stand out on the sidewalk and try to talk you into coming in to look around, which rather irritates me. Very few British-owned business establishments on the Kowloon side of the colony.

Saw quite a few British troops of various nationalities in Hong Kong—some of whom were stationed there and some on their way whither to or from Korea.

Also, an assortment of other European troops also going to or from Korea but not in any great numbers. But by far the great majority of people on the streets were Chinese. I don't believe that I have ever seen such terrific concentrations of people anywhere—not even in Japan. (Okinawa, by the way, has a greater population density than does Japan—which is aggravated by the fact that the military has a considerable proportion of the land on Okinawa and by the fact that the northern part of the island is quite mountainous and uninhabited, relatively.)

The Chinese definitely don't seem to like the Caucasians. I imagine that is attributable to the British—whom they seem to dislike intensely—and they immediately associate every Caucasian they see with the British. This was especially noticeable regarding the children. You couldn't get the kids to smile to save your soul. When children won't smile, it seems to be a pretty good indication that there definitely is a feeling of animosity.

Also, I went to a couple of movies while I was there. At the end of which a picture of Queen Elizabeth was shown and "God Save the Queen" was played. Quite a few hisses came from the main floor that I thought surprising and interesting.

Around the main part of both Kowloon and Hong Kong one did see quite a few British. The males appeared quite arrogant and aloof while the great majority of the British women appeared to be quite a scurvy lot. Very careless about their appearance, which the Chinese women definitely were not.

From what I was able to gather—and much from the tailor (a Chinese) I went to—there is a great deal of money in the colony which was brought in by the Chinese ahead of the Communists. Seems the British won't let anyone in unless they can show they have some means of support.

Of course, there are great numbers of very poor people there, also, but the concentration of wealthy Chinese is supposed to be high. They are supposed to own most of the business establishments and buildings, with the exception of colonial government buildings, some of the docks, and much of the main large finance and trade section on the Hong Kong side.

See quite a few young Chinese around the streets. While they profess not to like the Communists, neither do they seem especially eager to get to Taiwan where the center of the Nationalist Chinese government is. They don't seem too worried about the Communists taking over the colony.

Actually, all a person needs is one look at the harbor with all the shipping to realize that the Communists aren't going to kill the goose that lays the golden eggs. Hong Kong is much too good a deal for the Communists. Of course, one can never tell just what the Communists are going to do next, but they certainly are nobody's fools, and, at the present time, I can't see much chance of the Communists coming in there.

Of course, even if they did move in, the miserable British would undoubtedly find other places and methods for the continuation of trade with the Communists.

There is quite a bit of brass scrap smuggled out of the Ryukyus to the Communists through Hong Kong where it is transshipped. I met a couple of British sub-inspectors whose assignment is harbor control—checking on shipping in and out of the colony. I asked them about the smuggling carried on by the Ryukyuan (and also Okinawan) vessels and all they did was ask me what they were. Finally, out of desperation and in an effort to keep the conversation from dragging, I said, "Japanese ships" and they said, "Oh, yes, there are quite a few little Japanese ships in and out of the harbor." All of this in spite of the fact that there is a law against the possession of any type of munitions—even down to the possession of one empty brass cartridge case. Punishable by up to seven years in jail—or at least that is what they were saying.

Quite interesting in comparing the way the average Japanese walks down the street with the Chinese one sees in Hong Kong. The Japanese walks right along as if he had a purpose and good reason for going from one place to the other while the Chinese is merely strolling along the street without any apparent purpose other than walking.

Of course, one must not take Hong Kong and what one sees there as being typical of the Chinese but on the surface of things, they (the Chinese) don't show a great deal and I rather doubt if they are ever going to be in a position or frame of mind to do us a great deal of good—at least not for quite some time to come.

I am going to have to wait and bring the tablecloth on home with me as there is a great deal of red-tape in mailing any goods of that sort through the mails even though the linen did come from Ireland and the work was done in Hong Kong itself.

Saw quite a bit of American money floating around. Could pick it up any place.

I was quite surprised by the comparative absence of house flies over there. While the city is not repulsively dirty, neither is it the cleanest place I have ever been, and I would have thought that there would have been many flies all over the place.

Didn't have to have a passport to get to Hong Kong. Traveled on military orders in uniform, so it wasn't necessary.

Sorry to hear about your back, Pa, and your arthritis, Ma. You people should take care of yourselves and don't try to do too much in the yard. Let Casper take care of it and if he doesn't turn up regularly, can him and get someone else. No sense in adjusting your lives to suit the whims of the gardener.

I certainly was very sorry to hear about Aunt Clara's condition. I hope that a good rest in the hospital will straighten her out.[1]

Really a mess about Katherine's marital situation.[2] Quite strange

---

1. Clara Koerner Myers (1887–1955) was one of Peter's paternal aunts.

2. Katherine Koerner (1924–2012) was a paternal cousin and the older sister of Peter's contemporary, William ("Bill") Koerner (1928–2003). She married and later divorced Robert Chipperfield. Presumably the "marital situation" referred to relates to Chipperfield.

about the rest of the family's attitude toward the whole thing. As long as they are holding out on all of the information, I don't see why they even mentioned it in the first place. It would further seem to me that Bill and Mary had better get with the program and start doing a little something constructive for a change before they become complete bums. Quite a mess in all!

I was glad that the both of you got down to San Francisco, although I realize that Pa's trip was more business and not any pleasure mixed up in it—but at least he had a chance to check up on Ann's hovel—although at the rent they pay I guess that it couldn't rightly be called a hovel. Nice to hear about her advancement and pending pay increase. However, if it has anything more to do with the sending of things to the Flips (outside of thistle seeds, that is) I am definitely against the whole thing.

The weather here remains about the same—about 87 to 88 degrees maximum and around 78–79 degrees minimum. The days are beautiful. There is a line of big white clouds that continually hovers over the island—very beautiful and picturesque.

Last night I was invited to a party down at one of the tea houses given by one of the Okinawan prosecutors from the legal department at USCAR. Really a nice party with lots to eat (actually, too much; and the last course, the chicken, was a little tough) and some dancing, which was very interesting. The dances depicted various historical events of ancient Okinawa and were extremely colorful and some were quite graceful.

Too bad you banged up the car, Ma. I guess that the car is just too long and the engine too powerful for your reflexes. Take a little time to learn how to drive it safely, I guess.

Am glad that Phaon finally got to medical school. After trying as long as he has and after going to school as long as he has, it is about time. I rather imagine that the Gambees must have burned up about a carload of candles getting Phaon admitted. Rather a catty remark and I am rather ashamed of myself, but I couldn't resist.[3]

---

3. Phaon Gambee (1928–2008) and Peter were lifelong friends. Peter refers to the Roman Catholic practice of lighting "votive candles" while praying.

Just happened to think that next Friday is your anniversary. I hope that this gets to you in time. Happy anniversary!

I saw the article in *Time* magazine about the change at the bank. I hope the new president, whoever he is, will turn out to be a better person to work for than Belgrano.[4]

Tell Pearl not to work too hard and not to let her assistants get the best of her.

I guess that I have not mentioned the new roommate. He is a captain and a nice, congenial person. However, he (like everyone else) has his idiosyncrasies. He is presently keeping his reserve supply of soap and baby oil in the refrigerator. A rather new one on me but then I have many things to learn. He is also interested in making gun stocks. He made himself a workbench in his room out of part of an old shuffleboard. Along with his bed, dresser, desk, steamer trunk, two chairs, and two footlockers, there just isn't a hell of a lot of room left over.

Lots of snails out these days. Big African snails. They are really a pest to the farmers.

The rice around here is ripening fast and will be ready to cut around here in a week to ten days—about three weeks or more for the northern part of the island. Seems to be a pretty good crop this year and I only hope we don't have another typhoon until they get it harvested okay.

Well, I seem to have really outdone myself this time. Don't expect much for some time to come.

Take care of yourselves and don't try to do too much!!

Love,

Peter

---

4. Frank N. Belgrano, Jr. (1895–1959) was a prominent figure in banking circles on the West Coast.

"Really a mess about the business in Korea."

Monday, June 29, 1953
Kadena Air Base; Okinawa

Dear Ma and Pa,

Well, as I mentioned in the last letter, this one won't have very much to it—nothing left to say for a while. First of all, I want to thank you for the birthday wishes. Also, I received the candy that you sent from San Francisco, Ma, and it was very good. It was amazing that it arrived in such good condition as the weather here has been very warm this last week or so—up around 90 degrees maximum; typical of last summer's weather.

Thank you for taking care of the insurance installment for me, Pa. Also, thank you, Ma, for the money.

This last week has remained busy but rather uneventful. I have been spending much of my time getting the supply business straightened out. Seems that the Air Force is changing its supply set-up, which entails a great amount of paperwork.

From what I see of it, and from what I have heard from people who work full time with supply, there is no advantage to the new system, but I guess there must be something to be said for it; undoubtedly took a couple of dozen colonels weeks to figure out originally, who otherwise wouldn't have had a great deal to do.

I should be just about through with it in a couple of days.

The new man still hasn't come in although his car arrived down from Japan last week. Latest reports have him here day after tomorrow, but no one is expecting him until he arrives. So far, he has been delayed three times. Everyone will be relieved when he does finally arrive—and especially Pullen, the man presently in charge, as he doesn't like it a bit.

I was very pleased to hear about Bill Stevenson being elected as president of the bank. When you see him next, be sure to offer my congratulations. I'll be interested to hear of Pearl's reactions to any and all changes he institutes in the organization—assuming, of course, that he will.

Our Nisei interpreter-translator is leaving for a re-employment leave tomorrow back to the States and may be passing on through Portland. If he has an opportunity, he may give you a ring.

Your trip down the river and the barbeque sounds like it must have been very enjoyable. I think that would be a very pleasant way to spend a weekend.

Really a mess about the business in Korea. For a while it looked like the fighting might stop but now it looks like it is going to continue for another three years. Too bad that MacArthur still isn't in charge of the whole works. Even with all military considerations aside, he was respected and even admired by the Japanese and also well known.

Now, a man is just beginning to orient himself and he is rotated back to the States and another man is sent out and has to start over again. Of course, this two-year rotation has the effect of also rotating incompetents out of the area as well as those people who are doing a good job.

What with tomorrow being the last of the fiscal year, the local purchasing and contracting office had a big day spending the remaining funds they were allocated. Everyone is expecting four years of famine as far as the appropriations are concerned. Also, a cut in personnel. You should hear some of the complaining that is going on.

I guess that it was in *Time* where I read about Wilson's remarks about the services cutting out the essential expenditures and maintaining all of the deadwood.* Sometimes I think they could stand for two each of the three armed services in order to establish a little competition.

Well, I can't seem to think of a great deal else to report so I shall close.

Love,

Peter

---

* Charles E. Wilson (1890–1961) was Secretary of Defense from 1953 to 1957. As Peter's comments imply, Wilson was a strong supporter of cutbacks in defense spending in connection with the Eisenhower Administration's efforts to adopt a military strategy that depended more on nuclear weapons and less on conventional weapons—conventional weaponry being more expensive. Wilson was widely known as "Engine Charlie," a reference to his earlier career at General Motors.

The new CO

Sunday, July 5, 1953
Kadena Air Base; Okinawa

Dear Ma and Pa,

Well, again not a great deal to report this week. I don't know if I mentioned it or not but around last weekend someone discovered a typhoon about 800 miles off and all this last week the wheels around here have been in a panic; up until Friday night when they decided the storm wasn't going to come this way. In fact, the closest it got was about 400 miles to the south. They had all of the tents down by Tuesday and everyone assigned to concrete structures, etc. They even went so far as to close the PX and the clubs when the storm was 450 miles away. If they keep that up the rest of the summer and fall, everyone is going to be a nervous wreck. One reason, possibly, is that the Air Force general is bucking for a promotion (he is more than due) and the Army general just got a promotion (which judging from his various attitudes around here was pretty much a gift) and between the two of them, they weren't taking any chances on any bad publicity.

We didn't even get any rain from the storm, but it did get a little breezy (about 25 mph) on Saturday morning.

The new man arrived this last week and has been pretty busy getting squared away and will probably be quite busy for a couple more weeks. He speaks Japanese which is certainly a help. He has been stuck up in headquarters where his ability to speak Japanese hadn't been doing him any good. (Typical.) I hope that he is of a mind to get out and circulate.

Jake circulated all right but not many of the important local officials played golf, so it didn't always do a great deal of good as far as liaison with the Ryukyuans was concerned.

Had a couple of the regular monthly meetings this last week which were fairly interesting, as usual. Interesting as far as the methods these people [use to] hold meetings and as far as unofficial tidbits and gossip are concerned.

Someone (possibly USCAR or possibly the GRI—Government of the Ryukyu Islands—with the tacit consent of USCAR) sometime back promised the local Civil Police extra living, travel, etc., allowances in an effort to compensate them for their low living expenses. Well, comes the end of the fiscal year and the police department presents a bill for about Y6,000,000 and is told that there is no allowance for payment. Really quite a mess. Although the powers that be—USCAR—are trying to figure out some method of paying them, the police, needless to say, are rather unhappy.

That USCAR is undoubtedly the most confused and confusing outfit I have ever come across or heard about. Collectively, I don't believe those people have enough sense to pound sand in a rat hole.

Before I forget it, would you mind sending me some 'Ting' for my foot rot?[1] I am just about out of it and will be needing some more. It is a patent medicine and comes in a small white tube with red letters. You might also toss in a pair of tweezers if you happen to think of it. Thanks.

It has been a pretty busy week although I really haven't got a lot to show for it. Just one of those things. Yesterday afternoon I went down to Naha to look around a bit and then today I drove up north a little bit and looked around. The weather was really very nice, although a little warm.

These roommates of mine are really starting to get me down. They all refer to the Okinawans as 'gooks,' which irritates me a great deal.

Thought that you would be interested in the enclosed clipping. I was very happy to know that evidently, he doesn't find his responsibilities too heavy or his duties too wearisome to preclude his indulging in a bit of inane prattle occasionally.[2]

Well, I can't seem to think of a great deal else to comment on this evening, so I shall close. Take good care of yourselves.

Love, Peter

---

1. Ting is an anti-fungal cream, at that time manufactured by the Schering Corporation. A 21st Century product label says, "CURES MOST ATHLETE'S FOOT & JOCK ITCH."

2. Guy Cordon (1890–1969) was a Republican U.S. Senator from Oregon from 1942 to 1955. The article Peter mentions was from the June 6, 1953 issue of *The New Yorker*, which contains a colloquy among Senators Cordon, Paul Douglas (D-IL), and Lister Hill (D-AL) over the meaning of the word "meander."

More shoddy construction

Monday, July 13, 1953
Kadena Air Base; Okinawa

Dear Ma and Pa,

Well, this last week has been rather uneventful as far as anything unusual occurring is concerned. I have remained busy as usual but do little of any great interest. I had a nice, pleasant, dull weekend.

Saturday, I was duty agent and while I got a call in the middle of the night, it turned out to be of no consequence.

Sunday, I had planned to drive up north, but it rained most of the day, so I spent most of the time sleeping and doing a little reading. Actually, one of the more restful weekends I have spent.

Today—this morning especially—it rained quite hard, but the temperature didn't vary a great deal; a high of about 88 degrees. The rain helped settle the dust, which was starting to get very bad. Also, the farmers were starting to be hurt by the lack of rain for the past month. It is clear this evening, and, undoubtedly, will be clear and warm tomorrow.

What with a great deal of the construction completed, there is a great deal of difference this year from last as regards the dust problem. One big difference is the rock crusher and asphalt batch plant over on the other side of the hill. I believe that I must have mentioned it last year.

Now that they have the airstrip almost completely finished and about all of the roads paved, they have curtailed operation of the plant, much to the relief of everyone. It certainly spewed out a lot of smoke and dust last year.

Heard a couple of good ones about the local construction program this last week. In one of the new houses (cost, including grading, etc.: $37,000) a new occupant moved in the house and when he went to turn on the shower, no water came out. Seems that they put in all the fixtures without any trouble but neglected to install the pipes in the wall.

Another: there is a new commissary here on Kadena that has been completed for about two months now but it seems that when they were ordering all the material, some high-powered, high-priced engineer forgot to order the doors to the refrigerators. The general, in his weekly staff meeting last week, was quite perturbed about the appropriations that have already been necessary for maintenance and repair on the buildings that have just been completed within the past-few-months-to-a-year. A person just wouldn't believe it unless he saw it and even then would find it difficult to believe a short time later.

The new man is gradually getting oriented to the operation here but is quite slow in getting around to look at everything and make up his mind on various problems. Of course, he has only been here a little over a week and he has a lot of new plans and ideas, so it will take some time, I imagine, before he is completely at ease.

Went down to the tea house one night last week for dinner. Very pleasant as usual but we arrived later and left earlier than the time before, so the bill was much more reasonable. The time before, three of us ran up a bill of about $40. It was a good thing that our credit was good, or we would have wound up washing chopsticks.

Well, it looks again like they might arrange some kind of a truce in Korea. But then again, as long as we aren't going to be allowed to wage a war, they might just as well arrange a truce even though it doesn't arrive at any conclusion that could even faintly be considered to be lasting or final.

Although I realize that Eisenhower isn't a free agent, I'm afraid I'll have to confess that he is on the verge of disappointing me. . . . I really expected him to at least orally evidence a more realistic attitude toward the military situation in Korea than he has.

They are redoing the ceiling of the waiting room of the plane terminal for the fourth time (including the original construction) since they opened it. Average duration has been six to seven weeks. Not bad.

Love,
Peter

Major Reese, the new District Commander

Tuesday, July 21, 1953
Kadena Air Base; Okinawa

Dear Ma and Pa,

Well, I seem to be a couple of days late this week.

Sunday, I went on up to Motobu and it was fairly late when I returned, and I was quite tired, so I neglected getting a letter off to you.[1]

Yesterday evening, we went down to the tea house and it was after 11:00 p.m. by the time we got back, and I went to bed. Can't remember off-hand just what I did on Saturday, but it must not have been very important or interesting. I believe I napped as it rained in the afternoon.

The trip to Motobu was nice but we got caught in a couple of showers around Nago and then another heavy rain shower just before we got back to the base. Went through the middle of the Motobu peninsula where I had never been before. Very little traffic there. They grow quite a bit of pineapple up in the hill there along with quite a few bananas. Almost no military influence there.

While all the rice has been harvested around here, they were just starting to cut rice to the north of here. From all indications, the rice crop will be a pretty good one and the showers we are having now probably won't damage the crop any.

On top of that, the rain will fill up the rice paddies for the next crop.

The weather here last week has been rather unusual. Mostly clear in the morning and then around noon or a little before, it starts to cloud up and there are rather heavy scattered rain showers until around five in the evening when it clears up again.

It is actually rather uncomfortable as it is too hot to wear any kind of raincoat, even the lightweight plastic raincoats.

---

1. A town on the China Sea (eastern) side of Okinawa.

The new District Commander is a regular major by the name of Reese. I don't know if he went to West Point or not, but I rather doubt it. He is not on fly-in status, so it is not like having Jake around—here today and gone someplace tomorrow. He spends most of his time in the office. Even with all the time he spends in the office, I don't believe that he gets a great deal more done than Jake. Of course, Jake was pretty much a goldbrick when it came to work, and he would do the bare minimum in a great hurry so he could get out and circulate.

Reese is a great one for mulling things over in his mind and as a result, he doesn't get things done for a couple of days. However, he is a capable man from all reports and indications and will probably work out OK.

The grapevine has it that he didn't get along too well with the wheels in Headquarters (Far East Air Forces—Tokyo). If that is the case, that is only another indication in his favor. It would be very hard to completely trust anybody who was a member of that clique. Just like a pack of wild dogs circling, waiting for someone to step out of line and then pounce.

Saw the British *Comet* coming in for a landing Sunday morning.[2] Usually, it arrives about 3:00 a.m. and then leaves at 4:00 a.m. four times a week. But this time, apparently, it was quite a bit behind schedule. It certainly is a sleek looking aircraft. Has a low landing speed—or at least appeared so. Makes a terrific whine when it comes in for a landing or when taxiing.

Nothing very interesting this last week as far as the work is concerned. Didn't even pick up anything interesting along any other lines. The Ting and tweezers arrived in good shape and thanks a lot.

Well, I am duty agent tonight and I think that I shall drive around a bit. Stir up a little breeze and cool off. Quite warm and uncomfortable this evening.

Don't work too hard,

Love,

Peter

---

2. The de Havilland DH 106 *Comet* was the world's first commercial jet airliner.

". . . some sort of agreement in Korea."

Tuesday, July 28, 1953
Kadena Air Base; Okinawa

Dear Ma and Pa,
Well, I seem to be a day—rather two days—late again this week in getting a letter off to you. If remember my activities of last week, it is for the same reason.

Went for a ride Sunday—this time partly south along one side of the island, over to Naha and then back up. The weather was very pleasant but fairly warm. No rain at all for a change, which was nice. Took a few pictures. The PXs are just about all out of color film, which is going to be too bad what with the nice summer weather.

They have the same shortage every summer but never seem to learn from experience and stock up more film for the following year. It would be different if there were a film shortage but having no manufacturer's shortage, there is no excuse for it.

If you have the opportunity, I would appreciate your sending me about a half-dozen rolls of film. Kodak 'KODACHROME' Daylight type K135 (35mm) and twenty 20 exposures to the roll. Let me know how much it is, and I shall send you a check.

Had quite a bit of excitement at Naha last night, which fortunately I was not in on. Seems some . . . airman stole a rifle and was shooting it off in the village and hit and wounded an Okinawan. Someone called the MPs and when they closed in on him he killed an Army MP lieutenant and wounded another MP enlisted man before they wounded and captured him. He undoubtedly will claim he was drunk and (as he may have been—no info yet) and get off with about 20 years—serving about seven or eight. . . . Seemed a little strange that the MPs took the guy alive after he had killed one of their men. It will be interesting to see how the whole thing turns out.

Had a total eclipse of the Moon here Sunday evening, which was quite interesting. Looked more like a cloud of smoke covering the Moon than anything else as you could still see the outline of the Moon very plainly although it was definitely much darker than normal.

The tea house I go to most of the time is owned by some bird who works for USCAR and whose Okinawan wife manages. It is really a very nice building and the food is very good. They have both Japanese and American food. I eat the Japanese food, which is excellent, and I have heard the American food is also supposed to be very good. Of course, it is not as elaborate nor has it the wide variety of the Japanese tea houses, but it is still very good. However, last night I got a bottle of cold sake that was a little provoking. Had some roast eel a couple of weeks ago which was very good; quite sweet with no fish taste whatsoever.

Well, it seems that they finally reached some sort of agreement in Korea. I only hope that it is not typical of the agreements that we have historically seemed to participate in whereby we get taken to the cleaners. It will be interesting to see what progress they can make in the post-armistice negotiations with the Commies. Seems to me that they are in the driver's seat—as they always have been.

It will also be interesting to see what they do with all of the unemployed heroes here on the island. Goodness knows they can't do anything but fly the airplanes, and even that they can't seem to do with any degree of proficiency.

The GRI is planning on taxing all foreigners not employed by the military and who don't pay income taxes in another country. I think and hope that it applies to my roommate. He will undoubtedly scream like a stuck hog. Also applies to some of these foreign traders who have been freeloading around here long enough. Should prove to be a fairly good source of income to the GRI—sorely needed what with financial aid from the U.S. coming to an end within the foreseeable future. Next thing to do would be to export all the Flips and the islands would be in a bit better shape.

Love,
Peter

Leaving for Tokyo?

Thursday, July 30, 1953
Kadena Air Base; Okinawa

Dear Ma and Pa,
Just a note to let you know that I shall be leaving tomorrow (or at least Saturday) for Tokyo for about three days.

From there we will fly to Korea for a couple of more days and from there to San Francisco by boat. As yet, I know no more about the itinerary, but I shall let you know as soon as I hear about it. Probably next week from Japan. I don't know how much time I shall have in San Francisco or whether I shall be going any other place before I come back here again.

In all, I may be on the go for about 90 days.

In any event, I shall let you know more when I find out and will at least give you a ring from San Francisco even if I can't get a few days off to fly up to Portland.

Love,
Peter

CHAPTER NINE

South Korea and Japan

Operation Big Switch

Monday, August 10, 1953
Inchon, South Korea[1]

Dear Ma and Pa,

Well, we (Nielsen and I) managed to get off of Okinawa on Saturday morning (a week from two days ago) and arrived in Tokyo around one in the afternoon.

Supposed to have been a typhoon between Okinawa and Japan but we had a very smooth trip. Big last-minute hurry and we managed to bum a ride on some general's B-17. Nice and comfortable and not crowded.

We spent Sunday, Monday, and Tuesday getting "processed and briefed" (magic words in the military representing two days of paper shuffling—usually—that shouldn't take 30 minutes; briefing is especially a waste of time because I have yet to come across anyone who knew what he was talking about) and then were hustled on an airplane at 1:30 a.m. Wednesday that didn't take off until 2:45 a.m. Big rush. There were about 120 of us on the plane, a C-124. What a miserable damn airplane that is. Too big and heavy. Not too bad after it is in the air. It is the take-off that ages a person. The trip took about 4½ hours.

Weather in Japan wasn't too good, but we had other things to do and couldn't do any sight-seeing, so it didn't make much difference.

We landed at Seoul and after much confusion as regards our baggage, we were brought down here to Inchon—about 12–14 miles away. Unfortunately, we didn't get to see anything of Seoul but will probably have a chance to get up there sometime this week. Yesterday we walked around Inchon for several hours. It was very interesting.

I have never been any place that smelled as bad. It is really stifling. From what I have been able to find out, the whole country is just as bad if not worse. It can't be accounted for by the use of night soil as

---

1. Inchon is a romanization of Incheon, a South Korean city approximately 17 miles from Seoul.

Okinawa and Japan use the same fertilization methods and they smell like a bed of roses compared to this place.[2]

It is just an accumulation of filth. The people themselves are miserably dirty and seem to make no effort to do anything about it. While they don't have the best facilities in the world for keeping clean, they do have—at least around here—the equal to the Okinawan facilities.

They burn quite a bit of coal; as a result, the roads and streets in the villages are very dirty what with the accumulation of cinders. Seems that just about everything of no value is chucked out into the middle of the streets.

What amazed me most of all is the comparatively (to Okinawa) little damage done to the buildings around here by the war. Especially when you consider that this area has changed hands four times in the last three years.

Outside of several blocks around the port area, the buildings are in pretty good shape. Occasionally you will see a large building that was burned out, but the walls are all still in good shape; a few bullet scars but no big artillery shell holes. Much of the construction by the way is ordinary red brick for the larger buildings and adobe with various types of composition sheeting for the houses. Seldom any plain wood houses or buildings. Roofs are either thatched or cement-tiled—similar to the tiles on the Japanese roofs. Some of the older roofs are tiled with clay tiles similar to those on Okinawa but they are not nearly as well put on.

Saw quite a few different types of factories on the trip down from Seoul. About half were in operation.

Easy to see the Japanese influence around here—mainly in regard to the buildings and streets. The Koreans never had it so good as when the Japanese were running the country.

---

2. Night soil is fertilizer containing human excrement.

Our main purpose here is to act as counterintelligence interrogators for all Air Force personnel being returned in Operation Big Switch.[3] Any activity on our part will depend upon the numbers of Air Force repatriates received. So far, they have received less than a dozen.

If they do start receiving them in any numbers, I will be assigned a group of them to work with on the boat on the way back to San Francisco. The way things have been going so far, it looks as if I may be here until the first of September. No Air Force personnel coming through. Getting bed sores lying around. Big trouble is that this is strictly an Army operation and we are attached to the CIC, which, if it knows anything definite, which I rather doubt, is not letting us know.

About the only thing good so far is that we aren't having to pay a mess bill. But I expect that to end any day now.

We are quartered on the second floor of a two-story building—cement—being used by an Army replacement depot. Not too good but a lot better than it could be.

Well, will write later on in the week.

Love, Peter

---

3. Operation Big Switch was a prisoner-of-war exchange between the UN forces on the one hand and the Chinese and North Koreans on the other. Over 70,000 North Koreans and over 5000 Chinese troops were repatriated. Operation Big Switch lasted from August to December 1953.

Chinese troops, headed home

Sunday, August 16, 1953
Inchon, South Korea

Dear Ma and Pa,

As you see, I am still here—doing absolutely nothing and from the looks of things, I shall be here for some time yet, as still no Air Force prisoners have been returned. However, no one seems to know for sure when we will leave so you had better not try to write here.

Have been here for about a week-and-a-half now and have lost touch with the date. However, I see that you are having a birthday in a few days Ma, so I shall wish you a Happy Birthday now and hope this reaches you in time.

From what I hear, the mail service from Korea is pretty good so it may get to you in time. I hope so.

Due to the lack of activity, there really isn't a great deal to report. As yet I haven't been able to get in much sight-seeing but from what I hear, there isn't a great deal to see.

Went down to the port area a couple of times this last week, which was fairly interesting. Extremely filthy and smelly. Amazing to see all the old buildings and factories still standing. Even comparatively close to the docks themselves. However, given a few more years, I imagine the Koreans will let them completely fall apart. They really don't show me much!

We went down today and watched them transport Chinese Communist prisoners. There must have been several hundred. They seem to be in very good shape and were by far the best-disciplined troops I've seen for a couple of years.

Yesterday they were transporting them in trucks from the pier through the main streets of Inchon, but they were fairly badly stoned so today they shipped them by railroad cars, which was safe and rather disappointing.

Well, it is now Monday—got sidetracked and went over to an officers club in the port area. Nothing fancy but they do have cold beer and ice.

The water problem here is getting pretty serious. Seems the wells are running dry and you have to shower whenever they manage to pump a little water. Extremely inconvenient. Being [that this is] a replacement depot, one would think they would realize there is going to be a large demand for water and plan accordingly, but I guess that is logical and is expecting too much.

Well, can't seem to think of anything else to report so I shall close.

Love,

Peter

New HQ: Seoul University School of Medicine

Monday, August 24, 1953
5th Air Force HQ; Seoul, South Korea

Dear Ma and Pa,

Well, I'm still here but as you see from the return address we have moved up to Seoul and are now billeted in the transient quarters of HQ, 5th Air Force, just three to four of us in a room which makes it much nicer. Fairly clean but not much cooler.

The 5th Air Force HQ have occupied buildings that formerly were the Seoul University School of Medicine and are fairly modern and in good shape. Still the same program and still no idea as to when we will be moving out of here; getting quite tiring.

We moved here last Wednesday and since then it has been raining most of the time. This is their rainy season although they claim it is later than usual this year—starting just about two weeks ago.

Nice to get out from under Army control, even though there isn't much extra to do. They have a club nearby and movies every night, which helps to vary the routine somewhat.

What with the rain, haven't been going out at all so—coupled with the absence of any activity here—there really isn't much of anything to report.

Good possibility that we should be getting some idea this week when we may move out. Don't see how we could possibly be leaving here for a couple of weeks.

They sent some people over here from the States and they will be leaving here first. If they don't send enough of the expected replacements back on the ship we won't be needed—which is perfectly all right with me.

Well, as soon as I hear anything, I'll let you know. Take care of yourselves.

Love,

Peter

"The Army is still as disorganized as ever."

Monday, August 31, 1953
5th Air Force HQ; Seoul, South Korea

Dear Ma and Pa,

Well, I'm still here and as yet no word when we will be leaving. As of today, there are approximately 500 more American POW's to be repatriated, which—at the present rate—will take about four more days.

The number of Air Force personnel: that number will determine whether or not I shall go back to Japan and then to Okinawa or whether I'll be included in the operation. The way things stand now, it doesn't look like I'll have to go on the whole thing but will be released back to Air Force control. The Army is still as disorganized as ever.

The way things stand now—what with Air Force cutbacks, appropriations, and personnel—I shall be released from active duty once I get back to Okinawa and get things wound up there, mainly my supply account.

If I do happen to go on this operation, goodness knows what they will do. Perhaps even another trip back over again to dear Okinawa.

At any rate, I should be leaving before the end of October. But I won't believe it until I am actually released.

With luck, it will be about six weeks but I'm afraid that is a little optimistic. Just too many contingencies.

Well, nothing new around here. Took some pictures this last week and am having them sent home. After they are processed, I will explain them when I get home. Don't touch the pictures themselves and don't let them get damp. I hope they turn out OK.

I'll let you know of any plans when I hear anything new.

Love,

Peter

P.S. Please stop *The Saturday Evening Post*.

"I plan on leaving here Saturday . . ."

Thursday, September 10, 1953
Tokyo, Japan

Dear Ma and Pa,

I'm very sorry that I missed Sunday and am so late in getting this off to you. I left Seoul around midnight of last Saturday and on Sunday arrived out at the airbase around four in the morning and got into Tokyo around 6:30 a.m., and got billeted in one of the halls.

The day before I left Korea I managed to contract a cold and am just now beginning to get rid of it.

I have been getting a few things squared away here the past couple of days before I return to Okinawa. I plan on doing some shopping today but that shouldn't take too long as things are quite expensive— or at least the things that I am interested in and that are worth anything.

I plan on leaving here Saturday by plane for Okinawa and will probably be there two to three weeks before I can get a boat out. I assume that I will be leaving by boat, as that has been the case with everyone else leaving from down there. Actually, I'm stretching things a little, staying around here so long, but as long as they wasted five weeks of my time in Korea, I figure I can take a few days here.

Well, I'll write when I return to Okinawa.

Take care of yourselves.

Love,

Peter

CHAPTER TEN

Coming Home

The bad and the ugly: final thoughts on office politics

Wednesday, September 16, 1953
Kadena Air Base, Okinawa

Dear Ma and Pa,

Sorry I'm late again with the letter but this way I can tell you a little more about my plans and arrangements for leaving here.

I am scheduled to leave here on the 29th or 30th of the month on the *General Mitchell*. We go to Japan (Yokohama) for a day and from there to San Francisco, arriving there sometime about the 16th of next month.

Of course, all of this is still tentative regarding the stop in Japan and the dates of sailing but should be within a day or two of the actual times. There will be about five of us from the office who will be on the boat, which will make things a little more interesting, perhaps.

Two of them have their families. From what I gather, there will be a lot of people returning from here at Kadena. Quite a few of whom are getting out of the service one way or the other. Quite a few involuntary releases.

So far this week, I have been seeing about getting my finances straightened out and starting to see about getting my hold baggage sent off.

The trip to Korea was not without its compensations.I get about $27 per diem (which actually just about covers the extra expenses incurred) and about $80 in income tax refund seeing that for each month, or fraction thereof, a person spends in Korea, $200 is deducted from his taxable income.

Needless to say, this will be very welcome indeed as Japan was fairly expensive—even the few days I was there.

I have also been spending much time getting my supply account squared away so that I can pass it on. Major Reese is going to take it over. Actually, he has no business worrying about it, but he is doing a lot of things like that that normally a district commander wouldn't think about doing. Mainly, I think that he is scared stiff. Seems that he tried to get out of OSI before he came down here and his application was refused. The people in headquarters are laying for him [i.e., "out to get him"] and he doesn't want to give them a chance to get anything on him. They will pick up the most trivial things and make a big ado about the whole thing. I have never even heard of such a petty, back-stabbing outfit in all of my life. The letters that are coming down here to the district are perfect examples of the program they have instituted to harass Reese.

The attitude of headquarters is felt all over the theater. While I was in Japan and Korea, I had an opportunity to talk to quite a few people from some of the other districts and from what they had to say, there are very, very few people in the theater who are happy and satisfied with the way the organization is presently being handled.

But everyone is afraid to try to transfer out of the organization for fear of their effectiveness ratings. The dictatorial attitude on the part of the colonel in charge is being felt in the caliber of people they are getting in the headquarters.

At the present time, the man in charge of the counterintelligence branch doesn't know the difference between positive- and counter-intelligence information. This is a pretty sad commentary on the organization that is responsible for gathering these types of information for the Air Force in the Far East theater. Almost wish there were some way that I could keep in touch with the operations of the organization over here to see how the whole thing turns out. Eventually, it should prove to be extremely interesting.

Ran into a lot of people that I know when I was in Tokyo which made the stay there very pleasant. The weather was rather poor and as a result, I didn't have an opportunity to take any pictures, which was too bad as goodness knows when I'll ever get back here.

They have had a rather rainy season there this summer. Much more than is usual. Went down to Yokohama one day while I was there. Didn't see much of the main part of the town but it was very interesting.

Well, that is about all that I can seem to think of for the time being. I shall write next week—probably the last letter from here—and then again from Yokohama letting you know when the boat is due to arrive in San Francisco.

I will be processed and discharged at Camp Parks just south of Hayward, California.* From what I hear, this takes about a day or a little more. If you are planning on meeting the boat, please let me know so I can be on the lookout for you; also where you will be staying.

It would be a nice trip for you to drive down if you feel you can take the time.

Love,
Peter

---

* Camp Parks was a U.S. Army facility in Dublin, California, later renamed Parks Reserve Forces Training Area.

"Somehow, I seemed to have managed to accumulate a lot of stuff . . . "

Monday, September 21, 1953
Kadena Air Base, Okinawa

Dear Ma and Pa,

Well, this will have to be a quick one as I am writing during the noon hour. I went for a trip up to the northern part of the island yesterday and didn't get back until quite late and I went to bed without getting a letter off to you.

Well, this is going to be a busy week for me. I have to have my "hold baggage" in by Wednesday which means that I will have to pack tonight and tomorrow night. I hope that I won't have to get another footlocker.

Somehow, I seemed to have managed to accumulate a lot of stuff that I hate to leave behind. I am going to give as much as I can to the maid but even with that, I am going to have quite a bit of stuff to pack and send off.

On top of that, I have to get my supply account turned over to Major Reese this week. He is awfully difficult to get underway and I imagine that I'll be doing it the last minute.

Had firing practice this last week and one of the guns jammed up and was ruined and I am going to have to get the paperwork together to get it turned in even though Reese is supposed to take care of all that now that he is signed for the property.

My housemaid presented me with a kimono she made over the weekend along with some lacquer coasters, both as going away presents. As yet I have not been able to get her another job when I leave but I hope to be able to sometime this week. Otherwise, it might be sometime before she can get another job in this area as there aren't as many people living around here as previously and there aren't as many jobs available for the maids in the area.

I was certainly sorry to hear about Ann's tooth and hope that by this time she is feeling well again and is able to return to her job. She should have had it taken care of as soon as it started to bother her. I hope the tooth didn't die.

As yet, I have received no additional information as to when the boat will be arriving in San Francisco. I probably won't know for sure until after we actually leave here. I will try to get a note off to you from Japan concerning the arrival date if I can't find out before then.

There is always the chance that it will be delayed a day in Japan. From what I hear, the route home will follow the Great Northern Circle Route, so I imagine that it may be a little chilly most of the time.

Well, I have to get back down to work, so I shall close. Will write again next week.

Love,

Peter

"I'll be seeing you soon."

Tuesday, September 29, 1953
Kadena Air Base, Okinawa

Dear Ma and Pa,

Well, the boat arrived this morning on schedule, so it should be leaving on time in the morning. I have to assemble here at the base at 7:00 a.m. to get on the boat, which means that the boat won't be leaving until about 1:00 p.m. Or at least that is high tide. It is going on up to Yokohama for two or three days and from there to San Francisco.

It is now scheduled to arrive on or about the 16th of October at Fort Mason.* I believe that I wrote of this in a previous letter, but I thought that I would give you all of the information I have again in case the other letter didn't arrive.

Needless to say, I have been very busy these past few days, what with getting cleared from the base, getting my supply accounts squared away, etc. This morning they came and took my bedding which just about winds things up with the exception of a deposition that I have to give the legal department this afternoon at 1:00 p.m.

Those people are pretty disorganized. I finally had to go on up there and remind them that it would be needed. On a case last April. Certainly takes them a long time to get a case tried around here. So far, most of the witnesses have gone home. Happens every time. Half of the testimony is depositions.

Managed to sell my radio and fan. The rest of the stuff I am going to give to the maid. Put her in a taxi this afternoon and sent her home.

The weather has been very pleasant for the past couple of weeks but this morning it started to rain, and it is now just more than coming down. Hate to pack wet clothing but seems like I may have to.

---

* Fort Mason, officially the San Francisco Port of Embarkation, was a U.S. Army base in San Francisco, California. It later became part of the Golden Gate National Recreation Area, operated by the National Park Service.

Had a party down at the tea house Saturday night that turned out to be a very nice one although rather expensive. Quite funny. They really hooked up on the bill.

Well, I shall try to get a letter off to you from Yokohama. I believe that I mentioned that the ship is the *General Mitchell*. At least I think that is how it is spelled.

Well, I still have some odds and ends to take care of around the office here, so I shall close. I'll be seeing you soon.

Take care of yourselves.

Love,

Peter

The last letter

Saturday, October 3, 1953
Yokohama, Japan

Dear Ma and Pa,

Well, we arrived here in good shape yesterday morning at 10. We left Okinawa at eleven, Wednesday morning. It was raining when we left there and arrived here—and off and on between times.

We depart here sometime Monday morning and are due in San Francisco sometime on the 16th—or at least that is the last word out on the schedule.

The trip up here was calm and uneventful. Very little roll to the ship.

I got stuck as a compartment commander for one of the troop compartments with about 370 men. Not too much trouble but rather inconvenient at times. I drew the first day's duty in port—noon yesterday to noon today—and then I'm off until sailing time, which was the best time to have it.

Let about 300 men off last night and only 16 missing this morning, which isn't too bad; a couple of those are in jail ashore, so there are only about 14 unaccounted for.

An awful number of awful children aboard this ship. I don't know who is worse, the children or their parents.

It is mild and clear just now, and I have hopes of getting a few pictures up in Tokyo this afternoon. And also doing a little shopping.

Well, that is about all for now. Will see you soon.

Take care of yourselves.

Love,

Peter

CPSIA information can be obtained
at www.ICGtesting.com
Printed in the USA
LVHW091257021121
702237LV00004B/13